Changing Play

Changing Play

Play, media and commercial culture from the 1950s to the present day

Jackie Marsh and Julia C. Bishop

 Open University Press

Open University Press
McGraw-Hill Education
McGraw-Hill House
Shoppenhangers Road
Maidenhead
Berkshire
England
SL6 2QL

email: enquiries@openup.co.uk
world wide web: www.openup.co.uk

and Two Penn Plaza, New York, NY 10121-2289, USA

First published 2014

A catalogue record of this book is available from the British Library

ISBN-13: 978-0-33-524757-8 (pb)
ISBN-10: 0-33-524757-1 (pb)
eISBN: 978-0-33-524758-5

Library of Congress Cataloging-in-Publication Data
CIP data applied for

Typesetting and e-book compilations by
RefineCatch Limited, Bungay, Suffolk

The names of all interviewees and participants have been changed in order to protect their identity.

Praise for this book

"Changing Play recovers the groundbreaking work of Iona and Peter Opie, making it relevant and consequential for the contemporary study of children, play and media cultures. Marsh and Bishop convincingly demonstrate how children's play practices, when approached on their own terms, exhibit a persistent dynamism that cannot and should not be reduced to simple exclamations of panic or celebration."

Daniel Thomas Cook, Department of Childhood Studies,
Rutgers University USA

"Using the work of Iona and Peter Opie as a benchmark, Changing Play tracks the continuities in children's play and the changes that have taken place over the past half-century. The research juxtaposes the memories of children who grew up in the 1950s and 1960s with observations of and conversations with today's children in Sheffield and London; in doing so it allays much of the current anxiety about consumption and the media. Timely and topical, Changing Play will find its place alongside the Opies' classic volumes."

Hugh Cunningham, University of Kent, UK.
Author of The Invention of Childhood

"This important new text challenges the prevailing view that children's play has been contaminated by access to digital technologies. In exploring accounts of children's play from the 1950s and 60s to the present day against the backdrop of rapid changes within media and commercial markets, the authors skillfully reveal the particular ways in which children's play has changed and stayed the same. In so doing, they invite the reader to reject romantic notions of 'lost childhoods' and embrace the realities and richness of children's play in the 21st century. I highly recommend this book."

Professor Trisha Maynard, Director, Research Centre for Children,
Families and Communities, Canterbury Christ
Church University, UK

Contents

Notes on the authors

Julia C. Bishop is a researcher at the University of Sheffield and the University of Aberdeen, specializing in traditional music and children's folklore from historical and contemporary ethnographic perspectives. She leads the team working on a multi-volume critical edition of the James Madison Carpenter Collection of folk song and drama and is a past editor of the *Folk Music Journal*. Her publications include *Play Today in the Primary School Playground* (co-edited with Mavis Curtis, 2001), *Inclusion of Disabled Children in Primary School Playgrounds* (co-authored with Helen Woolley, Jane Ginsborg, Mavis Curtis and Marc Armitage, 2005) and *The New Penguin Book of English Folk Songs* (co-edited with Steve Roud, 2012).

Jackie Marsh is Professor of Education at the University of Sheffield. Her research is focused on the relationship between childhood cultures, play and literacy in the digital age. Recent publications include *Children's Virtual Play Worlds: Culture, Learning and Participation* (co-edited with Anne Burke, in press), *Handbook of Early Childhood Literacy*, 2nd edition (co-edited with Joanne Larson, 2013), and *Virtual Literacies: Interactive Spaces for Children and Young People* (co-edited with Guy Merchant, Julia Gillen and Julia Davies, 2012). She is an editor of the *Journal of Early Childhood Literacy* (Sage Publications).

Acknowledgements

We would like to thank warmly all of the participants who took part in the research studies reported in this book; your stories and experiences were so generously shared. A debt of gratitude is also owed to Nicola Shipman, headteacher of Monteney Primary School, and Peter Winter, the gifted ICT teacher at Monteney, who continue to collaborate with us on research projects and thus share their wisdom and experience with others. Thanks also to the headteachers of Ecclesfield Secondary School and St Winifrede's Primary School for being so enthusiastic about the project. We would also like to acknowledge the team who worked on the research project 'Children's Playground Games and Songs in the New Media Age', led by Andrew Burn at the Institute of Education, University of London. We enjoyed working with you and collaborating on all aspects of the 'Playgrounds Project' including the 'Playtimes' website (http://www.bl.uk/playtimes). We also express our gratitude to Steve Roud, who advised us on key aspects of the history of children's play, and Clive Hurst, Bodleian Libraries, who generously allowed us access to the Iona and Peter Opie archival collection on numerous occasions. The work of Iona and Peter Opie, and the many children and adults with whom they corresponded, has also proved crucial to our study. We gratefully acknowledge the support of Iona Opie and her kindness in providing us with additional information concerning the work of Peter and herself.

Finally, we thank the funders of the research projects that are discussed in this book: the Arts and Humanities Research Council, who funded the project 'Children's Playground Games and Songs in the New Media Age' (AH/G013640/1) and the British Academy, who funded the project 'A Study of the Relationship between Media, Commercial Markets and Children's Play in the UK between 1950 and 2011' (SG111215). We would also like to thank the British Academy for awarding British Academy Research Project status to the project 'Childhoods and Play: An Archive' (see http://www.opieproject.group.shef.ac.uk).

1 Introduction

This book explores changes in the nature of the relationship between play, media and commercial culture through a comparison of play in England in the 1950s/1960s and the present day, drawing on data from two separate research projects, in addition to the analysis of secondary data from a study conducted by Iona and Peter Opie in the mid-twentieth century. The starting point for the study is significant because this era was when the first large-scale surveys of play in Britain were undertaken by the Opies. In addition, the 1950s and 1960s saw the widespread take-up of television by families, which began a dynamic engagement with screen entertainment in the home. This, therefore, provides a pivotal point for the start of a study on changes in the relationship between media, play and consumer culture. In this introductory chapter, details of the research projects are provided and the methods used to explore this dynamic outlined. First, the need for such an exploration at all is considered.

One of society's recurrent myths, frequently circulated through media reports, relates to childhood and play. This particular 'moral panic' laments the decline of play but, of course, this is a claim that has a long history, with each generation documenting the perceived degeneration of the social and cultural practices of its youth and, at least over the past hundred years or so, blaming this degeneration on media and technology. This has prompted a range of scholars to challenge this assumption (e.g. Buckingham 2000; Bishop and Curtis 2001: Willett *et al.* 2013) and we situate the current book within this body of work. What distinguishes this book from others that have addressed this issue is that we look in depth at the way in which play has changed over the past sixty years, examining the changing relationship between play, media, technologies and commercial culture during this period. Specifically, we address the questions, 'What are the continuities and changes which emerge in a comparison of childhood play in the 1950s/1960s and the present day?' 'How do the nature and extent of these changes relate to concomitant developments in media, technology, and commercial culture?' Only by considering similarities and differences in play over time can we begin to address the constant cries concerning the perceived disappearance of childhood.

In order to answer the questions posed above, rich, qualitative datasets are drawn upon in order to identify the key issues that emerge in examinations of this area and to explore some of the most common myths and misunderstandings that surround discussions concerning children's play. Throughout the book, the concept of play is deliberately not closed down through the offering of a firm definition; instead, Brian Sutton-Smith's (1997) notion of the 'ambiguity of play' is drawn upon. Sutton-Smith outlined several discourses with regard to play, such as play as power, or play as development, discourses which are shaped by particular disciplinary and professional interests, or popular perceptions. He suggested that because of these shifting, and sometimes competing, discourses, which can be applied simultaneously to the same episodes of play, the nature of play is ambiguous and, therefore, attempts to constrain its meaning are misguided. A refusal to align with one particular concept of play is necessary in research projects such as those discussed in this book, which are interdisciplinary in nature. Therefore, notions of play as embedded across a range of disciplines informed the work, including childhood studies, folklore studies, education, anthropology, sociology, and media and cultural studies. The theoretical frameworks engaged with are, accordingly, diverse and, across the chapters, include theories that enable the relationship between play and other structural aspects of children's lives, such as social class and gender, to be examined.

The studies also draw on the 'new sociology of childhood', characterized in particular by the work of James *et al.* (1998). Recognizing that childhood is a social and cultural construct means acknowledging the way in which childhood is differently constituted in particular historical periods, economic circumstances and geographical locations. As Qvortrup *et al.* (2009: 8) argue, 'conceiving childhood as a unit in the social structure makes it possible to distinguish the individual development of children from the historical and cultural history of childhood'. One can read off from the experiences of individual children to the wider macro-structures that shape those experiences and, in this book, the accounts of children and adults with regard to their play are a starting point for a consideration of the particular historical and social contexts in which this play took place.

Two of the projects which inform this book took place between 2009 and 2012. The earlier of these was entitled 'Children's Playground Games and Songs in the New Media Age', conducted as part of the Arts and Humanities Research Council's 'Beyond Text' programme (Burn *et al.* 2011; Burn and Richards in press). The project was a partnership between the Universities of London, East London and Sheffield, and the British Library. The project included ethnographic studies of two primary school playgrounds, one in Sheffield and the second in London. The data collection took place over two years. The Sheffield school, Monteney Primary School, is located in an area of both public and private housing on an ex-public housing estate and the children came largely from white, working-class families. The area is one of socio-economic deprivation. The London school, Christopher Hatton Primary, is an inner-city, multicultural school located near King's Cross. Children aged from 5 to 11 were involved in the study. Researchers visited the schools on a weekly basis and undertook observations on the playground during playtimes and lunchtimes, using written field notes, digital video cameras, still cameras and digital audio recording equipment. Researchers observed play across both Key Stage 1 (aged 5–7) and Key Stage 2 (aged 8–11) playgrounds. Over the two years, various kinds of observations were made including a focus on a particular group of children playing, or the type of play occurring at the time of observation, or a specific use of space in the playground. Sometimes, one group of children was filmed throughout the playtime period as they moved from activity to activity and at other times children were asked to demonstrate songs and games from their repertoire for the purpose of recording them. Children also participated in interviews about the play that had been observed on occasion; sometimes these interviews took place straight after the play, at other times children reflected on video data. Therefore, as is the case in ethnographic work, observations were not systematic in the sense that there was no attempt to record everything that occurred, but the team ensured that over the period of study, comprehensive data were collected on a range of playground activities. Children completed surveys on their media ownership and use, and their knowledge of clapping games.

The study engaged children as active participants in the research process, recognizing their significant role as informants or 'knowledge brokers' of children's cultural practices (Marsh 2012). Each school selected members for a Children's Panel, which consisted of children who met with researchers on a regular basis throughout the project. The panels served as a means of involving the children in project management, as the meetings were used to discuss issues relating to data collection and analysis. Panel members used digital video and audio recording equipment to record playground rhymes and games, and panel members in the Sheffield school used notebooks to record observations. Panel members interviewed children about their play on the school playground. At the end of the project, a children's conference was held in Sheffield, during which children presented their research findings to children from other schools.

In this book, the data from the Sheffield school, Monteney Primary School, is focused upon. This is largely because, as we were the researchers who collected/co-constructed data in this school, we have a more intense engagement with the data than with that from Christopher Hatton Primary School, which was the focus of study for colleagues on the project, Rebekah Willett and

Chris Richards. The team has written elsewhere about the ethnographic studies as they were conducted in both schools (Willett *et al.* 2013), and about the project as a whole (Burn and Richards in press). In this book, the focus is on the data from the ethnographic study undertaken in Monteney Primary School, used as a starting point for the discussion of the relationship between play, media and commercial markets through time. These data were analysed using a range of approaches, discussed in Willett *et al.* (2013), primarily constituting a thematic analysis (Braun and Clarke 2006) and multimodal analysis (Jewitt 2009). The data are drawn upon to illustrate key points throughout the book and references to the relevant file numbers are included in the notes section so that the original files can be accessed if required (located at the British Library).

During the AHRC-funded study (known hereafter as the 'Playgrounds Project'), the British Library Sound Archive digitized sound files of interviews that the folklorist Iona Opie undertook with children across Britain in the period 1969–83 regarding their play (Jopson *et al.* in press). This led us to consult the papers of Iona Opie and her husband, Peter, held at the Bodleian Libraries, relating to the play and traditions of British children in the mid-twentieth century. Iona, writing in 2001, explains the origin of these papers (referred to hereafter as the 'Opie Play Papers'):

> When, in 1951, my husband Peter and I had finished *The Oxford Dictionary of Nursery Rhymes*, we began our quest for schoolchildren's lore. We ourselves were poorly educated in the traditions of the schoolyard, having been to private schools, though this had the advantage that most traditional childlore was new to us, and vitally interesting. As it was generally assumed at the time that such lore was on the wane, the purpose of our first survey was to find out how much of it still existed, if any, and whether it varied from place to place, either in quantity or in local association. We began by writing to *The Sunday Times*, in November 1951, saying what we wanted to do, and asking for help in doing it.
>
> (Opie 2001: x)

Iona notes that this survey and subsequent versions of it (conducted *c.*1950–80) engendered an overwhelming response and that teachers and others sent in data from all over the country, documenting the play cultures and customs of approximately 20,000 children. These data were supplemented by the Opies' own in-depth observations and sound recordings and the outcomes were published in a series of books (Opie 1993; Opie and Opie 1959, 1969, 1985, 1997) that document the rich play and cultural practices of children over the latter half of the twentieth century. In this book, the data from the Opies' work is drawn upon in order to analyse the relationship between play, media and commercial culture during this period and it is used as a baseline for considering subsequent changes that have taken place in this relationship.

Following completion of the 'Playgrounds Project', we undertook a study funded by the British Academy, based on the Opie Play Papers. The aim of the project was to attempt to trace some of the contributors to the Opies' surveys, now adults aged 50–70, and interview them about their memories of play, in order to explore some of the links between play, media and commercial culture in the 1950s and 1960s. This project is referred to as the 'Memories of Play Project'. The first step in the 'Memories of Play Project' was to identify two schools that we would work with. We searched the Opie Play Papers at the Bodleian Libraries to find schools that were geographically close to the schools in the 'Playgrounds Project' and which contained letters from children that indicated that they engaged in some media-related play. Ecclesfield Grammar, the only Sheffield school to contribute to the Opies' survey, was selected. Fortunately this school is geographically close to Monteney Primary School, which participated in the 'Playgrounds Project'. Indeed, many children from Monteney move to Ecclesfield School when they transfer to secondary, although it is now a comprehensive school. Both schools serve a demographically similar area. We also identified a school from among those represented in the Opies' research that was geographically close to Christopher Hatton School in London (although not as close as the two Sheffield schools), St Winefride's Catholic Primary School in Manor Park, Newham. The demography of the school's catchment area had changed since the time of the Opies' research, however. Whilst the original data were collected from children with names from a limited range of origins (including England, Ireland, Poland and the Caribbean), the current school has children whose families' ethnic identities originate from a wide range of other countries, including Asian countries.

We attempted to trace the original contributors to the Opie collection from Ecclesfield School and St Winefride's School through a number of sources including social networking sites (e.g. Facebook, Friends Reunited), local press, online directories and school alumni networks. This proved intensive and challenging work and we decided early on that we would extend the study to include individuals who had attended either these schools or schools close to them in the 1950s and 1960s, but who had not taken part in the Opies' surveys. Monteney Primary School was asked to distribute letters to the families of children who attended the school, asking grandparents to volunteer to be interviewed for the project. We decided not to distribute these letters at St Winifrede's School because of the population change; many grandparents would not have English as a first language and are recent immigrants to the area and the country. Instead, we approached those who had recently attended the school's recent centenary celebration, as well as contacting the East of London Family History Society. Through these various and multi-stranded strategies, we contacted twelve of the original contributors and twenty of their contemporaries, thirty-two people in total. All of the respondents identified themselves as white and working-class; ten were men and the rest women. The respondents were born between the years of 1937 and 1961, with an average age of 60, the majority enjoying their formative play years in the 1950s and 1960s.

Semi-structured interviews with twenty-eight of these respondents, including eight of the Opies' contributors, were conducted. In the interviews, the individual's memories of childhood play and its relation to media and commercial markets were probed. Interviews were conducted both face-to-face and over the telephone, according to logistics and individual choice, and were digitally recorded and transcribed, supplemented by written recollections by several interviewees. These data were analysed through a process of constant comparison (Strauss and Corbin 1998) and, using the qualitative data analysis package 'Hyper-research' to manage the data, the original 155 codes that emerged through the first level of analysis were organized into twenty larger clusters that, in turn, informed the identification of eight major themes that are addressed in the chapters of this book: forms of play; media and play; technology and play; commercial markets and play; gender, sexuality and play; space and play; parents, families and play, and changing childhoods. Throughout the book, the accounts of fifteen of the respondents are drawn upon to illustrate the themes raised in greater depth; this is not because these fifteen were the only ones to address those themes in their interviews, but because they were representative of the general issues raised (and one because his account was distinctive in nature, as we discuss in Chapter 6). Pseudonyms are used throughout.

The oral history interviews were richly detailed and respondents recalled a great deal about their play. There is now a widespread recognition that 'the functions and expressions of autobiographical memory are ... deeply embedded in our social world, in adult life as well as childhood' (Barnier *et al.* 2008: 35). As such, people do not so much recall in total accuracy the events of the past, as reconstruct them, drawing on a range of modes and senses as they do so. This process inevitably involves an element of nostalgia. No longer confined to modernist understandings of nostalgia as an intensely private and personal longing for an irretrievable past, it can be assumed that the nostalgic mindset is informed by broader social and cultural representations of the past that is the focus of study (Higson 2013). The older participants will have, no doubt, encountered numerous references over time to the period of their childhoods through a range of sources, such as television, film, the internet and books. This nostalgic glance backward also enables people to consider their current lives which, in the case of the respondents in the 'Memories of Play Project', was often as parents and grandparents engaged in reflecting on changing play. As Wright and McCleod (2012: 3) suggest, 'Nostalgia ... is pivotal to how participants construct a critique of their present and navigate the shifting relationship between past and present.' They note that rather than considering this process as diminishing the reliability of oral history data, we should understand the way in which the present shapes an understanding of the past. This was an important aspect of the study for the adult participants and, in all of the interviews, enabled respondents to reflect on their perceptions of the changing relationship between childhoods past and present.

In the chapters that follow, the datasets from both the 'Playgrounds Project' and the 'Memories of Play Project' are drawn upon in order to explore continuities and discontinuities in the relationship between play, media and commercial culture in the 1950s/1960s and 2010s, and we also engage with a secondary dataset, the material from the Opie publications and Opie Play Papers, based on the Opies' surveys. The Opies' corpus of work is used as a baseline for the consideration of changing play. In the 'Playgrounds Project' the classification system developed by Bishop and Curtis (2001) (see Table 1.1), which they based on the Opies' groupings, was adapted by the team. The classification identifies the content and form of activities and distinguishes them by physical, verbal, musical and imaginative content.

Placing the data arising from the observations and interviews at Monteney Primary School onto these categories enabled a direct comparison between the prevalence of particular forms of play in the contemporary playground and the

Table 1.1 Classification of children's games and play at school playtime (adapted from Bishop and Curtis 2001)

HIGH VERBAL CONTENT

- *Narratives* (e.g. ghost stories, personal experiences, dreams)
- *Jokes* (e.g. story jokes, riddle jokes, practical jokes)
- *Other verbal play* (e.g. jeers, taunts, tongue twisters, nonsense sentences, nicknames)

HIGH VERBAL AND MUSICAL CONTENT

- *Songs and rhymes (without associated physical activity)* (e.g. pop songs, parodies, 'rude' rhymes)

HIGH PHYSICAL AND HIGH VERBAL AND/OR MUSICAL CONTENT

- *Clapping (with song/rhyme/chant)*
- *Skipping (with song/rhyme/chant)*
- *Singing games*
- *Dancing with self-expressed music/song and/or with CD track*
- *Singing with accompanying moves*
- *Counting out rhymes*

(Continued)

Table 1.1 Continued

HIGH IMAGINATIVE CONTENT

Fantasy play (e.g. combat narratives)	• *Space-specific*
	• *Non-space-specific*
Socio-dramatic play (e.g. Mums and Dads)	• *Space-specific*
	• *Non-space-specific*
With playthings	• *Manufactured objects*
	• *Natural objects*

HIGH PHYSICAL CONTENT

Without playthings	• *Individual* (e.g. unsynchronized running about, handshakes)
	• *Group* (e.g. high-power It games such as 'Grandma's Footsteps'; low-power It games such as 'Tig', 'Racing')
	• *Team* (e.g. 'Kissy Catch')
	• *Play strategies* (e.g. race to decide who's It)
	• *Space-specific games* (e.g. using playground markings)
With playthings	• *Individual* – with balls, ropes (e.g. skipping), hula hoops, miscellaneous (e.g. loose playthings, crazes)
	• *Group* – with balls, long ropes (e.g. skipping, colours)
	• *Team* – with balls (e.g. football)
	• *Collecting and making things* (e.g. fortune tellers, nests, cards)
Body play	• *visual effect* (e.g. hand or body shadow figures)
	• *sensation* (e.g. Chinese burn, or those games where you perform a repeated action, often with the hands, and then are supposed to feel a resulting physical sensation)
	• *auditory effect* (e.g. 'burping' or other 'Rabelaisian' noises made with the body)

Source: Reprinted from: Willett, R., Richards, C., Marsh, J., Burn, A. and Bishop, J. (2013) *Children, Media and Playground Cultures: Ethnographic Studies of School Playtimes*. Basingstoke: Palgrave Macmillan. Reproduced with permission of Palgrave Macmillan.

forms of play present in the Opies' studies, although of course we were not comparing like with like, as the Opies' studies were national in scope. Nevertheless, by triangulating the patterns that emerged with reference to other studies of historical change in play (e.g. Roud 2010), key trends could be discerned. Thus, through a shifting kaleidoscope that variously brings into view data from all of these diverse sources, calibrated with reference to relevant research in the field, the key issues that emerge in any consideration of the relationship between play, media and commercial cultures over time are reviewed.

In approaching this task, it was felt to be important to provide an account of the contribution that Iona and Peter Opie made to studies of childhood and play and place it in historical perspective, given the significance of their work for both of the recent research projects discussed in this book. This account is provided in Chapter 2, where the significance of the Opies' studies for an understanding of children's folklore is identified. Although there has been documentation of children's play in Britain from the early nineteenth century, the work of the Opies in the second half of the twentieth century set new standards. Their surveys were conducted with children themselves and this written information was later supplemented by recordings made using the then new portable magnetic tape technology. The Opies' five publications on children's lore, language, play, customs and beliefs are distilled from this pioneering work and remain classics in their field. This chapter also considers the legacy of the Opies and the significance of their work for subsequent studies of childhood and play.

Chapter 3 compares and contrasts the forms of play described in the Opies' publications with the forms of play observed in the 'Playgrounds Project'. The focus here is on play in the street and school playground. The chapter illustrates continuity and change in children's game preferences as revealed by mapping the Monteney Primary School data onto that in the Opies' books. It then traces the history of specific forms of play encountered at Monteney Primary School and gives examples of ways in which they have developed over time and how changes in media and technology have impacted on them. This chapter provides a platform for subsequent discussions, as it emphasizes the numerous continuities in children's experiences over the past 60 years, as well as acknowledging the way in which play is always developing and changing in the light of transformations in social and cultural contexts.

In Chapter 4, the nature of the relationship between media, technologies and play is considered. The chapter provides a historical review of the differences in children's access to media and technology in the 1950s/1960s and 2010s. The ways in which the uses of media, cinema, television and radio, and their affordances, have changed are reviewed, and an examination undertaken of how these changes impact on children's play in playgrounds, homes and communities. The role of the media in the transmission and learning of play and games is examined and it is suggested that, in contemporary times, transmission of children's cultural practices has been augmented by the use of digital technologies.

Towards the end of the twentieth and the beginning of the twenty-first centuries, the positioning of children as economic subjects in the market became even more pronounced. In Chapter 5, how far the materiality of childhood has changed in the past sixty years is reviewed. The place of toys, artefacts and texts in children's play in the 1950s/1960s is compared and contrasted with data from the more recent project to examine both the continuities and discontinuities in the relationship between play and commercial markets. A consideration of how key tropes in relation to material childhoods have remained consistent is undertaken, such as the desire for collections and practices involving swapping, and the more complex relationships that contemporary children have with commercial cultures are outlined, focusing in particular on the place of brands in everyday play.

Chapter 6 reflects on play as it is instantiated in the separate institutions of home and school. The chapter begins with a consideration of how parental involvement in children's play has changed since the mid-twentieth century. Interviews with adults who reflected on their play in the 1950s/1960s suggested that parents did not generally engage with children's play unless it was to supervise and monitor the activities from a distance. In contemporary Britain, play is frequently viewed as a site for adult engagement as new forms of technologies, such as the Wii and X-Box Kinect, encourage greater diversity in forms of family play. The chapter considers these developments and identifies the way in which changes in constructions of the family in society have impacted upon play. In addition, over the last sixty years, there have also been key developments in the way in which playtimes are conceived of and constructed in primary schools. This chapter analyses school playgrounds of the 1950s/1960s from the viewpoints of the adults who were interviewed and contrasts this with an analysis of contemporary playgrounds. The chapter addresses themes such as the role of adults during playtimes, the material resources offered by school for play and issues of social exclusion and bullying.

There has been widespread discussion about the way in which contemporary childhoods are spatially constrained due to concerns about risks. In Chapter 7, this topic is reviewed, drawing on the accounts of the adult respondents in the 'Memories of Play Project', to consider the way in which previous generations were able to play in spaces and places that are not available to contemporary children. Developments in new technologies mean that spatial elements of play are different for children today because of access to both online and offline spaces. What these differences mean in terms of identities, the construction and maintenance of friendships, and the relationship between the local and global are considered.

Chapter 8 examines the similarities and differences between gender, sexuality and play in the 1950s/1960s and contemporary society. The chapter considers how far structural constraints that impact on this area have remained intact over the past sixty years. The patterns of heteronormative play that have been persistent over decades are discussed, along with reflections on the changing nature of constructions of sexualized identities in the 2010s.

In the concluding chapter, a reflection is undertaken on the main themes emerging from the analysis conducted across all of the chapters in terms of the continuities and discontinuities in the relationship between play, media and commercial culture between the 1950s/1960s and the present day. The chapter points to the need for further analysis of the changes in play across time and space. In this way, it is argued, a fuller understanding of children's play, past and present, will be developed and, thus, a challenge can be made to the kinds of assumptions that arise in some studies of the relationship between play, media and commercial markets, which propose that children in contemporary societies live toxic childhoods in comparison with the free and innocent childhoods of a mythic, romantic past. This, as we hope to demonstrate, is itself a myopic and misguided myth.

2 Early studies of children's play and the legacy of Iona and Peter Opie

> The most compelling reason for recording children's lore, for me, was to leave a picture, for future generations, of how the children of today amuse themselves in their own free time.
>
> (Opie 2001: xiii)

In Britain, and also in other parts of the English-speaking world, the names of Iona and Peter Opie are synonymous with the study of children's folklore, in the sense of folklore *for* children and the folklore *of* children. Yet, despite the stature of their work, there has been no detailed account or appraisal of their contribution. This chapter offers a preliminary account of the Opies' work on children's play, especially their methods, motivations, theoretical orientation and findings.[1] It begins by sketching some of the Opies' precursors in this field, especially those whose work is known to have had a significant influence on them and whose findings formed an important point of reference.

Eighteenth- and nineteenth-century scholarship

The earliest and most sustained research into children's play in the modern period took place within the context of folklore studies and its twin ante-cedents of antiquarianism and nineteenth-century Romanticism.[2] It therefore reflects various stages and theoretical orientations in the development of folklore as an academic discipline (Bishop and Curtis 2001). These include a concern with bounded and collectable forms – 'games', 'rhymes' and, later, 'singing games' – a predilection for amassing collections on a regional or national scale, and the influence of contemporary theory, such as the notion of unilinear cultural evolution and a Tylorian concept of survivals.

The work of Joseph Strutt (1747–1802), an engraver and antiquarian, is often cited as the first major historical study of play. Strutt combed documents in the British Library to bring together information on many aspects of English culture and tradition. Among his resulting publications was *The Sports and Pastimes of the People of England*, published in 1801. Strutt's main concern is with adult sports and amusements but his final chapter is devoted to 'popular manly pastimes imitated by children'. It describes the games of both boys and girls, including a number that would be familiar to children today, such as 'Ducks and Drakes', 'Puss in the Corner', skipping, 'Hide and Seek', and even 'hopping and standing on one leg' (several of these are discussed in Chapter 3). Strutt's book was reprinted many times due to 'the novelty of the subject, [which] attracted the notice and admiration of readers of almost every class' (quoted in Cox 1903: v). The Opies later praised Strutt's pioneering work as 'a remarkable undertaking that embodies considerable research' but criticized it for allotting too little space (14 pages out of 313) to the 'sports of children' (Opie and Opie 1969: vii).

The nineteenth century saw the publication of a steady stream of works concerning children's play which drew on oral rather than written evidence. Among these are Robert Chambers' *Popular Rhymes of Scotland* (1826) and James Orchard Halliwell's *Nursery Rhymes of England* (1842), and its sequel *Popular Rhymes and Nursery Tales* (1849). Both contain game descriptions and rhymes of school-aged children as well as 'nursery' or Mother Goose rhymes intended for younger children. The books by Chambers and Halliwell proved popular and went through many reprintings. Meanwhile, games collections began to appear relating to other countries in Europe, North America and elsewhere (see Chapter 2 Appendix).

The testimony of children and young people themselves can be glimpsed here and there in some of these nineteenth-century sources. Chambers' 'puerile rhymes' section contains an example said to have been 'scrawled and bawled everywhere in Edinburgh, by the boys attending the High School' (1826: 296), where Chambers himself went to school some ten years or so previously. Nevertheless, it is adults' memories of their younger days which predominate in these works. As such, they may be coloured by nostalgia and filtering and, as the Opies point out, a tendency to focus on the dramatic rather than mundane games and 'the amusing quips and jeers, the significant calls and superstitions, which mean so much in the life of a ten-year-old at the time, but have been too ordinary to be filed in memory's archive' (1959: vii).

William Wells Newell's *Games and Songs of American Children* (1883, revised and enlarged in 1903) draws principally on adults' recollections but some of the items presented are children's street games which he had observed in New York City whilst a teacher there (McNeil 1988: 11). His collection includes game descriptions, grouped by thematic content, main activity and material object used, and associated verbal texts and melodies. A central figure in the founding of the American Folklore Society in 1888, Newell's study is notable for its academic approach. Despite his belief that the games were dying out, he included essays on the 'invention' (particularly with reference to pretend play) and the 'conservatism' of children. He also sought out and highlighted the existence of parallel versions of games and songs elsewhere and at different historical periods. This comparative approach was in keeping with contemporary folkloristic scholarship into the folktale, proverb, riddle and ballad but Newell's study was the first time it had been applied to games and rhymes (Withers 1963: v–vi). The Opies commend Newell on this scholarship (Opie and Opie 1969: viii) and adopted the same technique themselves in much of their work.

In 1888, Henry Bolton, another founding member of the American Folklore Society and a chemist by profession, published an extensive collection of counting-out rhymes amassed from texts sent him by adult correspondents. Bolton adopted a survivalist approach to the 877 rhymes he amassed, seeking to relate them all to ancient forms of divination by lots (McNeil 1988: 14). The theory of survivals in culture was posited by the British anthropologist, E. B. Tylor, in his highly influential book *Primitive Culture* (1871).

This approach is also prominent in the landmark publication of Alice Bertha Gomme (1853–1938), *The Traditional Games of England, Scotland, and Ireland*, which appeared in two volumes (1894, 1898) and was intended as the first part of a dictionary of English folklore proposed but never brought to fruition by her husband, George Laurence Gomme. Based on information from 76 correspondents, relating to 112 locations, it contains detailed descriptions of around eight hundred games and their variants (Boyes 1990), divided into 'descriptive games' and 'singing or choral games' (1894: ix). Gomme has been criticized for relying too much on the memories of adult middle-class correspondents but she also drew on the observation and testimony of some children, including working-class children (Boyes 1990).

Gomme's adoption of a cultural evolutionist approach led her to search for parallels between Victorian children's games and rhymes and the rituals and beliefs of peoples regarded as being at the earlier, 'primitive' stage of civilization. These parallels were taken as evidence of the origins of the games which, according to the theory of survivals, had long outlived their original context but which could be 'read' in such as way as to reconstruct that context:

> Children do not invent, but they imitate or mimic very largely, and in many of these games we have, there is little doubt, unconscious folk-dramas of events and customs which were at one time being enacted as a part of the serious concerns of life before the eyes of children many generations ago.
>
> (Gomme 1894: ix)

Thus, Gomme sees in the singing game 'London Bridge is Falling Down' the remnants of the custom of foundation sacrifice (Gomme 1898: 501).

When Tylor's theory was discredited, Gomme's work became discredited too. Boyes, however, argues that she nonetheless produced 'the first major theoretical work by a woman folklorist' (Boyes 2001) and, as the Opies note, Gomme's descriptions are still valuable even if her theorizing is outmoded (1969: vii–viii). Her publication became the standard work for the next generation of researchers into play and it also gives extended attention to the distinctive game preferences of girls, particularly the 'singing game' (Gomme 1894/1898; Opie and Opie 1985).

Contemporary with Alice Gomme's work was a very different piece of research, focusing on a single place, a fishing village and seaside resort in northern Scotland on the east coast of Sutherland. Collated and edited by Edward W. B. Nicholson, the then Librarian of the Bodleian Library in Oxford, the contents of *Golspie: Contributions to its Folklore* were collected by seven children, aged between 12 and 15 (Nicholson 1897: 331), all named on the book's title page. Nicholson had been holidaying in Golspie when he saw children at school playing. He decided to instigate an essay-writing competition for which he offered a prize of a book and cash (Nicholson 1897: 2–3). The children were given a set of topics to cover, including local stories, songs, sayings, customs and superstitions, but also games and rhymes.

Nicholson drew on Gomme's work to annotate the children's examples and urged the Folklore Society to initiate collecting in every location in the UK, particularly by means of young people (1897: 7). His engagement of young people as researchers not only seems to anticipate the approach adopted by the Opies some sixty years later, it also provided them with a rare opportunity to follow up on this research. Thus, in 1952–53, the Opies gave the same questionnaire to pupils at Golspie Senior Secondary School and asked them about the items that their predecessors had noted (1959: vii).[3]

Twentieth-century scholarship

Not surprisingly, Gomme's work continued to be both a stimulus and reference point in much early twentieth-century play research (see Chapter 2 Appendix). Maclagan's *Games and Diversions of Argyleshire* (1901) focuses on 'pastimes found in use in Argyleshire *at the present day*' (1901: vi, emphasis added), suggesting that Maclagan's co-researchers noted items from their observation of, and perhaps interaction with, contemporary children. Memories of adults regarding their play are also included. Maclagan refers the reader to Gomme's work for further analogues (Maclagan 1901: vi).

Meanwhile, English folksong collectors, alerted to the importance of singing games through Gomme's work, also began to collect them, mainly from young people. Sharp and Gomme collaborated on a series of popular singing game publications together (1909–12) whilst Kidson, Gilchrist and

Gillington each published collections of this genre in the 1910s. In Wales, William George instigated a competition at the National Eisteddfod in 1911 'to do for Wales what the Alice Gomme collection has done for England' (quoted in Bishop and Curtis 2001: 5). Later, in the early 1930s, the American folksong scholar James Madison Carpenter became the first to make sound recordings of children's singing games in Britain. He recorded approximately fifty singing games in England and Scotland using the Dictaphone cylinder machine. These were mostly recorded from adults but there are six from 'Lincolnshire children singers'.[4]

It was, however, a slender volume entitled *London Street Games* (Douglas 1916) and partly pitched as a critical response to Gomme's work, that anticipated the direction of much play research since the Second World War and, in some cases, helped to inspire it. *London Street Games* is based entirely on the testimony of children, documented by means of 'scores of letters' (Bock 1993/2010) written for Norman Douglas, the book's compiler, by lower-class children. Douglas encountered these children playing on the streets in various parts of London, including Finsbury, Hackney, Islington, Whitechapel, Stepney, Limehouse, Poplar, Shoreditch, Bethnal Green, Deptford, Camberwell, Kennington, Bermondsey, Rotherhithe, and Shadwell (Douglas 1931: ix).

Douglas was a writer, most famous for his novel *South Wind* published in 1917. His one and only foray into children's games research was published first in 1913 as 'In Our Alley' in *The English Review*, a literary magazine of which he was also editor at the time (Mullin 2005). *London Street Games* was a longer version of this, published in book form in 1916 and reprinted in 1931 with a preface and index by Douglas. The preface gives an insight into Douglas's collecting methods:

> The following pages [were] published in 1916 . . . and I might have continued to note down Street Games till Doomsday, and compiled a veritable Corpus of them, but for the fact that, owing to other occupations, it became increasingly difficult to find the necessary time. Time! It required time, days and weeks, to stalk these children and win their confidence. Whoever doubts this – let him try.
>
> (1931: ix)

What Douglas does not mention is that, in the same year, he was charged with the sexual assault of a 16-year-old boy, followed some months later by two further offences involving boys aged 10 and 12. He jumped bail and left the country, subsequently living in various parts of Europe where he continued to write, as well as causing further controversy in his personal life as well as his written works (Mullin 2005). The specific circumstances under which Douglas obtained the game descriptions from the children have yet to be established but these contemporary events make *London Street Games* a problematic source.

Douglas claims that he intended to produce 'a social document' (1931: x) and the book consists largely of verbatim quotations from his child correspondents with connecting comments by him addressed to the reader in conversational style. The book has been criticized for being difficult to understand (e.g. Opie and Opie 1959: v).

The anti-academic stance adopted by Douglas is directed at Alice Gomme, of whom he is openly critical. Referring to her as 'Aunt Eliza', he remarks on her ability to 'explain everything', satirizing and dismissing her survivalist interpretations in startlingly misogynistic terms:

> Then she says that *Here we come gathering nuts in May* is a relic of 'Marriage by Capture', and some more stuff of that kind. No doubt; no doubt. Aunt Eliza thinks a good deal about Marriage by Capture – to judge by her talk, at least. Nobody ever tried to capture *her*, you know. And nobody ever will, I don't think.
>
> (Douglas 1916: 88)

By contrast, Douglas's stance was to avoid intellectualizing about the games and to demonstrate the inventiveness of the children (Douglas 1931: x). A recurrent theme in the book is the way in which children have to improvize when they do not have game equipment to hand:

> There's a difficulty about ball-games, which is this: that most of them generally need a ball; meaning you can't play with a ball unless you have a ball to play with. And you generally haven't got one – meaning the children. And then the trouble begins. Because then you have to start thinking about something that doesn't need a ball.
>
> Somebody or other may have a top . . .
>
> . . . And if you have not tops, you can make up games with your caps or boots or jackets . . .
>
> . . . And if you have no caps, which you sometimes haven't, you must just find something else to play with. Buttons, for instance . . .
>
> . . . But some of the best sports are those which they make up without anything at all, just out of their heads.
>
> (Douglas 1916: 4, 5, 6, 10)

Douglas thus emphasizes the way in which children's play is responsive to their immediate circumstances. In particular, he seems to adumbrate a practice which is characterized in play research today as 'bricolage' (Lichman 2001; Willett *et al.* 2013), in which children draw on whatever physical and cultural resources are available to them to orchestrate their play, especially resources not intended for such purposes. We will return to this point below.

Whilst the methods underlying Douglas's research raise significant ethical and social issues, his book is prophetic of future directions in the study of children's play. These include a focus on play in the urban environment and the dialectical relationship between play and environmental, material and cultural resources. Douglas also gives prominence to children's voices and the description of play from the perspective of those who are involved in it. We now turn to collectors active during and after the Second World War to trace these and other new directions further.

Play research from the Second World War and beyond

Play research in Britain in the interwar years was sparse, but notable projects were taking place elsewhere. One of these was the Schools' Folklore Scheme of 1937–38 in which around 100,000 children in some five thousand primary schools in Ireland collected folklore in their local communities over an eighteen-month period.[5] These young researchers primarily noted information, including 'old games', from older members of the community. In the same year, Harrisson, Madge and Jennings initiated 'Mass Observation', in which volunteers from all over Britain recorded their everyday life in diaries and in response to questionnaires.[6] The project continued into the early 1950s and was revived in the 1980s. Iona and Peter Opie later drew on 'reports prepared by Mass-Observation's panel of voluntary observers' (Opie and Opie 1959: xv).

Meanwhile, in the US, Dorothy Howard (1902–96), a teacher and educationist, was undertaking fieldwork for her doctorate 'Folk Jingles of American Children: A Collection and Study of Rhymes used by Children Today', which she completed in 1938 for the School of Education at New York University (Factor 2005). According to Factor, 'Howard may well have been the first person in the English-speaking world to gain a doctorate . . . for a study of contemporary children's "folk jingles"' (2005: 2). She went on to make the first in-depth survey of children's playlore in Australia in 1954–55 (Factor 2005). The Opies later corresponded with Howard and paid tribute to her as 'one of the originators of this field of study, who not only sent us her great thesis . . . the fruit of seven years' collecting in the 1930s, but a quantity of her subsequent collecting both in Maryland and in Australia' (1959: xvi).

In the period after the Second World War, a new generation of British researchers into children's play took to the field. Among these was Britain's first teacher–collector, Dr James T. R. Ritchie (1908–98). Ritchie was a science teacher at Norton Park School, a junior secondary school on the Edinburgh–Leith border. He was also a poet and an ardent advocate of Scottish language and culture (Bishop 2011). Already familiar with the work of Chambers and Douglas, he became aware that his own students were living exponents of games and songs in their native Scots. Ritchie began to note these down and got the students to do likewise (Bishop 2011). This resulted in several radio broadcasts for the Scottish Home Service from the late 1940s, a pioneering film entitled *The Singing Street*, made with fellow school teachers Raymond Townsend and Nigel McIsaac in 1951, and Ritchie's books *The Singing Street* (1964) and *Golden City* (1965), which focus on play and games in the street and the back-green respectively.[7] The film attracted the attention of the Opies who were just embarking on their research into school-aged children's folklore. Peter Opie wrote to Ritchie expressing their interest but Ritchie preferred to continue his work independently of contemporary researchers into children's play.[8]

This is in contrast with Father Damian Webb (1918–90), a Catholic priest of the Benedictine Order, whose interest in children's games and songs grew out of his work, his talents as an amateur photographer and his love of travel (Brumfield 2011). He first documented children playing singing games whilst on a holiday in Portugal in the early 1950s, going on to photograph and tape-record children's games and songs in various parts of northern England, Scotland and Ireland as well as other parts of Europe and Kenya during the 1960s to 1980s (Webb 1984).[9] This resulted in an extensive collection of recordings, including thirty-six made in Britain, and high-quality photographs.[10] Webb became acquainted with the Opies in the early 1960s, and provided photographs for all of their joint publications except *The Lore and Language of Schoolchildren* (Brumfield 2011). The Opies also drew on his notes and recordings for *The Singing Game* (1985).

Brian Sutton-Smith (1924–) was a teacher who became interested in children's play and games in his native New Zealand, gaining a PhD thesis on the subject in 1954. He later emigrated to the United States, where he has spent a lifetime researching into the play of children and adults, emerging as the foremost theorist in this area of study. His work has been characterized by an interdisciplinary approach, particularly located within psychology but also folklore studies, anthropology and sociology. He lectured to the Folklore Society in Britain and met Peter and Iona Opie with whom he became friends, as he later recalled:

> On the 1952 visit, I also met and befriended the great folklorist Peter Opie in a London pub, and we both declared we would write our next book on games. Eventually we both did so, but the difference was this: *The Lore and Language of Schoolchildren*, which Peter and his wife Iona published in 1959, caused a great stir especially among those interested in worldwide communication theory; my book, *The Games of New Zealand Children*, published by the University

of California–Berkeley Press, also in 1959, landed with a resounding thud in the academic remainder bin.

(Sutton-Smith 2008: 88–9)

It is to the Opies' lives and work that we now turn.

Iona (1923–) and Peter (1918–82) Opie

Iona describes Peter and herself as 'children of Empire' (1988: 203).[11] Peter was born in Egypt, where his father was serving as an army doctor before being posted to India. Educated at Eton College, Peter joined the army at the start of the Second World War but was invalided out in 1941. After a number of jobs, including working for the BBC and for a publisher, he became a full-time writer.

Iona was born in Colchester, Essex, the daughter of an expert in tropical diseases who worked in Africa. She went to Sandecotes School, Parkstone, and later joined the meteorological section of the Women's Auxiliary Air Force. They met and became friends after Iona, on reading his youthful autobiography, *I Want to Be a Success*, had written to him and they struck up a correspondence with each other. They married in 1943 and had their first child, James, the following year. Soon after, the London publishing company for whom Peter was working moved to Bedfordshire to escape the bombs and the Opie family followed. It was here, during a walk, that the future direction of their lives was 'decided by a ladybird':

> Idly one of us picked it up, put it on his finger . . . and said to it: 'Ladybird, ladybird, fly away home,/Your house is on fire and your children all gone.' The ladybird obeyed, as they always do – and yet it always seems like magic; and we were left wondering about this rhyme we had known since childhood and had never questioned until now. What did it mean? Where did it come from? Who wrote it?
>
> (Opie 1988: 208)

Their search for answers to these questions led them first to Halliwell's *Nursery Rhymes of England* and thence to the British Library, resulting in 'a treasure hunt which was to last forty years' (Opie 1988: 208).

Peter had been writing since he was a child. A later autobiographical work, *The Case of Being a Young Man*, published in 1946, won a literary award and the prize money allowed Peter to devote himself to writing. With the help of her mother-in-law, Iona juggled childcare and acting as Peter's research assistant. The first fruits of their labour was *I Saw Esau*, a 'pocketbook' of schoolchildren's chants and rhymes, published in 1947, the same year as their second child, Robert, was born.

Meanwhile, they were involved in the larger project of compiling a definitive dictionary of nursery rhymes which traced their histories and described the variant forms in which they had been found. At Peter's suggestion, Iona joined the Folklore Society, with Peter attending meetings as her guest (1988: 209). They also began to buy children's books at this time, gradually building up what became the largest privately held collection of children's books. At work in the Bodleian Library, Oxford, they were noticed by Richard Hunt, the Keeper of Western Manuscripts. Through him, they were introduced to Oxford University Press who went on to publish all of the Opies' major works, beginning with the *Oxford Dictionary of Nursery Rhymes* in 1951, which was an instant success. It was followed by *The Oxford Nursery Rhyme Book* (1955) and *The Puffin Book of Nursery Rhymes* (1963).

Of that time, Iona later wrote:

> We could see the road ahead almost too plainly. We knew, by now, that there were rhymes that belonged to older children – rhymes that were not passed from adult to child, but from child to child. We had been sent such rhymes by correspondents who remembered them from their childhood. However, we decided that instead of gathering these schoolchild rhymes from people who could remember them only imperfectly from many years before, we would go to the people who were using the rhymes in the present day – the schoolchildren themselves.
>
> (1988: 213)

Thus, the Opies turned in earnest to children's own lore and play and took on the role of empirical researchers as well as historical and comparative ones. A letter to the *Sunday Times*, published on 6 November 1951, asking for information, resulted in a plethora of responses including 151 from teachers offering to get information from children in their own schools and to contact colleagues elsewhere (Opie and Opie 1997: v; Opie 2001: x). The Opies' aim was to obtain material from children aged 7–11 years, particularly those aged 8–9, and from a reasonably even distribution of places in Britain, in both rural and urban locations (2001: x), although a study of the demographics of the schools that were involved has yet to be undertaken. For their first book, they were in touch with approximately five thousand children at seventy different schools (1959: vii). Their next publication added a further 112 schools and another five thousand children (Opie and Opie 1969: v–vi). Iona Opie later estimated that, over a period of some thirty years (*c*.1950–80), they were in touch with about 20,000 children, although this was still only a tenth of the children in the 8–10 age group in 1960 (Opie 2001: xi). These contributions were supplemented by the network that the Opies built up of friends, family (including, as time went on, their own children, James, Robert and Letitia), and other correspondents.

The Opies' methods

The Opies' intention was to build up a synchronic view of children's play throughout Britain (Opie and Opie 1959: viii; Opie 1989: 60). The survey approach was the obvious way to gain this breadth and there was precedent for the use of questionnaires in earlier studies by folklorists as well as in such contemporary related research as Mass Observation, mentioned above, and dialect studies:[12]

> Our innovation was to collect children's folklore directly from chil-
> dren, in their own words and on a national scale, either by direct
> communication or through informal questionnaires that suggested
> topics and invited opinions rather than requiring answers of 'Yes' or
> 'No' or lists, or descriptions of named games (which might not be
> known under that name locally).
>
> (Opie 1989: 60)

The Opies' initial questionnaires went through several different versions. The first is entitled 'The Oral Lore of School Children' and explains the aims of the survey and the kinds of material they wished to document. The Opies stress that they are 'not merely making a collection of oral lore, but studying its transmission, distribution, age, origins, and implications to the child himself'. They also give advice on how to administer the questionnaire, with either the teacher writing down the children's oral responses or the children writing them down themselves. It is aimed at children aged about 7 to 14. The questions cover skipping, ball games, counting out rhymes, singing games, other rhymes, jokes, tricks and conundrums, and crazes, as well as words and sayings.

A 'supplement' to the first questionnaire was also distributed during the 1950s.[13] This requests information on further and more specific games and areas of language, custom and belief. In the preamble, the Opies comment;

> there appears to be almost as much knowledge of traditional matter
> as there ever was, although the emphasis, particularly in children's
> play, seems to have shifted in the past half century. Some of the
> expressions and rhymes sent in have clearly been of post-war inven-
> tion (mentioning pre-fabs, nylons, flying saucers, the Skylon, etc.),
> while other games, customs and terms, which children have written
> down, are known to be old, and had, sometimes, been thought to be
> obsolete.[14]

In what appears to be a telling shift from the first questionnaire, the Opies tactfully state that 'the most satisfactory results have usually been obtained when each child in the class wrote down his replies himself'. They also suggest asking children to write essays on 'my favourite game in the playground (or round about my home)', customs, and magic and fortune-telling.

Following the publication of their first book on children's play, *The Lore and Language of Schoolchildren* (1959), based on the responses to their first surveys, the Opies devised a new questionnaire to collect further information towards their next publication which focused on street and playground games played without the use of play equipment.[15] The questionnaires and the children's responses to them, together with the correspondence with the relevant teachers, were deposited at the Bodleian Libraries in the 1990s by Iona Opie, where they form part of the Opie Working Papers, and the material on custom and belief was deposited in the Folklore Society Archives.[16]

Iona also did fieldwork, sometimes in the company of fellow play researchers such as Damian Webb. From 1969–83, she made tape recordings of children from around the country performing songs and singing games, and talking about their play (Jopson *et al.* in press).[17] These recordings were made in schools, council estates, and country villages around the country, including the Southwest, Welsh borders, Midlands, the Northwest, Yorkshire, Scotland and London. This work was an attempt to round out the geographical spread of their research and helped to reinforce the impression that cities were as rich in material as the countryside (Opie 1988: 213).

Iona also made regular visits to the primary school in Liss, Hampshire, where the Opie family had settled. Here she made notes on her observations over some years, a portion of which she published in 1993 as *The People in the Playground* (see Burn and Richards (in press) for a discussion of Iona Opie's methodological approach). The Opies compiled, compared and annotated their data at their home by virtue of a spartan lifestyle imposed by Peter. They were meticulous in gaining clarification of the children's responses where needed, writing back to the teacher or child in question to request these, or visiting the school themselves.

Aware of the immense task they had set themselves, they aimed not only to complete each book but to make it a classic in order to have sufficient income while they produced the next book. They received no grant funding and would not accept publishers' advances (Opie 1989: 57). They conducted their work in adjoining offices in the manner of a small business, Iona as clerk and Peter as manager or, in the academic model, as research assistant and principal investigator respectively:

> During the years in which we were engaged in our surveys of schoolchildren, the first job was to open any packages of material and to write to acknowledge their safe arrival. We each had our own correspondents, who became valued personal friends. I would then

> take through to Peter the next section of whatever book we were
> writing – the next game, perhaps, consisting of 30 or more sheets of
> notes in chronological order, with outline explanations. While he
> wrote that section, which might take days or weeks, I continued to
> analyse and file the material, to back it up with further reading, to
> write in more detail to the head teachers taking part in the survey, or
> to individual children, to transcribe tapes, and to fend off visitors.
> When he had done his best with a piece, he brought it through to me
> for written comment, and then I handed it back to him. Only after he
> had considered all my suggestions and objections and had adjusted
> the piece accordingly, did we discuss it face to face, which meant, in
> fact, resolving those points on which we did not agree. If neither of us
> would give way, we had an arbiter – Doreen Gullen, then on the staff
> of the Scottish Educational Supplement, without whose help, I am
> convinced, none of our books would ever have seen the light of day.
>
> (Opie 1989: 57)

By means of this process, they gradually produced their books, beginning
with *The Lore and Language of Schoolchildren* in 1959, followed by *Children's
Games in Street and Playground* in 1969. These contain a careful distillation of the
data, illustrated with representative examples sifted out from the mass of
material they had collected. During this same period, Peter's role in the Folklore
Society expanded and he served on the council during the years 1951–69 and as
President in 1963–64. He was also President of the anthropology section of the
British Association in 1962–63 and did occasional talks and radio broadcasts.

While they were working on their third play volume, concerning singing
games, Peter's health began to fail and, in 1982, he died of a heart attack.
Despite having to cope with the loss of Peter, and the lack of his input in the
final stages of the book, Iona brought *The Singing Game* to completion in 1985
and continued to work on the final volume they had planned, *Children's Games
with Things* (1997), 'really just as a joke . . . to astonish Peter's obituarists' (Opie
and Opie 1997: vi). Iona also wrote a number of articles about the work of 'the
Opies' following Peter's death (1988, 1989) and continued to visit the school
playground at Liss. After Peter's death, Iona gave their collection of children's
literature to the Bodleian Library. This collection included 'juvenile books on
games,' which the Opies were the first to explore systematically when writing
the history of the games and texts in their works on play (1969: viii).

The legacy of the Opies

The results of the Opies' research were published in their five books on
children's play – four joint volumes (Opie and Opie 1959, 1969, 1985, 1997),

the last two of these being brought to fruition by Iona, and one solo volume by Iona (Opie 1993). Although a rigorous comparison of their archival collection with their books has yet to be undertaken, it is clear that there were many areas on which they amassed information but did not publish. Their books cover games and forms of play with either historical antecedents or widespread contemporary popularity. Overall, the books were well received, not only in academic circles but with a general readership as well, and they have become classics in the field, remaining in print for long periods. There is not space here to undertake an evaluation of each of their books. Instead, we focus on their contributions to the field in three areas:

- children and children's culture;
- continuity and change in play, games and texts; and
- the influence of contemporary media on children's play, games and texts.

Children and children's culture

In their books, the Opies combine their position as adults and as anthropological, historical and comparative folklorists with the perspectives of the many children from whom they had received information and who were participants in the very culture that the books set out to describe. In drawing on this 'insider knowledge' as well as their own scholarly perspective, they sought to document the everyday culture of children, with attention to the ordinary and often overlooked (by adults) aspects, and without romanticizing it or becoming nostalgic about it. Many view them as having achieved this successfully. Warner observes that their first book is:

> remarkably poised, brimful of genuine, vibrant affection for the children, but empty of melancholic comparison with adult destinies, of compensatory yearning for children's 'savage energies' or 'ecstatic tribal innocence,' their supposed liberty and anarchy.
>
> (Warner 2001: xi)[18]

In portraying the culture of children, and peer transmission among them, they have been aligned with a notion of the 'tribal child' (James *et al.* 1998: 214), the study of childhood as a separate and distinct sphere from the adult world. This, perhaps, is not surprising when one reads the rather startling statement in *The Language and Lore of Schoolchildren*:

> And the folklorist and anthropologist can, without travelling a mile from his door, examine a thriving unselfconscious culture . . . which is as unnoticed by the sophisticated world, and quite as

little affected by it, as is the culture of some dwindling aboriginal tribe living out its helpless existence in the hinterland of a native reserve.

(Opie and Opie 1959: 2)

However, placing this comment within the scope of the Opies' work as a whole, we would suggest that it is not wholly representative of their overall assessment of play and childlore. Indeed, throughout their work, they are at great pains to indicate how children are affected by the wider world, accounting for the way in which media permeates children's games and rhymes, as is discussed in Chapter 3. Nevertheless, there is undoubtedly a notion that the child and adult worlds are somewhat divided in the Opies' work and, as Warner argues, 'the Opies probably overestimate this division, since transmission of all kinds takes place between grownups and youngsters' (2001: x). However, she makes the important point that this 'does no harm to the matter or the spirit of their enterprise; it rather brightens the focus on children themselves' (2001: x). We would argue that this aspect of the Opies' work needs to be placed within the context in which they were working. In the mid-twentieth century, the voice of the child was largely absent from stories of their everyday lives and the Opies' work is notable for its recognition of the significance of the direct accounts of children. As James *et al.* suggest (1998: 215), work such as this 'is not part of a supportive social pyramid constructed in the worship of the rational adult world' and, in this regard, is an important precursor to more recent developments in the recognition of the agency of children.

Continuity and change

Underlying the Opies' work was a fascination with continuity and change, the endurance of certain forms and texts of play, and their adaptation. We suggest that it is important to understand the views they expressed in relationship to the scholarship of their predecessors. In their first book, for example, they emphasize the high level of continuity that they have observed, characterizing children as preservers (Opie and Opie 1959: 12), 'respecters, even venerators, of custom' in whose 'self-contained community their basic lore and language seems scarcely to alter from generation to generation' (Opie and Opie 1959: 2). They nevertheless acknowledge that 'oral lore is subject to a continual process of wear and repair, for folklore, like everything else in nature, must adapt itself to new conditions if it is to survive' (Opie and Opie 1959: 9). They thus stress the dynamism of folklore even though this leads them to write of it in super-organic terms that do not acknowledge the agency of children, which the Opies so emphatically champion in other ways. It suggests, however, that they have in mind a macro view of folkloric change, what we might nowadays term the sedimentation of certain texts and practices over time and space, and they give examples of 'updating' at the level of text (by the substitution of certain words), in object used (substitution of cigarette cards by milk bottle top 'flying saucers'), in the timing of calendar customs (Halloween bonfires taking place on 5th November) and in function, illustrating this last through a playground rhyme taken from an eighteenth-century ballad, which has been used for counting out, skipping, and as a nursery rhyme, with concomitant textual changes (Opie and Opie 1959: 9–11). They likewise chart changes in game rules and preferences in their second book (Opie and Opie 1969: 8–10).

The point to note here is that their reference to folklore's survival in the dictum quoted above can be read as a response to Gomme's survivalist study. Indeed, the wording of the Opies' statement in 1959 anticipates their second book on play, in which they characterize Gomme's approach to her collectanea thus: 'They were examined as if they were archaeological remains, rather than living organisms which are constantly evolving, adapting to new situations, and renewing themselves or being replaced' (Opie and Opie 1969: vii–viii). The Opies' emphasis on continuity and children as 'preservers' allows them to account for the persistence of certain texts and forms over long periods of time, as found by Gomme, whilst their emphasis on adaptation to new circumstances enables the Opies to counter Gomme's survivalist approach and stress the function of these texts and forms for contemporary children.

Despite their acknowledgement of the changes introduced by children in their play and texts, the Opies are consistent in their view that these do not constitute children's creativity or inventiveness (Opie and Opie 1959: 8, 12; 1993: 3). Variations, especially textual ones, are viewed as occurring 'more often by accident than design' (Opie and Opie 1959: 8), as 'hopeful experiments, and minor games which last no more than a day, or at the most a few weeks' (Opie 1993: 12) and as due to mishearing, misunderstanding, rationalization, and abridgement (Opie and Opie 1959: 8–9). These remarks need to be seen in the light of the Opies' concern to understand the sources of children's songs and rhymes. They are a reaction to the recurrent claim among children that they have 'made up' these songs and rhymes, and a result of the fact that the Opies never encountered evidence of children having been the ultimate creator of them (Opie and Opie 1959: 12). They continue, 'the unromantic truth . . . is that children do not "go on inventing games out of their heads all the time", as Norman Douglas believed; for the type of person who is a preserver is rarely also creative' (Opie and Opie 1959: 12). Instead, they suspect that earlier fashions of adult popular culture are the ultimate source of many of the rhymes and they draw attention to the fact that 'this process of children adopting or adapting popular songs for use in their games continues . . . in the present day' (Opie and Opie 1959: 14).[19] We would suggest that this process can be understood as bricolage (Lévi-Strauss 1966) and is comparable, although with different cultural resources, to that described by Douglas, as argued above.

Media influence

The influence of media is discussed in two interlinked ways in the Opies' published works, first in relation to the deleterious effect of media on children's propensity to play in general (Opie and Opie 1959: v) and secondly as a source of content and frame of reference for some of their games and texts (understood multimodally as potentially including words, music, gesture and other modes of kinetic communication and performance; cf. Bishop and Curtis 2006; Bishop and Burn, 2013). Wherever the media are invoked, such as in rhymes (those used for skipping, clapping and counting out, or chanted just for entertainment), jokes, gestures, catch phrases, nicknames, pretend play, physical play, and musical play, the Opies highlight and explain this as far as they can, an achievement not to be underestimated in the days before the internet and its associated resources for research into the minutiae of popular culture. Their detective work shows that children draw on such sources as advertising jingles, news reports, popular song and dance, talent shows and competitions, and drama (as portrayed in television and film). Their account of the publicity surrounding the release of the film *Davy Crockett, King of the Wild Frontier* in 1956 (Opie and Opie 1959: 118–20, described in more detail in Chapter 5) reveals that they were ready to document current events and use them as case studies to inform their views on the relationship between children's play and the media.

Their cognizance of media influences may stem from their suspicion that the origin of many rhymes may originate in the popular culture of yesteryear. On the whole, however, they concluded that much media-referenced play was relatively ephemeral and they opted to include it only where it could be shown to have lasted or to have taken the form of a widespread but temporary 'craze' (Opie and Opie 1959: 138; 1969: 340; 1985: 414–15, 445; 1997: 212–13). Yet, as Jopson *et al.* (in press) point out in relation to Iona Opies' tape-recorded fieldwork:

> the fundamental purpose of these interviews was to capture traditional singing games; not to document the children's popular media cultures. Nevertheless, the recordings demonstrate clearly that Iona Opie did take the time to capture, often in some detail, many instances in which children refer to their engagement with contemporary media.

The Opies' documentation of children's engagements with media are discussed in more detail in the ensuing chapters of this book.

Conclusion

The Opies' work on children's folklore successfully mapped out this field of study in the UK and became a reference point for others to draw on as they needed in their research. It is the case that, as a number of scholars have pointed out, the Opies did not pursue in much depth a more socially and culturally contextualized approach (Grugeon 1988; Boyes 1995), but it is hard to imagine how they could have done so and retained the geographical breadth and historical depth of their research. It is now up to others to supply this lacuna retrospectively. Meanwhile, the Opies' work continues to put the case for the importance of the historical view in studies of contemporary culture for, as Peter Opie observed, 'it is practically impossible to understand and evaluate the present if we are not familiar with the past' (1964: 75). In this sense, their work contributes fundamentally to the task we have set ourselves in this book and informs the chapters which follow.

Appendix
Chronology of the principal children's game and song collections prior to the publications of Iona and Peter Opie

1801	J. Strutt, *The Sports and Pastimes of the People of England* (also new edition by William Hone, 1830)
1826	R. Chambers, *Popular Rhymes of Scotland* (and later editions)
1842	J. O. Halliwell, *The Nursery Rhymes of England*
1849	J. O. Halliwell, *Popular Rhymes and Nursery Tales of England*
1857	E. L. Rochholz, *Allemannisches Kinderlied und Kinderspiel aus der Schweiz*
1879	F. Zimmer, *Volkstümliche Spiellieder und Liedespiele*
1883	G. Pitré, *Giuochi fanciulleschi siciliani*, in *Biblioteca delle tradizioni popolari siciliane* 13
1883	E. Rolland, *Rimes et jeux de l'enfance*
1883	William Wells Newell, *Games and Songs of American Children*
1888	Henry C. Bolton, *The Counting-Out Rhymes of Children*
1891	A. Kiss, *Magyar gyermekjátékgyüjtemény*
1891	W. Gregor, *Counting-out Rhymes of Children*
1894	Alice Bertha Gomme, *Children's Singing Games*
1894, 1898	Alice Bertha Gomme, *The Traditional Games of England, Scotland, and Ireland*, 2 vols
1895	E. A. Pokovskrij, *Dětskie igry*
1895	R. S. Culin, *Korean Games, with Notes on the Corresponding Games of China and Japan*
1896	E. T. Kristiansen, *Danske Börnerim, Remser og Lege*
1897	E. W. B. Nicholson, *Golspie: Contributions to Its Folklore*
1897	F. M. Böhme, *Deutsches Kinderlied und Kinderspiel*
c.1898	A. G. Gilchrist, MS collection of singing games
1899	B. Støylen, *Norske Barnerim og Leikar*
1899	R. S. Culin, 'Hawaiian Games', *American Anthropologist*
1900	R. S. Culin, 'Philippine Games', *American Anthropologist*
1901	R. C. Mclagan, *The Games and Diversions of Argyleshire*
1902–08	A. de Cock and I. Teirlinck, *Kinderspel en Kinderlust in Zuid-Nederland*
1907	R. S. Culin, *Games of the North American Indians*

1909–12	A. B. Gomme and C. J. Sharp, *Children's Singing Games*
1909	A. E. Gillington, *Old Isle of Wight Singing Games, Old Surrey Singing Games and Skipping Rope Rhymes, Old Hampshire Singing Games*
1913	A. E. Gillington, *Old Dorset Singing Games*
1915	'Notes on Children's Game-Songs by Annie G. Gilchrist and Lucy E. Broadwood', *Journal of the Folk-Song Society*
1916	F. Kidson, *One Hundred Singing Games, Old, New and Adapted*
1916	N. Douglas, *London Street Games*
1922	M. W. Beckwith, *Folk-Games of Jamaica*
1929–35	J. M. Carpenter Collection
1938	D. Howard, 'Folk jingles of American children' (Ed. D. thesis)
1946	H. Halpert, 'Folk rhymes of New York City children' (MA thesis)
1952	P. G. Brewster, 'Children's games and rhymes' in *The Frank C. Brown Collection of North Carolina Folklore*
1953	P. G. Brewster, *American Non-Singing Games*
1959	B. Sutton-Smith, *The Games of New Zealand Children*
1959	I. and P. Opie, *The Lore and Language of Schoolchildren*
1964	J. T. R. Ritchie, *The Singing Street*
1965	J. T. R. Ritchie, *Golden City*
1969	I. and P. Opie, *Children's Games in Street and Playground*
1985	I. and P. Opie, *The Singing Game*
1993	I. Opie, *The People in the Playground*
1997	I. and P. Opie, *Children's Games with Things*

3 Forms of play

> If a present-day schoolchild was wafted back to any previous century he would probably find himself more at home with the games being played than with any other social custom.
>
> (Opie and Opie 1969: 7)

The breadth and scale of the Opies' work, coupled with their interest in the historical trajectories of texts and forms of play, make it inevitable that it should be used as a baseline for comparison with play in the future. In this chapter, a selection of the data that were gathered at Monteney Primary School, one of the schools in the 'Playgrounds Project', is outlined and compared with the findings of the Opies. The aim is to gain a sense of changes and continuities in play from the time of the Opies' surveys (c.1950–80) to the present. Although the data were gathered under very different circumstances, over different lengths of time and using different methods, they are suggestive of trends whose validity can then be investigated in more depth by means of other studies from the last fifteen years or so, such as Roud (2010).

In order to facilitate comparison in this chapter, our data have been mapped onto the categories by which the Opies' publications are organized (see Chapter 3 Appendix). This shows at a glance the presence or otherwise of examples in the contemporary context at this particular school. It is important to note that the material in the Opies' published oeuvre is only a partial representation of the material that they amassed, both in terms of examples and the range of games evidenced. Furthermore, extensive though their collection is, it is, in turn, only a partial representation of children's play at the time of their research. Despite these caveats, some general patterns can be discerned with regard to continuity and change and examples of these are discussed below. Each of the Opies' publications are considered in turn and observations triangulated with the findings of other relevant research.

The Lore and Language of Schoolchildren (1959)

The verbal dimension of play and games was an important emphasis throughout the Opies' research and verbal play largely forms the focus of their first book relating to school-aged children's folklore. Verbal play, at least as encapsulated into texts, is particularly amenable to documentation via questionnaire and this data collection method also allowed the Opies to tap into children's wider knowledge of play as well as their current practices. By contrast, the fieldwork at Monteney was primarily based on observation and audio-visual recording of what the children were doing at the time and we only elicited information relating to lore and language when this was prompted by play that we had witnessed.

Nevertheless, examples of many of the genres described in *The Lore and Language of Schoolchildren* were documented. These included miniature forms like nicknames, such as 'Frankenstein' (Francesca), 'Earthling' (Ellie), and 'Emu' (Emily), and epithets for red-haired children, such as 'Gingerbread Man' (cf. Opie and Opie 1959: 170) and 'Ginger Ninja Turtle' (JB fieldnotes, 16.6.09), a neologism presumably inspired by the American animated television series *Teenage Mutant Ninja Turtles*. Interestingly, the key word 'ninja', which obviously lends itself to combination with the rhyming word 'ginger', was censored and replaced by the word 'hero' when the series was first shown in the UK (*c.* 1990), the word 'ninja' not being allowed until the 2003 television series. It may be significant that the earlier television series were released on dvd with the ninja branding in 2009, the year that our fieldwork commenced.[20]

The many forms of verbal one-upmanship that pervade the Opies' chapters on children's wit, repartee and guile were not very evident among our data from Monteney, although the mock threats to 'tell of' someone are directly paralleled among the Opies' examples (Opie and Opie 1959: 49). On the other hand, trick questions and punning riddles were told by both boys and girls and came from jokebooks and comics, as in the Opies' day (Opie 1993: 14), and a new source, the internet (JB fieldnotes, 21.1.10).

We encountered few 'jeers and torments' at Monteney, suggesting these are on the decrease in recent times, but this would need further investigation. Certainly, it is likely *a priori* that anti-bullying campaigns and different behaviour expected of both teachers and pupils have been effective in discouraging the use of this kind of lore (Warner 2001: xv). Likewise, we found, as did Roud (2010: 438), that examples of anti-school lore were almost completely absent, presumably reflecting a different atmosphere in schools, despite the fact that adult authority and adult-imposed structures are still very much present in this context (see Chapter 6). These may be challenged in other ways, such as via song parodies and risqué rhymes. The Year

6 girls who contributed the following examples said that they combined the classroom topic of the planets with SRE (sex and relationships education):

> Old MacDonald went to Saturn
> Then he went to Uranus
> All the children on earth
> Had sore bums for ages.

> Old MacDonald went to Mars
> Then he went to Venus
> A shooting star went up his arse
> And paralysed his penis.

(MPJB2010-05-26a00137)

It remains to be seen if the Opies collected anything as scatological as this but, as Iona Opie later made clear, publishers in the 1950s would not print anything more risqué than 'knickers' (Boyes 1995). Recent research has also found that parodic elements, often conveyed through movement and gesture, also occur in some of the children's performances of popular songs and dances (cf. Marsh 2008).

Finally, with regard to verbal play, the same Year 6 girls who contributed the scatological rhymes and a boy in their circle of friends also had a repertoire of ghost stories.[21] Some of these had been learnt from the previous Year 6 children. They included a number of legends relating to the school toilets and other sites in the school, including the Bloody Mary stories also found by Armitage (2006) (see Chapter 6). Several stories contain the motif of the disembodied voice of a ghost or monster getting closer and closer, including the well-known 'Johnny, I want my liver back', a story that Wilson dates back at least fifty years (1997: 109–18). The technique of building suspense through the disembodied voice drawing ever nearer is described by the Opies and noted in other ghost stories collected in the nineteenth century (1959: 36).

Children's Games in Street and Playground (1969)

Starting a game

The data from Monteney shows that there are a variety of methods used for handling the selection of who will first be 'it' or 'on' (both terms were used at Monteney, apparently interchangeably) prior to the game proper beginning. As the Opies note, the role of 'it' is often an unpopular one so that an array of strategies has developed by which children choose, ostensibly fairly, who will first take on the 'it' role (cf. Goldstein 1971; Arleo 1991; Roud 2010: 346–8). These can become a game in and of themselves. At Monteney, there was a full range of ways in which the children decided who would be 'it', from someone taking the role on voluntarily,[22] through verbal strategies and racing, to counting out. This included the direct verbal (and gestural) strategy nominating someone else ('Tig, you're on')[23] and relying on anticipation and quick reaction time once a game had been mooted. The strategy of verbally exempting oneself ('Bagsy not it'), noted as widespread by the Opies (1969: 18–19) and Roud (2010: 376) and found at the London school in The 'Playgrounds Project',[24] was not encountered at Monteney. The verbal strategy of nominating 'newcomer's it' (JB fieldnotes, 4.6.09), however, was used there and is paralleled in the Opies' description of the 'time-honoured precedent, [in which] the last person to arrive for the game finds himself welcomed with genuine warmth, for it is he who has to take the unwanted role', a custom which appears to have been known in the seventeenth century (Opie and Opie 1969: 19). A mini physical contest was another common strategy by which 'it' was decided at the time of the Opies' research, and this is paralleled in the 'last one to the red post is it' race preceding games of Tig under and around the canopy (see below) at Monteney (JB fieldnotes, 4.6.09), also found contemporaneously in Essex and London by Roud (2010: 341).

Despite the reduced amount of playtime during the school day that has occurred since the time of the Opies' research (see Chapter 6), there is clearly still felt to be time for 'dipping' or counting out at Monteney as a method of selection (cf. Opie and Opie 1969: 28–61). The data illustrate a diversity of methods and accompanying texts within this one school, although certain dips appear to have been preferred among specific friendship groups while others are in general use by the majority of children (cf. Curtis 2001). As in the verbal strategies, the choice may be made directly or by a process of elimination. Fingers, fists or feet are used in the counting out procedure in which the children cluster into a ring alongside the person doing the dipping.

Of the counting out games found at Monteney, 'Banana, banana, banana, Split' and 'Coconut, coconut, coconut, Crack' were frequently reported there[25] and appear to be among the best known of counting out texts in the UK (Roud 2010: 348–9, 356). Yet, they are newcomers to the repertoire since 1969 when the Opies' book was published and constitute a new departure in that they are rhythmic chants rather than a rhymed verse. Roud found that 'some children delight in making up other suitable words' (2010: 349) and we likewise encountered at least eight reworkings at Monteney, some clearly made up on the spot in response to our interest, and several with media-referenced content deriving from the Disney television channel. Each retained the basic syntactic pattern of three-fold repetition plus climactic beat but the rhythm of each is subtly different:

> Coconut coconut coconut Crack!
> Banana banana banana Split!
> Camp camp camp Rock![26]
> Handy handy handy Manny![27]
> Bubble bubble bubble Pop![28]

In terms of the accompanying movements, these counting out games are clearly related to those using fists noted by the Opies as widespread in Europe and found especially in conjunction with the 'One potato, two potato' rhyme in Britain and America (Opie and Opie 1969: 54).

'Black shoe, black shoe, Change your black shoe' was recorded at both the Sheffield and London schools in the 'Playgrounds Project'[29] and is also currently very widespread in the UK (Roud 2010: 349). Again, this seems to be a recent development as the Opies do not list the words among their 'most-used dips'. Curtis, doing fieldwork in the 1990s, only encountered this rhyme in three of the nine schools where she researched, although it was widely known among children at these three schools (2001: 74, 77). Writing in the 1960s, the Opies note that counting out players' feet is a popular, but not long-documented practice in England, although well known elsewhere, such as on the continent (Opie and Opie 1969: 56).

Of the remaining seven counting out games encountered at Monteney, all but one were current in the 1950s and '60s and there is evidence that most were already in circulation in the nineteenth century.[30] Two friends in Year 1, for example, Kate and Carl, each knew a slightly different version of 'Eeny meeny miney mo', very close to the text quoted by the Opies:

Kate (MPJB2009-10-08at00092)	Carl (MPJB2009-10-08at00092)	Opie and Opie (1969: 36)
Eeny, meeny, miney, mo	Eeny, meeny, miney, mo	Eeny, meeny, miney, mo
Drop the baby on the po	Put the baby on the po	Sit the baby on the po
Wipe the baby's bum	When it's done	When he's done
With some chewing gum	Wipe its bum	Wipe his bum
Eeny, meeny, miney mo.	Eeny, meeny, miney, mo.	Tell his mummy what he's done.
	You are it.	*Current since the nineteenth century*

Only two examples of a 'participation rhyme', in which players contribute elements to the game which appear to randomize the process still further, were found at Monteney. This involved counting out with fists using the following verse:

> Racing car, racing car, number nine
> How many dimes did you lose this time?

Seven.
1, 2, 3, 4, 5, 6, 7.[31]

The sequence of movements for each player's fists, coupled with the rhyme and the participatory element, made this one of the most complex counting out games documented at Monteney. It is a close parallel to the text quoted by the Opies:

> Engine, engine on the line
> Wasting petrol all the time
> How many gallons does it take
> Five, six, seven, or eight?
>
> (1969: 58, cf. 1969: 38)

Curtis found this rhyme in all nine schools involved in her fieldwork in West Yorkshire in the 1990s (2001: 74). It is also widely disseminated in America (Abrahams and Rankin 1980: no. 161) and the reference to 'dime' in the Monteney boys' version suggests an American influence or source for their version.

The other participation rhyme was:

> Little little monkey
> Ran across the country
> Fell down a dark hole
> Split his little arse hole
> What colour was his blood?
>
> . . . Somebody picks a colour and you need to go round and . . . if [they] say 'blue' I need to go B-L-U-E and if it landed on them, they weren't it.[32]

The Opies found variants of this rhyme all over the country, especially in Scotland where a text from Edinburgh was published in the early twentieth century (Opie and Opie 1969: 59).

Kate in Year 1, mentioned above, and her friends counted out with their fingers to the rhyme 'Put your cigarettes in, Yes or no, Let me hear you cough, sir (*player coughs*), Very nice indeed, sir!'[33] (also found in Belfast, 1996–97, see Lanclos 2003: 78). Although not a fully-fledged participation rhyme, in that the player's response does not affect the counting out, it has been found with additional lines, such as 'How many blankets do you need?' which transform it into a participation rhyme (Opie and Opie 1969: 59). The Opies point to a version printed by Robert Graves in 1926 (1969: 37) and the rhyme, in various iterations, has also been widely associated with ball-bouncing and stocking ball (cf. Opie and Opie 1997: 158–9; Roud 2010: 197–8).

Physical games without playthings

The categories of games discussed in the Opies' 1969 book are of two basic types, games with high physical content, without playthings, and games with high imaginative content. With regard to the former, we can see from the Chapter 3 Appendix below that at Monteney Primary School there were examples in all the categories except hunting games and exerting games. The absence of hunting games is fairly easily accounted for. They involve a team of players hiding from the seeking team but leaving clues as to their whereabouts and some of these take place over a large area whilst others are played after dark, so are not conducive to the context of the schoolyard. Exerting games, on the other hand, are those requiring above all stamina and strength. They include tug of war and 'Red Rover' as well as 'tussles' and chain swing. It is possible that these are less tolerated on the contemporary school playground due to school rules (see Chapter 6).

Chasing games

The names of 28 chasing games were noted at Monteney. Some of these refer to the same game by a different name (cf. Curtis 2001), such as 'Tiggy Target'[34] and 'Tiggy Pole'[35] (see below), but the proliferation of names is also indicative of slight variations between games which, in the children's eyes, makes them a distinct game even though adults may regard them as versions of the same game. Many of these games revolve around the strategy by which immunity from 'touch' or being 'tigged' can be gained, such as 'Tiggy Bob Down',[36] or the fact that there is no 'safe haven' ('Tiggy Anywhere').[37]

'Tiggy Frog', in which the children gain immunity from the chaser by stepping on a frog painted onto the tarmac of the playground, and 'Alien', in which the safe place was some steps, were played among the Key Stage 1 children. We see these two games as analogues of 'Tom Tiddler's Ground', which the Opies show has circulated widely in Europe and North America with earliest references going back to 1780 in Britain and possibly earlier on the continent (1969: 84–6).[38] As the Opies stress (1969: 84), the thrill of the game is in the quick dashes into the territory of the 'alien' (or however the person who is 'it' is personified), the deft footwork needed to step in and out without being caught, and the taunting of the 'alien'.[39]

The canopied areas in the back and front playgrounds of Monteney school are important sites of Tiggy games among the Key Stage 1 and Key Stage 2 children respectively and illustrate the relationship between play and the affordances of the space and structures where it is played. The canopied areas are demarcated by four poles of different colours (red, blue, green and yellow) to form a covered square. They give rise to four Tiggy games which are all subtly different and reflect the children's ingenuity with respect to their use of the same space (a fifth game is discussed in Chapter 7). The basic chase game conducted there is called 'Tiggy Pole' or 'Tiggy Target', in which the players can run anywhere and all the poles are safe havens.[40] In 'Tiggy Redpost' (Bluepost, etc.),[41] all the poles are safe but the players have to get to the pole of the designated colour. A further twist on the game is 'Colours' in which the player who is 'it' tells the others which colour pole to run to; again, they are immune at other poles but must make their way to the designated colour.[42] Still another form is 'If you like . . .' in which only certain players must go to the pole dictated by the chaser. The selection is done by joining the colour instruction to a conditional phrase, such as 'Run to blue if you like Sheffield Wednesday [football team]'.[43] The chaser chooses criteria such as 'liking' school, a particular pop star or other celebrity, or a particular fruit. Both the older and younger players had a rule which meant that they could assist another player to get to the designated pole by holding hands in a line, the person nearest the pole holding on to it in order to claim immunity for themselves and the others in the line which stretches out to the player in need and pulls them in or allows them to reach across to an adjacent pole. Not all the children had a name for this, but one name cited was 'connects'.[44]

The historical evidence for tig in Britain dates from the seventeenth century (Roud 2010: 16). The tig games involving these specific features of the playground landscape – the canopy and coloured poles at Monteney – are versions of 'Tiggy Touch Iron' (or Wood or Colour) which were mentioned throughout the nineteenth century, including in Sheffield in the 1880s (Opie and Opie 1969: 78–80; Addy, quoted in Roud 2010: 34). Unlike the Monteney canopy games, though, 'Tiggy Touch Wood' was not necessarily confined to a square playing area and in this sense the Monteney games are also related to another old game, namely, 'Puss in the Corner', which the Opies classify as a racing game (1969: 207–09). This involved five players, one being 'on' and each of the other four being positioned at a corner. In the older versions of the game, the players taunt the 'cat' in order to allow two players at adjacent corners to swap places without being caught. The earliest reference to the game cited by the Opies is 1688 and it has been widely reported ever since, not only in Britain but also North America (Opie and Opie 1969: 207–09; Roud 2010: 3–5). In fact, the children at Monteney were also playing this same game, but without reference to the 'puss'. They called it 'Four Square' or 'Squares',[45] a reference to the fact it was usually played on the number square marking painted onto the playground, located beside the canopy in the Key Stage 2 playground.

Duelling games

Duelling games are defined by the Opies as those in which 'two players place themselves in direct conflict with each other'. They were not frequently encountered during our fieldwork at Monteney but arm wrestling and 'Slaps', plus a rougher version of Slaps which at times resembled 'Knuckles' (Opie and Opie 1969: 223; Roud 2010: 124), were known and occasionally played, by boys and girls in the case of arm wrestling,[46] and by boys in Year 5 in the case of Slaps and Knuckles.[47] In the course of our fieldwork, a craze for thumb wrestling also occurred. This craze has been found elsewhere in the country in recent years (Roud 2010: 124) and was possibly prompted by the advent of the American children's television programme *Thumb Wrestling Federation*, a live-action series modelled on professional wrestling promotions. Launched in 2006, this programme was shown on BBC1, BBC2 and the young people's BBC channel, CBBC. Although thumb wrestling is a form not mentioned in the Opies' publications, it was certainly known at the time that they were collecting (Roud 2010: 124) and is recollected as being played in the US and Britain in the 1930s and 1940s, according to a number of newspaper sources.[48] Roud gives several variants of the second couplet of the verse, usually said when the opponent's thumb has been pinned down (2010: 124). The Monteney version is worded differently, however, with both couplets preceding the start of the duel:

> 1, 2, 3, 4
> I declare a thumb war
> 5, 6, 7, 8
> Who will win the thumb fight?[49]

It is notable that *eight* and *fight* have a distinctive pronunciation in Sheffield dialect, with *eight* as /ɛɪt/ and *fight* as /fɛɪt/ (cf. Opie and Opie 1959: 197). This enables them to rhyme. The Monteney pronunciations are confirmed by evidence in the *Survey of English Dialects* (Orton *et al.* 1962–71).[50]

Daring games

Early on in our fieldwork at Monteney, two girls related to Julia that they were playing 'Truth or Dare':

> Angela and Maddy [in Year 4] tell me that they are playing Truth or Dare . . . Angela has dared Maddy to 'kiss the tree'. If someone won't do the dare, the other one says something that's not really true about them. She won't kiss the tree so Angela tells me that Maddy has got diarrhoea which Maddy then denies. Maddy tells me that you can say to someone 'Have you got five boyfriends?' and they have to answer. Angela then proceeds to tell me that she has three boyfriends and names them all.
>
> (JB fieldnotes, 26.6.09)

The game, which is principally played by girls at Monteney, can also be orchestrated within a larger group, as one Year 6 girl explained:

> *If we just want to, like, relax at breaks, we go to the benches, and . . . we play Dares there and we tell jokes and secrets and stories . . . and, well, it's, like, the person that's getting dared, they have to stay, like, quite far away from you so you don't hear. And then everyone else decides on a dare together. And then they get told and then if they don't do the dare what we told them to do, then they get a forfeit. And they either have to do the dare or the forfeit or they're out.[51]*

The kind of forfeit levied is to be called 'Chicken' for the rest of the day (cf. Opie and Opie 1969: 270–2).

This game was widespread during the time that the Opies were conducting their surveys and may entail more alternatives, such as 'truth, dare, promise, or opinion' or 'truth, dare, warning, love, kiss, or marriage' (1969: 264–6). The game appears to have its antecedents in such games as 'Questions and Commands' and 'King I Am', played by children, young people and adults, with obvious potential for more risqué suggestions (Opie and Opie 1969: 266–7; Roud 2010: 104). The same potential is reflected in recently developed smartphone and android Truth or Dare apps.

Physical skills and space-specific physical play

We added two further categories to our own classification – space-specific physical games, such as those using a particular feature of the playground or marking, and physical skills – which were not covered in the Opies' books. Physical skills were usually practised on an individual basis and involved gymnastic feats, such as cartwheels, headstands and 'the crab'.[52] Others involved picking each other up (although this was said to be 'not allowed')[53] and rolling down the slopes which flanked the grass play area at two points.

Physical skills also included handstands, practised by individuals but also developed among the Year 5 and 6 children into a competitive group game. It was played by both boys and girls but the girls were more numerous and more skilled at it. Played on the grass banks, the leader stood at the top of the slope and those doing the handstands in a row along the bottom, facing the leader. By means of a rhyme, the players were cued by the leader to perform a handstand at the same time. The one observed by the leader to stay up for the longest then took over as leader. In order to synchronize those doing the handstands, the leader sometimes counted them in, saying '3-2-1', but more often drew on a repertoire of verses associated with the handstand competitions. One of these took the form of a call-and-response pattern, sung with a strongly defined rhythm and associated gestures:

(Leader) I am the strongest (*jumping up and down, flexing alternately right then left arms*)

(Others) Not for the longest (*shake index finger from side to side*)
Under, over (*clap under lifted leg, clap over while putting it down again*)
Pepsi Cola (*rolling hands*)
Un deux trois (*first hand up by head, second hand up, followed by handstand*).[54]

In the event of a tie, the players who had tied shouted out 'Un, deux, trois' again and did a further handstand to decide who should win.

Another chant was performed by all the players simultaneously:

Salt pepper (*salt cellar twisting movement*)
Scooby dooby doo (*crossing arms one at a time over chest*)
The boys go (*kiss kiss*) (*first arm up, second arm up*)
The girls go 'Woo' (*handstand*).[55]

The game, played in much the same way (though with the players apparently standing in a circle around the leader) and with close variants of these same two rhymes, is described by Roud as taking place in Cambridgeshire in the same year as we noted it at Monteney (2010: 69–70). Some of the Monteney children had amplified the repertoire of associated rhymes with three further chants, all apparently influenced by media:

(Leader) This is a warning!

(Others) You what, you what?

(All) Got my berries (*hands on chest as if holding breasts*)
Got my cherries (*hands on bottom*)
Got my biscuit (*hands crossed in front of crotch*)
Got my crunch (*arms up by head ready to do handstand*)
Munch (*hands lowered*)
Bunch (*hands lowered further*)
Crunch (*handstand*).

(All) Get down on your knees
If you want to marry me
Cos my name is, my name is, my name is (*shout out own name and do handstand*).

'This is a warning' is taken from the lyrics of 'You Wot!', a commercial single released by DJ Q and MC Bonez, exponents of 'bassline' music.[56] Bassline developed in Sheffield in the early 2000s at the Niche nightclub. 'You Wot!' got to number 50 in the UK Singles Chart in 2008 and was widely played as part of the club scene.[57] One of the Year 5 girls using this chant for handstands mentioned a 'breakdance group' at the Niche and the fact that her mum had a CD of bassline tracks. The 'Got my berries' song taken from an advertisement, illustrates the way in which media inflects children's play, which is discussed in detail in Chapter 4.

The Opies did not come across any handstand games of this kind (Roud, personal communication) but Roud cites an example from Hampshire, 1982, with a different verse, and notes that Sutton-Smith found handstand games being played in the schools of Dunedin, New Zealand, in 1949 (2010: 69–70). Some sixty years later, in 2009, these handstand games were regularly played in the summer months at Monteney. The following year, however, handstand games seemed less popular (cf. Roud 2010: 68).

Pretend play

In *Children's Games in Street and Playground* (1969), the Opies identify eight categories of 'pretending games':

- Mothers and Fathers
- Playing Schools
- Road Accidents (boys feign injury; girls make-believe they are nurses)
- Playing Horses (children pretend to be or to possess animals)
- Storybook World (children make-believe they would be able to manage in abnormal situations)
- War Games (children engage in pretence battles either against an imaginary enemy or an opposing group of children)
- Cops and Robbers (players on one side chase or seek the other side)
- Fairies and Witches (girls enact the everlasting fight between good and evil) (1969: xxv–xxvi).

The socio-dramatic play found at Monteney centred on the same scenarios as noted by the Opies, including mums, dads and babies,[58] school,[59] horse and rider,[60] and dogs (including a Puppy Dalmatians game in which the children made a home and food using grass clippings).[61] The only exception in the list above is 'road accidents', of which we found no evidence due, perhaps, to road safety advice being less prominent in school teaching nowadays. Playthings were also used by younger children as props in pretend play, such as a skipping rope in horse and rider as a kind of reins or a dog lead[62] and one of a pair of pot stilts as a stethoscope.[63] Play equipment such as the 'log trail' was incorporated into pretend play too, such as in a jungle game.[64]

One of the key changes discerned in relation to fantasy play at Monteney was the extent to which media influenced the play, which we will discuss in further detail in Chapter 4. Among our findings was the use by the older children at Monteney of a new genre of television programme, that of the confrontational talk show, specifically the *Jeremy Kyle Show*.[65] We suggest that it is possible to view these enactments as up-to-date substitutes for 'acting games'. Acting games are defined by the Opies as those in which the children are 'allotted parts, they enact a particular story, and for the most part they repeat the words that were spoken when the game was last played' (1969: 304). In the older tradition, the children enact storylines involving the supernatural and acts of mutilation and cannibalism which, the Opies argue, provide children with the opportunity to 'act out their fears' or revel in 'the pretence of being frightened' (1969: 304). The frightening moments are relieved by 'interludes for slapstick, when parental or ghostly authority is flouted, when children get spanked . . . or when pure nonsense is spoken' (Opie and Opie 1969: 304). As we argue elsewhere (Marsh and Bishop 2012), the *Jeremy Kyle Show*, as shown on television and re-enacted by the children, contains parallel elements of pantomime which provide relief from the reflection on serious issues which affect their lives, such as drug use and teenage pregnancy.

Children's Games with Things (1997)

It is immediately obvious from the Chapter 3 Appendix that games depending on certain playthings were not found during the 'Playgrounds Project' research at Monteney school. Marbles, five stones and tops were not encountered there and the school did not provide them, although it did provide many other playthings.[66] The playworkers who worked at the school would be seen some minutes before an outdoor playtime placing stilts, pot stilts, skipping ropes, pedal racers, balance boards and hula hoops, as well as a variety of balls, including footballs, basketballs and tennis balls.[67] Table top games, such as Jenga, and the equipment for other sports, such as hockey, were also provided, depending on the weather conditions and the availability of playing areas such as the grass.

A number of the children that we interviewed at Monteney Primary School, especially boys in Key Stage 2, expressed a distinct preference for organized team games, such as dodge ball and football, but other sports, such as hockey and cricket, were also mentioned.[68] The playworkers were regularly involved in these games, providing equipment and often taking part themselves in order to keep order.[69] Those who were not attracted to the physical aspects of football sometimes took on other roles such as television commentator.[70]

Skipping

Skipping is often seen as one of the iconic 'traditional' games of children. Yet, as the Opies show, it is not demonstrably ancient, the first references in Britain deriving from the eighteenth century. There is historical evidence for both boys and girls participating in skipping (Opie and Opie 1997: 207–08; Roud 2010: 173–4) although the popular perception today, as in the mid-twentieth century, is that it is the province of girls. At Monteney Primary School, individual skipping was popular amongst girls and boys in the Key Stage 1 playground, where there was clearly a lot of effort going into learning to skip and becoming proficient at it.[71] Longrope skipping was not as prevalent as single skipping but was evident among the younger children and also the older children up to Year 5.[72] It was often organized by one of the playworkers who assisted in turning the rope, something which the younger children found difficult to do effectively due to its length and their shorter stature. Boys as well as girls joined in the longrope skipping but the girls tended to be more proficient. Children did not run into the rope to start, however, but began skipping from a stationary position by the rope. Many appeared to be at the stage of trying to keep up skipping in the longrope without tripping and so tended simply to count the number of skips. Others skipped to a verse, however, which was almost invariably:

> Cinderella
> Dressed in yella
> Went to the ball and kissed a fellow
> How many kisses did she get?
> 1-2-3 . . . (etc.)[73]

They counted on until they tripped on the rope, whereupon the skipper took one end and another began skipping. This is a well-known rhyme in the class of rhymes which the Opies note as divinatory. As they comment, many of the rhymes which end in this kind of counting have the potential for humorous results. The Cinderella rhyme was very popular in the 1960s (Opie and Opie 1997: 254) and was apparently given a boost in popularity by 'the otherwise unrelated pop-song "Cinderella Rockafella"' (1997: 253). The rhyme apparently derives from the United States where the earliest references date from the 1920s (Abrahams 1969: 30–2).

Some Year 3 children were observed trying 'double dutch' skipping (with two ropes turning simultaneously) with adult assistance.[74] It is possible that the television film made for the Disney channel, *Jump In* (2007), may have encouraged this interest in double dutch, although the form goes back to at least the late nineteenth century in Britain and the United States (Opie and Opie 1997: 196–7). Other games using a skipping rope were also noted at

Monteney. There was the wiggling of the rope on the ground for players to jump over (noted as 'snakes' by Douglas 1916: 49).[75] The other game, observed in the Key Stage 2 yard, was where one player swirls the skipping rope around while the others jump over it.[76] The jumping players do this on the spot or running in a circle in the opposite direction to the rope, jumping over the rope as they go (noted as 'Witches and Fairies' in Roud 2010: 182–3; cf. Opie and Opie 1997: 198).

Hoops

Somewhat surprisingly, the Opies do not discuss hoops in *Children's Games with Things* (1997) but their archival collection (Box 205) at the Bodleian Libraries contains a folder of information relating to hoops and hula hooping. The first references to the 'hula hoop' date from 1958, the reference to 'hula dancing' probably referring to the motion of the hips needed to keep the hoop in place (Oxford English Dictionary). This was the start of a new wave of interest in hoops which were triggered by their mass-production in 1958. The craze for hula hooping hit Britain in the same year.

Plastic hula hoops were very popular among boys and girls of all ages at Monteney Primary School, perhaps because they could be put to a variety of uses. Not only did children hula hoop with them in the conventional way, they extended this to include hula hooping to popular music,[77] using multiple hoops round their waist at the same time,[78] and hula hooping with the hoops around their neck, their ankle, and their leg.[79] We also saw hoops being rolled up the flight of five steps to the school building, and children rolling the hoop away from them with a twist of the wrist so that it could come back again.[80] Children could also skip with the hoops, spin them, and throw them up in the air horizontally, trying to position their body so that the hoop would land around them.[81] The material in the Opie archival collection contains descriptions of similar feats, plus record-breaking numbers of twirls accomplished before the hoop dropped, and beliefs about hazards to health of hula hooping with the hoop around one's neck or doing too many twirls in one go.

Another use of hula hoops was in ankle skipping,[82] a variant of the ankle skipping craze described by the Opies in which a tennis ball or cotton reel was fastened to the end of a piece of string knotted into a loop at the other end and placed round the ankle (Opie and Opie 1997: 203–04). The impact of television coverage of this game during the 1960s makes this a fascinating case study and precipitated the manufacture of ankle skipping toys:

> The game apparently came to England from Belgium. Early in May 1966 a girl who had learned 'Ippy Hoep' on holiday in Belgium wrote to the BBC children's programme 'Blue Peter' and said she would

like to show viewers how it was played. She said she thought it would become popular over here, and she was right. By the end of the month it had swept the playgrounds of Britain, usually with the name 'Belgian Skipping'. The craze grew so strong that some schools had to forbid it because the children were getting bruises on their ankles.

(Opie and Opie 1997: 203)

Dedicated toys were being manufactured within months, one being the Roto-skip, which became the predominant name. The hoops in use for this purpose at Monteney did not have a ball attached but the principle of jumping over the hoop with one foot as it was rotated on the ankle of the other leg was the same.

The Singing Game (1985)

The difference between play of the Opies' period and contemporary forms is perhaps most marked in the case of musical play (see Chapter 3 Appendix). Singing games were already on the wane at the time that they were writing and their decline in the playground has continued. The only examples that have survived into the early twenty-first century at Monteney school have been taught to younger children in nursery ('Ring-a-roses'),[83] or by playworkers or music teachers ('In and Out the Dusty Bluebells').[84]

What has taken their place, however, is a significant upsurge in musical play, particularly dance routines and clapping games. The former are described by the opies as 'song-dances' which are pop songs 'sung in the playground either with the actions believed to have been performed by the pop groups singing them on television, or, more often, with actions fitted to them by the children' (Opie and Opie 1985: 414). The Opies regarded these as ephemeral, however, going out of fashion when the pop song itself was superseded. The 'dance-song' examples the Opies give, therefore, are those which have 'taken root in oral tradition and often both words and movements have grown over the years' (Opie and Opie 1985: 415). The data from Monteney contains a raft of new examples deriving from current popular culture, which are likely to be as ephemeral as the earlier examples encountered by the Opies.

The Opies observed that it was predominantly girls who undertook 'impersonations', dance routines and clapping (1985: 414). An important change observed at Monteney was that many more boys were participating in performing pop songs and dance routines. These issues are discussed in further detail in Chapter 4, when we consider the relationship between media and play. Unlike the dance routines, the clapping play at Monteney was still very much the preserve of girls, as the Opies found (cf. Grugeon 1993). There seems to be an awareness of this among the older boys and girls and various explanations were put forward, such as girls clap more gently[85] and girls are better coordinated than boys,[86] as well as the observation that clapping rhymes are often more appropriate for girls than boys (see examples discussed in Chapter 4). This did not deter a handful of boys from joining in on some occasions, although their attempts were usually less fluent and slow compared to the girls and the accompanying gestures incongruous in the case of certain rhymes. The topic of gender differences in play is discussed further in Chapter 8.

The trend of textual continuities with the clapping games found by the Opies, exemplified in Chapter 4, was found in roughly one-third of the thirty clapping games documented at Monteney Primary School. In some cases the rhyme was clearly a variant of one noted by the Opies but found there as an entertainment, ball-bouncing or counting out rhyme. In gestural terms, the repertoire of movements can be seen to have expanded. The basic pat-a-cake and three-way clapping patterns (Down-Up, Clap-Partner, Clap Own) were still very much in evidence but other moves using the backs and sides of the hands and a greater range of mimetic gestures were employed across the repertoire as a whole.

The Opies characterize clapping games as 'the most zestful, speedy, and energetic of the singing games, and, in the modern phrase, one of the chief growth areas' (Opie and Opie 1985: 446). This is borne out by Roud, writing some twenty-five years later (2010: 296). It has also been noted, from the time of the Opies on, that clapping games have had a productive relationship with the verbal, musical and kinetic aspects of popular music and dance, television programmes, and film (Bishop *et al.* 2006; Gaunt 2006; Marsh 2008), and it seems to be no coincidence that this form of play has burgeoned in the last fifty years alongside the development of these forms and their dissemination via electronic media. Kathryn Marsh draws attention to the recursive and reciprocal cycles of appropriation and reappropriation of verbal, musical and kinetic elements of clapping games in the media and vernacular contexts (2008: 185). Gaunt has also highlighted the dialogical relationship between black girls' informal musical culture and black popular music 'in which both spheres are creating and refashioning new musical ideas, based on pre-existing material from the other realm' (2006: 107). Bishop has studied in depth the history and international distribution of the clapping game 'Eeny Meeny Dessameeny', documented at Monteney, showing that it was probably brought to the UK by children at the American School in London, in the 1970s. It seems to have its origins in a counting out rhyme found in nineteenth-century America and has featured in no fewer than five US popular songs in the period 1946–99 and included in hillbilly, doo-wop, women's rap and alternative music styles. Some of these, in turn, appear to have influenced the vernacular clapping game, especially the doo-wop numbers (Bishop 2010).

Another important development found at Monteney Primary School was the use of amateur films of clapping games uploaded to YouTube as a source of repertoire for offline clapping play (and other forms of musical play). These films are primarily made by children and young people for the purposes of demonstrating clapping games to others and in many ways they function similarly to learning situations in the playground, allowing close observation of peers outside one's friendship circle modelling the games, and multimodal presentation of the game, with added affordance that the performance is unvarying and available and repeatable on demand. On the other hand, they lack the affordance of physical contact which is employed when children learn clapping play (Marsh 2008: 138). YouTube is, then, of particular use to those with some competence in clapping play who are seeking to improve their skill, find fresh challenges, and extend their repertoire (Bishop in press).

Conclusion

In summary, it is clear that there is a good deal of continuity between the forms of play observed at Monteney school and those recorded as current in the 1950/1960s period by the Opies. This is most marked in the realm of physical play without playthings, with forms of chasing and catching games that are traceable much farther back in time, in one case as much as 330 years. There is also less obvious media influence in the content of these games, perhaps because they are primarily responsive to the physical space in which they are played. Nevertheless, we can see media-referenced play in such games as POLO, in which brands and celebrity names may occur,[87] and we suggest that media coverage or media reference to specific games, such as thumb wrestling, can dramatically impact on the popularity of games as played among children in face-to-face contexts, as seen in the Opies' example of ankle skipping.

Physical games with playthings appear to be relatively unchanging in the last fifty to sixty years, although there is clearly a high provision of play equipment at Monteney Primary School. We have noted examples of the unconventional and occasionally subversive use of such equipment in play. In relation to verbal play, we have noted that the repertoire of rhymes with a particular function within a game, such as accompanying a clapping game or to regulate counting out, is expanding to include new items alongside those which have been in circulation since the 1950s/1960s and sometimes before. We have also noted an example of dialectal usage in the rhyme which starts thumb wrestling, but on the whole it may be that regional usage is changing with more age-related usage on the increase (cf. Opie and Opie 1959: 14–15). This area requires further investigation.

Musical play has moved almost completely away from the older singing game forms, the children at Monteney favouring clapping play and dance routines based on popular styles. While clapping play has retained its association with girls, dance routines have become the preserve of both boys and girls.

New sources of repertoire have opened up and the possibility of global transmission through YouTube and other video-sharing websites, the impact of which was just beginning to be felt in the playground at Monteney Primary School during the time of our fieldwork. Television programmes, films and advertisements also feature briefer sets of 'moves', such as handshakes, which were imitated by the children, for example as the prelude and coordinator of their handstand games or simply for the fun of performing the moves. In this latter sense, these routines appear to be taking the place of rhymes used purely for entertainment, as distinct from those which function to support or regulate a game. Finally, socio-dramatic play at Monteney closely resembles that described by the Opies, but fantasy play, already strongly influenced by the audio-visual media forms of the 1950s and 1960s, has responded to the increase in available media, notably computer games (discussed in Chapter 4).

It is clear, then, that changes have taken place in children's play in the last sixty years or so. A detailed comparison such as we have undertaken here, however, has helped to develop a more nuanced understanding of the nature and extent of these changes, in respect of the different kinds of play, and their dialectical relationship with the changing context of childhoods in the UK. We now examine aspects of these contexts in more detail in the following chapters, exploring in particular the relationship between play, media and commercial cultures.

Appendix

Data from Monteney Primary School mapped onto play categories in the books of Iona and Peter Opie

Lore and Language of Schoolchildren (1959)	Selected Examples from Monteney Primary School (2009–11)
Just for fun [satirical and nonsense rhymes, tangletalk, puns, tongue-twisters, never-ending tales, ghoulish rhymes and songs, ghost stories and rhymes, Scout and Guide songs]	Rhyme: '[Boy's name] and [Girl's name], Snogging in a tree . . .' (JB fieldnotes, 23.6.09) Ghost stories (MPJB2010-05-26v01558) Songs taught in music lessons ('Grandma, grandma, sick in bed', MPJB2009-11-26v01102) and phonics songs ('Disco hair', MPJB2009-07-14v00054) learnt in class
Wit and repartee	'I'm telling of you, you dirty kangaroo . . .' (MPJB2009-11-26v01102)
Guile	No examples
Riddles	Trick questions ('Susan's mum had four kids . . .', MPJB2010-06-17v01567) Riddles ('Two crisps walking down the road . . .', MPJB2010-11-23v01656)
Parody and impropriety	Song parodies ('Jingle bells, Batman smells . . .', MPJB2009-12-08v01377)
Topical rhymes	Clapping rhyme referring to volcanic ash (MPJB2010-05-25v01554)
Code of oral legislation	Truce terms – Time out (MPCB2009-11-02v01314)
Nicknames and epithets	Nicknames (JB fieldnotes, 4.6.09) Epithets ('Ginger Ninja Turtle') (JB fieldnotes, 16.6.09)
Jeers and torments	'Loser, loser' (MPJB2009-09-24v00225)
Half belief/Customs	No examples
Curiosities	'This is Buddy' (BLJB2009-11-24v01086)

Friendship and fortune	Fortune tellers (MPJB2010-03-30v01466)
Partisanship	Cheerleading and football supporter chants (MPJB2009-09-24v00225)
Child and authority	No examples
Pranks	Practical jokes (MPJB2010-06-17v01567)
Chasing games	Repertoire of Tiggy games
Catching games	'British Bulldog', 'Sharky Sharky', 'Cat and Mouse' (MPJB2009-10-13at00099)
Seeking games	'Hide and Seek' (MPJB2009-10-01v00240)
Hunting games	No examples
Racing games	'Grandma' ['Peep behind the Curtain'] (MPJB2010-11-02v01646)
	'Squares' ['Puss in Corner'] (MPJB2009-06-11v00012)
	'Mario Karts' (MPJB2010-05-20v01524)
Duelling games	Thumb wrestling (MPJB2010-05-11v01515)
	Slaps (MPJB2010-07-15v01574)
Exerting games	No examples
Daring games	'Truth or Dare' (JB fieldnotes, 26.6.09)
Guessing games	POLO (MPJB2009-06-11v00010)
Space-specific physical play	Hopscotch (played without a stone) on play-ground marking (MPJB2009-06-11v00015)
	Jumping up to touch a particular brick in the wall (MPJB2009-07-14v00048)
Physical skills without playthings	Gymnastic moves (headstand, MPJB2009-07-09v00031)
	Handshakes (MPJB2009-07-01v00025)
	Group handstand competition with chant (MPJB2009-07-09v00032)
Acting games	No examples
	The *Jeremy Kyle Show*? (MPJB2009-07-09v00040)
Pretending games	Mums, dads and babies (MPJB2009-11-05v01034)
	School (MPJB2010-03-11v01438)
	War games ('The Battle of Sheffield', MPJB2009-10-13v00259)
	Media-inspired play
	Pretend play relating to 'log trail' play equipment (MPCB2009-09-29v00672)

The Singing Game (1985)	Monteney (2009–11)
Chains and captives	No examples
Match-making	No examples
Mating	No examples
Wedding rings	No examples
Cushion dances	No examples
Longways	No examples
Downfall of the ring	Ring-a-ring-a-roses (MPJM2010-05-20v01607)
Witch dances	No examples
Dramas	No examples
Contests	No examples
Mimicry	No examples
Bachelor games	No examples

Children's Games in Street and Playground (1969)	Monteney (2009–11)
Starting a game	Repertoire of counting out rhymes and methods Racing (JB fieldnotes, 4.6.09) 'Newcomer's It' (JB fieldnotes, 4.6.09)
Calls of friendship	No examples
Up against wall	No examples
Static circles	'In and Out the Dusty Bluebells' (with adult) (MPJB2010-07-20v01592)
Eccentric circles	No examples
Buffoonery	No examples
Impersonations and dance routines	Movement routines ('Don't make me put my fingers in the Zee formation', MPJB2009-07-16v00056, 'Boom click clap', BLJB2009-11-24v01099) Pop songs (Hannah Montana 'Hoedown Throwdown', MPJB2009-07-16v00056)
Clapping (incl. 12 less popular)	Repertoire of clapping games and associated rhymes

Games with Things (1997)	Monteney (2009–11)
Marbles	No examples
Five stones	No examples
Throwing and catching	'Dodge Ball' (MPCB2009-11-02v01347)
	Spot (MPJB2010-05-11v01518)
Gambling	No examples
Hopscotch	Hopscotch played without a stone (see above)
Chucking and pitching	Number cards and hoops game (MPCB2009-11-02v01370)
Ball-bouncing	No examples
Skipping	Individual skipping (MPJB2010-03-11v01442)
	Group skipping (sometimes with 'Cinderella dressed in yella', MPJM2010-03-30v01473)
Tops and tipcat	No examples
Physical skills with fixed play equipment and playthings	The 'log trail' (MPJB2010-05-25v01550)
	Stilts, hula hoops, pedal racers, swingball, bat and ball
	Football, cricket, hockey, tennis, basketball

4   Media, technologies and play

The media and technological landscape of childhood has changed dramatically over the past sixty years. Not only has the range of media and technologies to which children have access grown exponentially, but the way in which play and technology relate to each other is also very different in contemporary society to previous generations. In the first part of this chapter, we outline the nature of the older informants' engagement with media and technologies in the 1950s and 1960s, using their accounts to highlight how their experiences reflected the social and cultural uses of technology at the time. This use is contrasted with the use of media and technologies by contemporary children, drawing on a survey completed by children in Monteney Primary School and the observational and interview data from the ethnographic study. In the second part of the chapter, continuities and discontinuities in these experiences are considered in relation to the ways in which media and technology impact upon children's play.

Radio, television and cinema: developments in use

For the majority of the contributors to the 'Memories of Play Project' and their contemporaries, media and technologies did not feature widely in their childhoods. The most commonly reported media used were radio and television. This was a generation that was caught between the post-war dependence upon the radio for light entertainment and the emerging consumption of television. For many, listening to the radio was a family activity and it did not have universal appeal. Neil, born in 1954, recalled his lack of excitement for the radio:

> Well, basically before we had the telly we had the wireless and you all used to huddle round the wireless, because we had a coal fire as well, it was all, you know, that sort of era. And it was basically the parents wanted to hear

the news, you know, so it was all mainly the news every hour, and there wasn't a lot on the radio in those days, what I thought was of interest, you know. So we'd hear the news and then maybe a play or something like that, or The Archers *would be on, or something like that, but it wasn't very exciting.*

In addition to *The Archers*, respondents recalled listening to a number of programmes with their parents, such as *Dick Barton Special Agent, Family Favourites, Mrs Dale's Diary, Sing Something Simple* and *Workers' Playtime*. There were radio programmes for children, but the interviewees mentioned those programmes, such as *Listen with Mother* and the *Children's Hour*, less frequently. This may have been due to the fact that these programmes could have been part of children's very early listening experiences and thus less amenable to recall, or it may be that the programmes were of less interest to the respondents than radio shows aimed at a broader audience. Certainly, the appeal of early radio programmes aimed at children was not universal. The stated aim of early radio broadcasting for children was to contribute to their moral education and the content was decided upon by middle-class broadcasters intent on instilling particular virtues, such as good citizenship, in their audience. Oswell (2002) notes that broadcasters' objectives aligned with those of welfare institutions at the time, focused as they were on the health and well-being of children. He also suggests that:

> Children's programming was designed, not merely to present material of interest to listeners and not simply to provide a space for children's voices, but to represent the life of the child population to government: namely, to make children visible within broadcasting and to invent the child audience as an object of government.
>
> (Oswell 2002: 24)

Perhaps because of this overt intention to shape the formation of child citizens and the development of programmes that spoke to the experiences of middle-class children, it became clear in the 1950s that children's radio was not widely popular, that it had failed to properly address the interests of many children and that it could not compete with the emergence of television as a media form. As a result, the *Children's Hour* was discontinued in 1964.

Radio featured in the lives of the participants largely as a means of accessing popular music as they moved into their teenage years. They reported that, as they matured, they began to listen to pirate stations that played popular music. Neil recalls:

Oh but later on I think, I'm not sure, you'll have to check this, Radio Luxembourg I believe came out, and you know the pirate radio stations? . . . that was the pop era, then when we were getting, you know, before the Beatles came out, you know, the Beatles came out in the '60s, wasn't it? So that's when it was all starting to kick off, and you had Tony Blackburn, Kenny Everett and all those guys, you know . . . As I say, we had Caroline, Radio Caroline, that was it, that was out on the North Sea wasn't it, the boat. And I used to listen, I think it was Luxembourg, but you used to have a little . . . used to be in the bed, under the bed clothes, because you didn't have a duvet in those days, you had blankets and sheets, and you'd have a little transistor in the bed with your torch, you've got a little crackly little song coming out. But it was brilliant for us in those days.

BBC held a monopoly on domestic radio in this period and, thus, pirate stations such as Radio Caroline and Radio Luxembourg catered for the growing interest in popular music in the 1960s. Indeed, it was only with the Broadcasting Act in 1990 that commercial radio was legally allowed to flourish. Radio still plays an important role in the lives of some children in contemporary society, with 42 per cent of 5- to 15-year-olds in the UK reporting listening to the radio at home in 2012 (Ofcom 2012a: 36). They are more likely to listen to music programmes than any other genre, however, even in the younger age groups, and they access radio across a range of platforms, not just a radio set, including the internet. These patterns largely reflect the significant transformation in the children's music industry over recent decades, with the emergence of popular music aimed specifically at young children, including, for example, the *High School Musical* movies (Bickford 2012). The rise in the number of teenage stars (such as Justin Bieber, Miley Cyrus and Selena Gomez) has also been noticeable, fuelled by Disney's entry into this market and the ability for artists to build a considerable fan base through showcasing their talents on sites such as YouTube or Vimeo. This trend in the music industry has had the effect of levelling out the differences in musical choice across age groups, with some 3- and 4-year-olds having the same musical tastes as tweens and adults (Marsh *et al.* 2009).

In addition, radio has become a less significant source of music in recent decades because of the growth of internet sites such as iTunes, Spotify and peer-to-peer file-sharing sites. Young children can now access music readily on MP3 players, mobile phones and sites such as YouTube, which makes the need for poor quality listening opportunities, such as those reported by Neil, redundant. In a survey of 180 children aged 5–11 at Monteney Primary School in 2010, 68 per cent reported using YouTube on a regular basis. One of the activities undertaken by children of this age is viewing the videos of favourite pop singers, although it was also the case that children reported searching YouTube for musical videos made by other children and young people. For example, children stated that they searched YouTube for Club Penguin Music Videos (CPMV), which are machinima made in the Disney virtual world, *Club Penguin.*

They are constructed by synchronizing the music and lyrics of pop songs to the actions of penguin avatars in the virtual world. Children also searched YouTube for clapping games in order to learn the clapping sequences and related songs, as discussed in Chapter 3. The developments in radio and music consumption for children over the past sixty years, therefore, can be seen to focus on a diversification of platforms to access radio and an increasing appetite for popular music among younger children. The move to seeking out peer productions online is also characteristic of a 'produser' (Bruns 2006) society, which entails citizens being both consumers of mass media and contributors to media culture through the production and dissemination of digital texts and artefacts.

The older respondents were children in a decade in which television was overtaking radio as the preferred leisure audience experience. Whilst John Logie Baird produced the first commercial television set in 1930, it was not until the early 1950s that some families could afford to access them. For many working-class families, visiting those neighbours who were lucky enough to have a television set at home was the only opportunity to view it. Lillian (born 1941) was a member of one of the fortunate families who acquired a television for the Coronation in 1953, and remembered that:

> We did have some people come to watch. I can remember my father kicking it and it was a great big box and it wouldn't spring into life, it did with a kick and we did see the Coronation, but I can remember feeling as though we were quite special because we'd got a television.

Marion (born 1952) reported how her family rented a television from Radio Rentals when she was 8 years old. Renting was a common practice in that era, given the relative expense of television sets. However, because of the small size of screens, viewing for anyone with sight difficulties was challenging. Marion remembered watching television with the 'rich family' on the street:

> The rich family – by which we meant the family where there was only one child – they all had bad eyesight and they invited me over . . . And when I went over there they had the tiniest . . . mean, it must have [been] whatever the first-sized television was, and I was of course desperately looking forward to watching a television. They had a magnifying glass on a stand in front of this television. And my first image of a television was quite grotesque, and I often think of the image of these parents and this little girl with her thick-lensed glasses in this room with this tiny television with a stand and a magnifying glass. So it was obviously very distorted and unpleasant.

In contrast, of course, children at Monteney Primary School in the 2010s can enjoy large screens, high-definition colour images, surround-sound and even, in some cases, 3D television. Beyond the viewing experience itself, other aspects of television viewing have, inevitably, changed over the years, including programming.

Many of the older respondents were aged between 9 and 12 when they first watched television, and so their early childhood experiences were not shaped by it. Those born in the late 1950s or early 1960s, however, reported watching the *Children's Hour, Muffin the Mule* and *Watch with Mother* as infants, *Thunderbirds, Dr Who* and *Captain Pugwash* as older children, and then viewing programmes such as *Raw Hide, Bonanza* and *Sunday Night at the Palladium* with their families. For the majority, television viewing was not a predominant activity, as May (born 1953) recalled:

> *The televisions then were a little . . . were just little black things and you couldn't have it on. I mean there were no children's programmes, it used to be the Test Card, didn't it, all through the day, and I think we used to be allowed, if we weren't at school, if you were off poorly you could watch* Watch with Mother, *which were like* Bill and Ben, *and* Andy Pandy, *and* The Wooden Tops *and things like that. So I wouldn't have been influenced by the television then. But I don't think Yorkshire were out, there was only one channel, the BBC, weren't there? . . . We weren't allowed in our front room, you like lived in these kitchens and your front room was always immaculate. And it were only, like, on special occasions that you were allowed to go in there and watch telly, do you know what I mean?*

In addition to restrictions to access, as May notes, some of the respondents pointed to the way in which the tendency to play outdoors after school meant that there simply was no time for television viewing. Jeanette (born 1944) noted that:

> *We went to bed after* The Archers *on a winter, which [meant] we were in bed for half seven, so you didn't see much television because you were outside. When you came in for your tea it wouldn't go on while you were eating, that weren't . . . we didn't do that, so you might only glimpse television for half an hour, if that, a day. Because if it were light outside you were out, and if it were light at 8 o'clock you were allowed that extra play then. You were never in. It never drew you.*

Jeanette's comment regarding television's lack of appeal may be a result of the nature of programming for children during that period. Whilst some programmes for children were created by the BBC from the 1930s, it was only when Freda Lingstrom was appointed as the head of Children's TV in 1950 that sustained funding for programming could be accessed. Oswell (2002: 48) argues that, from the outset, Lingstrom and her team intended to offer a wide range of programmes for a diverse audience, with the desire to broadcast drama, films, animations, serials and educational programmes. Many of the early programmes watched by some of the respondents featured puppets such as Muffin the Mule, Andy Pandy and Mr Turnip and Hank in *Whirligig*. Oswell, in a close analysis of the discursive space constructed in *Andy Pandy* through the use of voice-over, the placing of the activity within the domestic space and the movement of camera to represent the maternal gaze, outlines how television for children was constructed as 'safe, maternal and homely' (2002: 64).

In the mid-1950s, broadcasters began to consider more carefully the needs of young audiences and the scheduling of programmes aimed at specific, distinct age groups was more firmly addressed. In the 1960s and 1970s, budgeting for children's programming improved and led to an era in which some iconic shows were broadcast, including *Blue Peter* (1958–), *Grange Hill* (1978–2008), *Jackanory* (1965–1996) *and Play School* (1964–88), and both the BBC and ITV offered a wide variety of programmes for children (Home 1993). It may be the case, however, that the golden days of television programming for children are in the past, given developments in recent years. In an overview of the history of television programming for children, Ofcom (2007) note that there were fewer than 1000 hours of output for children per year in the 1950s and 1960s, which grew to over 20,000 hours in 1998 and to 113,000 hours in 2006. By 2012, however, this figure had increased by only 2 per cent, and Ofcom (2012b) also identifies that spending on children's programmes had declined by 23 per cent over the period 2006–11. In addition, in 2007, only 1 per cent of programmes watched by children were first broadcasts, made in the UK; the rest were repeats and/or imports (Ofcom 2007). Having apparently enjoyed a renaissance period in the late twentieth century, therefore, it would appear that children's television programming currently faces many challenges, not least because of a lack of funding and a concomitant reduction in the commissioning of new UK-based programmes. The restrictions around advertising 'junk' food during children's schedules meant that ITV, facing significant reductions in advertising revenue, withdrew from broadcasting children's programmes on ITV1 and introduced CITV, which froze the commissioning of new programmes in 2006 for two years and now only commissions new programmes if producers can engage third-party funding, e.g. from the toy industry, a phenomenon which began in earnest in the 1980s. This tie-in of television with toys and other artefacts is not new, of course. Oswell (2002) reports that *Muffin the Mule*, broadcast from 1946, generated £0.75m in 1952 from various spin-offs but, as Steemers (2010:150–1) notes, at that time such licensing of merchandise was supplementary income, whereas in the 1980s it became a key source of money for production funding.

Product placement, therefore, began to impact upon the production process and content of programmes. Further differences in the experiences with television enjoyed by the older and younger participants in our studies relate to choice and diversity of channels. As May recalled, '*But I don't think Yorkshire [Television] were out, there was only one channel, the BBC, weren't there?*' In the 2010s, there is a proliferation of satellite and cable channels for children. Lury (2002) has detailed how these channels feature endless repeats, or draw programmes together in themes, such as *Tom and Jerry* marathons or science-fiction themes. This kind of viewing practice, she suggests, is very different from earlier generations as it signals a move from an emphasis on time to space i.e. predictable chronology is surpassed by a focus on a channel as a place to go to, a brand to access.

In addition, whilst the programmes in the 1950s were largely simple puppet shows, storytelling programmes, magazine series and live drama, today's choices include a variety of animation, factual series and news and current affairs programmes. The aesthetic qualities of children's television are also very different for contemporary children. Walters and Steemers (2010: 210) note the 'depth, subtlety and complexity' of the aesthetics of preschool television and it is certainly the case that the editing techniques, language, narrative structure, pace and sound are all much more complex and beguiling in much of contemporary children's television programmes than can be said for *Muffin the Mule* or *Watch with Mother*. Oswell (2002) comments that in the early programmes, the mother's perspective/gaze was predominant, the characters themselves were voiceless and the majority of programmes were located within the domestic space. This is in contrast to contemporary programming, which features a broad range of perspectives and contexts, and includes children as narrators. Inevitably, developments in technology have enabled immense improvements to be made in the aesthetic qualities of television, given the capacity for external broadcasting, complex editing techniques, multi-layered soundtracks, special effects and computer-generated images.

The final change to be noted in relation to television is that of the mode of viewing. No longer do the majority of children have only one television set on access to them in family homes. For some of the older respondents, this restriction to having to watch television in the living room caused frustration, as May outlined:

> *And then once the telly arrived, I mean I suppose you'd call it a family event, but like most families, I mean I had a very poor childhood and . . . you know, materially it was not in any way a wealthy childhood, the television was mainly controlled by my older brother and my older sister. And then my father religiously watched the news at nine o'clock and then he went to bed. And obviously . . . well not obviously, but there was a pecking order, so you had no . . . I mean, I was one of the younger ones, you know, I had no rights to choose what was on or what wasn't on.*

Whilst this might still be the case for the viewing of a television placed in the living room, children in contemporary society are more likely to have access to multiple sets and thus may have more agency in relation to their media consumption. Ofcom (2012a) reports that 43 per cent of 5- to 7-year-olds, 58 per cent of 8- to 11-year-olds and 73 per cent of 12- to 15-year-olds have access to a TV in their bedroom. Livingstone comments that this is an established trend for all electronic media:

> In this manner, television followed the trend established for electronic media throughout the past century: the gramophone from the start of the 20th century, telephone from the 1920s, radio from the 1930s, television from the 1950s, VCR from the 1970s, the computer in the 1980s, and now the Internet. Each has begun its career in the main collective family space of the living room, but as prices fall and multiplication and mobility of goods become feasible, each has moved into more individualised, personalised and, for children, unsupervised spaces.
>
> (2009: 156)

Further to this, children are now able to watch television across a range of platforms, including laptops and tablets. Increased mobility in television viewing is also possible through the use of smart phones, including iPhones. This gives rise to the possibility of moving viewing across platforms in a seamless manner, as characterized in a series of television advertisements in 2013 featuring the actor Kevin Bacon extolling the virtues of the 4G network Everything, Everywhere (EE), which enables subscribers to view content on their mobile phones as they stroll home and then transfer this onto a screen in the living room as they arrive. How far children will actually adopt this potential in the future is unclear, however, given the costs involved in streaming data on phones. One of the most popular recent developments for young children is the potential to watch excerpts from favourite television programmes on YouTube, or access content on catch-up players, reinforcing the point that mobility, choice and personalization are key themes in the construction of the modern child viewer.

This trend can also be seen in the history of children's film viewing. Whilst films ostensibly made for children first appeared in the early 20th century, such as adaptations of *Cinderella* (Georges Méliès, 1901) and *Alice's Adventures in Wonderland* (Cecil Hepworth, 1903), in general, the films children watched in special showings, such as in travelling cinematograph shows or in temporary auditoriums that served at other times as skating rinks or dance halls, were the same as the ones that adults viewed in the evenings (Staples 1997: 5). By the 1950s, films made for a child audience were well established, with Disney being the lead producer for this age group. In the UK, Rank began to make films for children that featured child characters in English locations, unknown before this time. These films were essential fodder for the viewers in the increasingly popular Saturday matinees for children. Going to the cinema on Saturdays was a regular occurrence for many of the respondents. Not everyone attempted to enter the cinema in the conventional manner, as Marion recalled:

> *Saturday morning pictures. You queued up and one person got in and then they let as many as they could creep through the fire door. I think it was a penny, I mean I could be wrong, I mean that's obviously a matter of records. But you queued up for Saturday morning pictures and then, you know, with a bit of luck, whoever it was was doing it that week would go and let as many people in at the side door as they could, for nothing, until someone found you and hit you over . . . you know, gave you a clip round the ear and you had to go round the front again to get in, you know.*

May remembered that once children were seated, they were engaged in a range of activities, not just watching films:

> *Everybody went. You know, mums would drop you off and you'd go into the pictures and things, and even . . . they used to have competitions, how many things you can fit into a matchbox, and a yo-yo man to show you tricks what you could do on a yo-yo, and probably pick three or four kids out and let you have a go, do you know what I mean, just different little things like that that they did.*

In his review of the history of children's cinema, Staples (1997) noted that cinema chains:

> quickly latched onto the yo-yo craze of the early fifties. It figured in numerous stage presentations all over the country. A common format was someone who was good at yo-yoing to do a demonstration, and then judge a competition.
>
> (1997: 182–3)

This early attempt by media institutions to use popular culture to draw in child audiences has been developed in recent decades to include links between films and toys for children in fast-food meals, for example. For many of the older respondents, it was not the films that were the main attraction, but the rituals engaged in playing games and singing before the film started and the edible treats available on the way home, as Jeanette suggested:

> *There were the Ritz on there, down at the bottom there, and we used to walk down, it used to cost us sixpence for Saturday afternoon matinee, matinee*

> *it were. And it was absolutely heaving full of kids, absolutely heaving full
> of kids. So we'd go down there, get in, and there were a man – and they
> called him Ivan, I remember his name, and he used to get all the kids
> singing. Before the film would start you all had to sing before the film
> started, when it was a 'Cowboy and Indian'. And he got you singing all
> these songs and then the film would start and then you'd watch that.
> And you were in quite a while I think. We used to start about one o'clock
> if I remember, and you used to come out about four, because that other
> were took up with this singing. And then we used to walk back home, and
> always when you came out – in fact it reminds me of the ice cream man of
> today – there used to be a fruit cart, horse and dray with fruit, and they
> used to sell speckled apples. And we always had the money to buy a speckled
> apple coming out. And if you were lucky, they were only little, you got two.
> And we used to walk up the road then eating these apples we'd bought. But
> he were always there, like an ice cream man is outside schools now – which
> I don't agree with at all, I think they should be banned – but he were there
> with fruit. But it were a horse and dray, because he let you pat his horse,
> and we used to get us apple and walk up.*

During the 1960s and 1970s, the association of food and films within
the matinee experience intensified, with the provision of popcorn, hot
dogs, sausages, sweets and drinks. Indeed, the British Film Institute noted
that without this income from food and confectionery sales, the Saturday
matinees may well have ended several years before they actually did (Staples
1997: 202).

The demise of Saturday cinema attendance occurred in the early 1970s due
to the growing influence of television. In particular, Staples (1997) suggests
that it was the introduction of *Tiswas* by ITV and *Saturday Swap Shop* by the
BBC that had a particular detrimental effect because of the use of outside
broadcasts, phone-ins and the inclusion of children in the studio. The
programmes thus:

> created that sense of access and participation and solidarity which
> had previously been one of the matinees' strong suits in their contest
> with television. Moreover, it offered all this free, and without the
> consumer having to get up at a particular time, or get dressed or have
> breakfast first, or sustain concentration on one story for any length
> of time.
>
> (Staples 1997: 230)

For children in contemporary society, cinema attendance is much more
likely to be a family affair than it was for the older participants, with regular
viewings of family 'blockbusters'. There are also several other significant

differences in the viewing practices of the 1950s and 1960s and the 2010s. Children today have ready access to films that can be watched on demand using services from providers such as Sky and Virgin and they can view films on a range of screens, from television sets, to computer and laptop screens, mobile phones and portable DVD players. YouTube and other video sharing sites enable children to watch trailers for films. iPad and tablet developments provide further opportunities to engage with films. Film producers now normally release a trailer on an app, which can be downloaded onto an iPad or android tablet. Some children's films also have a related app that enables users to play games based on the film narrative. Further, in the same way that television viewers are able to produce texts related to their favourite television programmes and then post these onto video sharing sites, film fans can create their own productions related to popular films. Indeed, as Graham (2010) notes, in a discussion of student Jeff Loveness's popular fan film *Wes Anderson Spider-Man*,[88] this phenomenon is blurring the boundaries between amateur and professional filmmakers.

Having reviewed the changes in children's engagement in radio, television and film from the 1950s to the 2010s, one area deserves additional consideration. There is an obvious difference in the use of electronic media by children in contemporary societies from the generations of children who grew up in the mid–20th century, and that is in the use of the internet. Not available to the general public until the 1980s, respondents in the 'Memories of Play Project' were unable to engage in online practices. For the children in the 'Playgrounds Project', use of the internet was a central part of their daily media practices. At Monteney Primary School, 70 per cent of children reported using the internet regularly (once a week or more frequently) and the range of sites they accessed was very broad, including game sites (Miniclip; Bored.com), social networking sites (YouTube; Facebook; Bebo), Massive Multiplayer Online Games (MMOGs) *(Runescape; Sacred Seasons; Evony)*; music sites (Limewire; Grooveshark; Monstrosity) and virtual worlds (*Club Penguin; Moshi Monsters; Farmville*). Inevitably, children drew on their online activities in their play in ways that were similar to their use of film and television. In the next section of the chapter, we move on to consider the changing relationship between children's use of media and technologies and their play over the past sixty years.

Media, technologies and play

In this section of the chapter, we will focus in turn on the media discussed previously in order to consider their relationship to play. This is not to suggest that children separate out their use of the media or their play based upon it in this way, but it enables an in-depth review of the affordances of each of the media for play.

Radio

Considering the subject matter in this way creates immediate challenges in relation to the radio, given that there has been very little research that has reviewed the relationship between radio and play. In one of the few examples we have encountered, Palmer Bonte and Musgrove (1943) report on a study of war play in Hawaiian preschools, which took place six months after the attack on Pearl Harbor. They recall a play episode which involved children constructing a ship and during which a boy made the sound of a siren and shouted, 'This is an air raid alarm! Take cover!' which was an exact imitation of the warning played on radio at the time. A further example is the children's rhymes from around 1950, documented by Iona and Peter Opie, in which the names of the radio comedians Charlie Chester and Dick Bentley appeared (1959: 117). These are rare examples, however, and apart from a consideration of young children's orientation to radio for musical interest (Young 2008), research on radio and play has not been undertaken in any meaningful way. The evidence from the interviews we conducted with the older correspondents indicates that radio influenced their play, but not as extensively as television and film. Only isolated cases were reported. Beryl (born 1943), for example, recalled the adoption of political slogans:

> *And another thing that we used to sing when we were skipping – and it's only because we'd heard adults talking because we'd no telly, so if we'd heard it we'd heard it on the wireless and we'd heard adults, 'Vote, vote, vote for Mr Churchill, calling Eden at the door.' Now Anthony Eden, he was a Prime Minister. 'Eden is the one that we all love best, so we don't want Churchill any more.' So they were all chants to do with political things that we'd heard. We didn't know what they were about but we'd heard the names mentioned, so we incorporated them into a song.*[89]

Writing in 1959, the Opies comment that:

> undoubtedly schoochildren were more actively employed in nineteenth-century parliamentary elections than they are today . . . Election time which used to be . . . a period of high spirits as well as high words, is now dominated by the family television set. 'I remember how in the old days', recalled Sir Anthony Eden in 1955, 'the boys used to go round singing in chorus: "Vote, vote, vote for So-and-so."'

(1959: 348)

The rhyme is certainly older than the 1950s, however, as it was used as a skipping song prior to the First World War and its tune ('Tramp, tramp, tramp, the boys are marching') is an American civil war song from 1865 (Opie and Opie 1997: 270).

There was also evidence from the 'Memories of Play Project' that the adults enjoyed pretending to be the pop stars they heard on the radio in their early teenage years, a practice the Opies categorized as 'impersonations and dance routines'. It is not surprising that these radio-inspired referents are evidenced in the use of text and sound, such as the use of names, sound effects and music, given the aural affordances of the medium. As we discuss below, in the 2010s, this form of play is more dependent on television and YouTube for its sources.

Television and film

Much of the research on media and play has focused on television. There has been a long tradition of research on children's play and television, conducted most notably by Dorothy and Jerome Singer (2005). This research has identified the way in which television can provide a rich source of material for play. A study conducted in 1982 by James and McCain reviewed the way in which preschool children drew from television in their play. They found that there were three elements of television-based materials that children used including: (i) the identities, behaviours, speech patterns and symbols of both fictional and real-life characters/personalities; (ii) plots and presentational formats of a range of television programmes including drama, comedy, news and talk shows, cartoons etc., and (iii) other forms of information derived from television (1982: 787). The researchers found that children use these materials in five different forms of play: gross motor play, construction play, language play, dramatic play and social play (1982: 788).

It is interesting to compare these findings with those of Palmer (1986) in her study of 8- to 9-year-old and 11- to 12-year-old children in Sydney, Australia. She examined a range of interactions which occur in relation to the television while it is being watched, as well as researching the influence of it on children's behaviour at other times. Many of these behaviours can be termed play, although Palmer does not always do so. Such interactions include 'performance', which involves acting out, singing or talking about television content whilst it is on (1986: 72–3). Of particular interest is her category of 're-make' in which children use television content 'when they are playing or looking for things to do':

> 'Re-make' can be a small reference or event within an otherwise conventional game or play sequence. At the other extreme, it could

describe a long episode in which children attempt deliberately to reconstruct what they remember seeing on TV. The 'making' can be in the form of words, gestures or acting out. It may even be material, the creation or use of objects based on TV shows.

(1986: 77–8)

Drawing on Palmer and their own observations in several schools in Yorkshire, UK, during 2002–03, Bishop and Curtis (2006), in a review of the relationship between television and play, suggested that there were three primary ways in which children drew from television. The first of these was allusion. Children can refer to the names of television programme characters, celebrities or brand names (onomastic allusion), copy gestures drawn from television (gestural allusion) or refer to topics they have viewed on television (topical allusion). The second way in which children can draw from television is referred to as the process of syncretism or hybridization. This can account for the way in which children can blend characters and plots drawn from television with more traditional play practices e.g. cops and robber play which might draw on *The Bill* (cf. Opie and Opie 1969: 340). The third way in which children can draw on television is through the process of mimesis. Whilst mimesis can refer to instances in which children copy characters or storylines faithfully, it can also refer to more creative adaptations in which children develop the original plots and characters in new and innovative ways. This third category can include parody. Bishop and Curtis (2006) also make the point that the influence can be generalized or specific to a particular programme.

It is clear that the ways in which television and film can influence play, as identified by Bishop and Curtis (2006), can be mapped onto data both from the mid-twentieth century and the twenty-first century. For example, we noted allusion, particularly onomastic allusion, in which children referenced media brand names, characters and celebrities in their play, across all of the datasets. 'Got my berries', introduced in Chapter 3, was used by the Monteney school children as the prelude to a handstands game and is adapted from a Müller Corner (yoghurt) advertisement which was aired on UK television in 2009. The advertisement featured people in an idyllic rural setting carrying placards, each depicting a different fruit. The lyrics of the accompanying song were as follows, a different voice singing each half line:

> I've got my berries, got my cherries
> Got my biscuits, got me [sic] crunch,
> Got my peach, got my shortcake
> And my blueberries
> I've got my cherries . . . (etc.)

(http://www.youtube.com/watch?v=d7GCtldU_PY)

The advertisement is itself a rewritten version of the chorus in the Nina Simone song 'Ain't Got No/I Got Life'. This was first released in 1968 but was remixed and re-released in 2006. In the handstands game, the children retained the rhythm and tune of the advertisement/song as well as the (adapted) words. The slightly risqué accompanying gestures (noted in Chapter 3) appear to be the children's own innovation. The revoicing (cf. Maybin 2013) of snippets from media sources was also evident on another occasion during our fieldwork when a Year 4 girl was trying out further chants every time she became leader of a group playing handstands.[90] These included:

> (Leader) Mamma mia.
>
> (Others) Here I go again.
> > > (Referent: the musical and film *Mamma Mia* (2008))
>
> (Leader) Hasta la vista
>
> (Others) Baby.
> (Referent: the catch-phrase made popular by Arnold Schwarzenegger
> > in the film *Terminator 2: Judgement Day* (1991))

Throughout the Opies' studies, the data from the respondents in the 'Memories of Play Project' and the 'Playgrounds Project', onomastic allusion was prevalent in relation to pop stars, film stars and television characters. Whilst media stars come and go, the data indicates that other aspects of the play were more persistent. One of the forms of play that we did not find in the Monteney playground was what the Opies call 'impersonations':

> certain songs in which a character is described have been made into miniature dramas, and are acted by each girl in turn in the centre of the simplest stage known to man – a circle of dancers who are also the chorus. Some of the songs are of known authorship; most if modern, are traditional.
>
> > > > > > > > > > (1985: 414)

Whilst we did not observe this kind of circle performance at Monteney, various parts of the text of one of the Opies' examples, 'Diana Dors', appeared in combination with a clapping song there, 'My Mummy Sent Me Shopping', more commonly known as 'I Went to a Chinese Restaurant' (1985: 465–7). In the Monteney version, the opening verse, with a three-beat clapping pattern, was concatenated with an updated version of the 'Diana Dors' game, with actions illustrating the meaning of the words:

My Mummy Sent Me Shopping (MPJB2009-07-09v00031)	Diana Dors (Opie and Opie 1985: 416)	I Went to a Chinese Restaurant (Opie and Opie 1985: 465)
My mummy sent me shopping		I went to a Chinese restaurant
To buy a loaf of bread, bread, bread		To buy a loaf of bread, bread, bread
She wrapped it up in a five pound note		They wrapped it up in a five pound note
And this is what she said, said, said:		And this is what they said, said, said:
My name is Tracy Beaker	My name is Diana Dors	My name is Alli alli . . .
I'm a movie star	And I'm a movie star	
I've got the curly wurly knickers And the see-through bra	I've got a cute cute face And a monkey guitar	
I've got the hips, the lips, the sexy legs	I've got the lips (kiss, kiss) I've got the hips, boom, boom I've got the le-egs, sexy le-egs	
If you want to marry me then count to three One, two, three.	. . . .	

The Opies observe that games and texts at the height of their popularity attract accretions and additions, as 'My Mummy Sent Me Shopping' has done here (1969: 8–9). Roud found a significant number of examples from the last ten years or so in which whole portions of text 'float' from the text of one clapping game to another in this way (2010: 315). In some performances by the same children, the movie star name used was 'Katy Perry',[91] a pop singer, and another group of girls who performed the game interpolated 'Britney Spears' here, another pop singer.[92] The name of Tracy Beaker is a more intriguing choice in that she is a fictional character, created by the award-winning children's writer Jacqueline Wilson, who has to live in a care home. She is rebellious rather than glamorous and sexy, although she believes that her mother is a film star. A film and a television series based on the books was popular at the time of the 'Playgrounds Project'.

In addition to onomastic allusion, gestural allusion was also present across the datasets. Emily (born 1955) reported playing games based on *The Man from Uncle* and *Thunderbirds* in the 1960s and described how the children copied the actions of characters:

*You got a pen or a pencil then or whatever, and you used to talk down to it,
because that's what they did on the television.*

Similarly, as we discussed in Chapter 3, a group of children in Monteney
Primary School re-enacted episodes from the *Jeremy Kyle Show* in the playground. The child who adopted the role of Jeremy Kyle at one point bent down
on his knees in the 'studio', elbow on knee, as he chatted to the 'guests'.
Another group of children replayed elements from the film *Avatar* (James
Cameron, 2009) and copied the gestures of the American forces as they
attempted to chop the sacred tree down. Taylor (2012) has referred to this practice as 'postural intertextuality', prevalent in the classroom meaning-making
practices of the children she studied.

Topical allusion was also embedded across all of the datasets, as indicated
in the example given by Brenda above, when she reported that she and her
peers incorporated the names of politicians such as Churchill into their chants,
influenced by the political landscape. Although we encountered few topical
rhymes at Monteney, we did observe one adaptation, by a Year 6 girl, of the
clapping game 'My Boyfriend Gave Me an Apple', to incorporate a reference to
a contemporary event. In this case, a cloud of volcanic ash, caused by the erup-
tion of the Eyjafjallajökull volcano in Iceland, brought European airlines to a
standstill for several days in April and again in May 2010. The event found its
way into the playground:

> My boyfriend give me an apple
> My boyfriend give me a pear
> My boyfriend give me a kiss on the lips
> And I threw him down the stairs.
>
> I kicked him over France
> I kicked him over Spain
> I kicked him over Iceland
> And he got burnt by the flames.

(MPJB2010–05–25v01554)

The Opies found rhymes which had been similarly adapted to make reference
to current affairs (1959: 98–106).

The process of syncretism, or hybridization, was also discernible across the
projects. Children blended characters and plots drawn from television and film
with more traditional play practices. Television- and film-influenced play
could be found across the majority of the categories of pretend play discussed
in Chapter 3, such as children playing 'Cowboys and Indians' war games in the
1950s and 1960s, based on programmes such as *Bonanza*, and children playing

witches and wizards in the 2010s, drawing from programmes such as *Wizards of Waverley Place* or the film *Hocus Pocus*. This process has been a persistent theme over the decades. As James and McCain report in their study of television and play in 1982, 'there was no game theme identified that was not somewhat related to the themes in games identified in previous research on the folklore of children's play' (1982: 799). This process of syncretization is complex and multi-layered and certainly challenges any notion that children simply 'copy' the source text (cf. Sutton-Smith 1997).

Similarly, in relation to mimesis, the adults in the oral history interviews reported replaying stories from favourite television programmes and films, just as we observed this pattern of activity in the contemporary playgrounds. Of course, it was the case in the 1950s and 1960s that children could assume that everyone had watched the same programmes before participating in the play. Neil described how he and his friends would play on the street after watching the same programme:

Julia: *You obviously had a TV in your home then, were you watching those at your own house?*

Neil: *Mainly yeah. We tended to sort of come in, play during the day, come in in the afternoon – I think it was 4 o'clock we finished or something like that, I'm not too sure now. We'd get in and then we'd have our tea and then watch a bit of telly, and those sort of . . . the 4 to 5 time would be kids' programmes, really, I think.*

Julia: *Yeah, OK. And did you sort of share those programmes with your friends, did you like talk about them or anything, or did you just assume they watched the same ones as well?*

Neil: *Well I think we just sort of assumed they watched them, because every time we came out . . . normally what . . . it's quite strange, what would happen, if there was, say, a football match on – not many in those days – but all the kids, after the football was over, they'd all come running out in the street with a ball. And if Robin Hood was on, when the programme had finished they'd all come running out in the street with their bows and arrows. So everyone sort of knew, I suppose we'd all been watching the same and they all . . . didn't sort of talk about it, just got, you know, starting playing what was ever on the telly.*

Julia: *That's really interesting. Yeah, so it's like you were all watching it at the same time, and then after it had finished you would come out and you would be inspired to play those.*

Neil: *Yeah, it just sort of . . . well, you sub-consciously knew they were watching whatever was on because they'd all come out with the same kit, you know. And then you're sort of debating, we'd sort of just get on with it, you know, 'Right you're on that side, we're on this side, you're going to start the fight' and off we go, you know, and that's how it went, you know.*

Whilst the majority of children in the 1950s and 1960s would generally all have watched the same programmes because of the limited number of channels (BBC1 and ITV in the 1950s, BB2 from 1964), as Neil's testimony above indicates, this is not the case in the 2010s. Multiple channels proliferate now, with a number aimed at children, such as CBBC/CBeebies, CITV, Disney and Nickelodeon. This means that it is not certain that all children will share knowledge of the same programmes in order to inform their play. Griffiths and Machin (2003) argue that it is the shared aspect that is important and, in the 'Playgrounds Project', children did report sharing information about media texts with each other in order to be inclusive in their play. Kathryn Marsh (2006) suggests that whilst one or more children may get content from television to inform their play, it is often transmitted and learnt by subsequent children in the same way as other play, e.g. by oral transmission and customary example. She also points out that the influence can be reciprocal inasmuch as children's play and rhymes may be appropriated by television (K. Marsh 2006, 2008).

A further difference between the two datasets was identified in relation to the way in which technologies now enable children to stop, pause and rewind moving image sequences. The children in the 'Playgrounds Project' reported using some of the modern features of media technologies to pause and rewind television sequences so that they could copy particular aspects of texts in their play. For example, Emma, in Year 6 (aged 10–11) explained to Julia how it is possible to copy a clapping rhyme and sequence from *I Carly*, a programme on the Nickelodeon channel, which Emma had identified as originating from the Disney channel:

Julia: *I've never watched* I Carly, *in fact I don't think we get the Disney channel so you're talking to someone who completely . . . it wasn't around when I was young. So just take me back a step here. OK. So you're watching the Disney channel, we're watching* I Carly, *so what happens? Do you see like a . . . does it come into the story or how . . .*

Emma: *You see a clapping game and then if you camera wind it and fast forward it you watch it a couple of times and you start doing it. It sinks into your head and then you know it. And you go to school and you're like, 'Oh, I've got a new clapping game, I've watched this at . . .' Like, 'Look at this that I've just learnt off* I Carly.' *And then you start doing it and it spreads all around school.*[93]

The viewing figures for these sorts of clips suggest that the routines are intensively viewed and circulated among children for a short while. For example, three Year 6 girls at Monteney performed 'What's that, a hat' from the Disney channel teen fantasy sitcom *The Wizards of Waverly Place* (2007–12), a 9-second routine performed in the television series each time one of the characters sees a hat.[94] This group also performed a number of cheerleading routines from

'Mascot Love', an episode of the Disney channel television series *Hannah Montana* (2006). A group of three Year 4 girls at Monteney also drew on the *Hannah Montana* series for inspiration, but in some cases adapting the texts to suit their friendship group, who called themselves the Party Princesses. One example was a chant, 'I'm going to Europe' (with stirring movement), which became 'I'm going to your house'.[95]

Another way in which contemporary social and cultural contexts impacted upon play today was in the way in which it was not always possible to identify if play was based on television, film or other media. Children drew on narratives that spanned beyond television into other media, such as computer games and toys. *Hannah Montana*, for example, is a Disney channel television series, but it has spawned a range of spin-offs, such as films, CDs, clothing and games and therefore the narrative influence cannot always be traced back to television alone. Therefore, the data from the 'Playgrounds Project' illustrated the continued significance of television and film in children's lives but also pointed to the way that they were only aspects of the complex 'medisascapes' (Appadurai 1996) impacting upon their daily existence. Television and film thus influenced fantasy and physical play in the 'Playgrounds Project', but they also influenced play with playthings as children traded cards related to television themes, or clutched *Hannah Montana* CDs as they sang and danced.

As discussed in Chapter 3, musical play was much more extensive in the Monteney playground than was evident either from the Opies' data or the accounts of the respondents. The Opies observed that it was predominantly girls who undertook 'impersonations', dance routines and clapping (1985: 414, 440). However, at Monteney we found that many more boys were participating in performing pop songs and dance routines. These were often inspired by male rap and hip hop artists, such as the streetdance group, Diversity, who won the third series of the ITV talent show *Britain's Got Talent* in 2009.[96] Michael Jackson-style breakdance moves were also imitated on the playground[97] as were raps, such as one by the American wrestler, John Cena, learnt from a YouTube clip.[98] Ritualized greeting routines comprising a sequence of gestures and body moves, termed 'handshakes' by the children but sometimes known as the 'dap greeting', were also made up and practised among both boys and girls and their friends.[99] Some of these appeared to be intended as homage to particular performers or performance items; others, such as the chants and songs associated with handstand games, contained elements of more parodic imitation of popular culture, similar to that found by Marsh (2008).

Electronic media and the internet

Inevitably, as developments in technology and media mean that children in the 2010s have access to a greater range of electronic play spaces, we found in the 'Playgrounds Project' that the online world permeated children's offline play (see Marsh, in press, a and b). Narratives, characters and themes from computer games found their way into imaginative and physical play and games such as *Call of Duty: Modern Warfare, Pokémon* and *Super Mario* informed a range of playful activities. At times, children imported structural features of computer games into their imaginative play, such as the levels that players normally have to progress through to win, a process identified as 'ludic bricolage' by Burn (2013). There were even instances in which children copied elements of Wii Fit in their play:

> Two Y1 girls . . . and a Y1 boy . . . are sitting down on the playground inside the hoops which are laid flat on the ground. They are sitting cross-legged and holding up their hands, elbows bent, in the manner of a meditating Buddhist monk. I ask them what they are doing. They say they are meditating. I ask them if they've learnt about this in class. Luke tells me, 'I've got a meditate on my mummy's Wii Fit.' He plays with this. The two girls tell me they got it from a book.
>
> (JB fieldnotes, 23.06.09)

Console games impacted on a range of types of play, including musical play. We have already noted the interest in music and dance at Monteney Primary School and children enjoyed replaying in the playgrounds dance moves they had learned from games such as X-Box's *Dance Central*. Inevitably, given children's growing interests in online virtual worlds (Burke and Marsh in press), they also shaped children's play, as Nina suggests:

> *Like, do you know Moshi Monsters? People in our class go on Moshi Monsters but I don't because I don't really like it. So people go on Moshi Monsters and Doctor Who games and they come back to school and say, 'Oh, shall we play Moshi Monsters or Doctor Who?' So they start playing Moshi Monsters and Doctor Who. Like, go to the shops and buy stuff and grow plants so they can get pets.*[100]

Moshi Monsters is a popular virtual world, which enables children to look after virtual pets and purchase virtual items in an online shop. We discuss the relationship between online and offline play further in Chapter 7, when we consider the way in which the spaces of play have changed over the past sixty years.

Conclusion

Across both of the studies reported here, media influenced play in a range of ways. Table 4.1 identifies how radio, television- and film- and computer-related

Table 4.1 Media, technologies and play, 1950s/1960s and 2010s

HIGH VERBAL CONTENT

- *Jokes* (e.g. based on television and film characters and plots)
- *Other verbal play* (e.g. partisanship chants, drawing from television viewing, such as premiership matches)

HIGH VERBAL AND MUSICAL CONTENT

- *Songs and rhymes (without associated physical activity)* (e.g. pop songs heard on the radio or viewed on television/YouTube; rhymes adapted from radio and television adverts; songs from films, such as Mamma Mia)

HIGH PHYSICAL AND HIGH VERBAL AND/OR MUSICAL CONTENT

- *Clapping and skipping* (e.g. with rhymes referencing television characters and film stars, or clapping songs adapted from media sources)
- *Dancing with self-expressed music/song and/or with CD track, copying dancing seen on television* (e.g. Diversity on Britain's Got Talent) *and film, or practised on computer games* (e.g. X-Box Dance Central)
- *Singing with accompanying moves* (e.g. pop songs viewed on television/YouTube)

HIGH IMAGINATIVE CONTENT

Fantasy play	• *Play drawing from generic radio, television and film or computer game characters* (e.g. fantasy play involving cowboys and Indians, princesses, witches, fighters)
	• *Play drawing on specific television, film and computer game characters and plots* (e.g. Hocus Pocus, Dr Who, Avatar, Call of Duty: Modern Warfare)
Socio-dramatic play	• *Play based on television programmes* (e.g. reality television, such as The Jeremy Kyle Show), *films* (e.g. The Incredibles) *and computer games* (The Sims)
With playthings	• *Play using objects to replicate items in television, film and computer-game related play* (e.g. sticks for wands)

HIGH PHYSICAL CONTENT

Without playthings	• *Running about games* (e.g. linked to television and film characters, or characters from virtual worlds, such as Club Penguin, or computer games such as Mario Karts, chasing each other)
With playthings	• *Football* (e.g. children emulating football characters seen on television)
Body play	• No television/film/computer game-related play observed/reported

play across the studies mapped on to the classification system discussed in Chapter 1.

Whilst the influence of media on play has grown since the 1950s, this largely relates to the extent to which such play can be noted in children's cultural practices. We found more evidence of play that is influenced by media in contemporary children's lives, as discussed in Chapter 3. Despite these perceived differences, in some ways little has changed in relation to the influence of media on play since the 1950s. As the Opies noted:

> [Children's] pretending games turn out to be little more than reflections (often distorted reflections) of how they themselves live, and of how their mothers and fathers live, and of the books they read, and the TV programmes they watch. Whatever has latest caught their fancy is tested on their perpetual stage.
>
> (1969: 330–1)

This remains the same today as it did for children playing sixty years ago, when television was just entering into the lives of the general population. Play for children is a continual process of remixing all forms of texts and therefore their textual poaching (Jenkins 1992) has always included the different electronic media since their various points of entry into the lives of the general public. This continuous process of appropriation, accommodation, assimilation and/or adaptation will continue to take place in the future, no matter how far developments in technology change the range of media available to children.

As we have identified, television and media are increasingly embroiled in the commercial world of childhood. In the next chapter, we move on to consider the material culture of children in the 1950s and 1960s and compare that with the present day, examining the way in which, whilst children might have access to a wider range of goods in contemporary society, this does not necessarily always change the way in which commercialism intersects with their play.

5   The material cultures of childhood

Towards the end of the twentieth and the beginning of the twenty-first centuries, the positioning of children as economic subjects in the market became even more pronounced. This chapter examines how the materiality of childhood has changed in the past sixty years, focusing on an analysis of one brand, LEGO, as a case study of changing commercial and related play practices. The continuities in the relationship between play and material culture are also considered, featuring a discussion of the practice of collecting and swapping objects.

History of the child as consumer

It is generally assumed that it is only in modern childhoods that we can identify the presence of consumerism, yet marketing goods aimed at children is a practice that is centuries old. Buckingham (2011), in a review of the history of the emergence of the child consumer, points out that as early as the sixteenth century, instructional primers and playthings for children were being produced, although it was not until the eighteenth century that products designed for children, including books and toys, were produced on a large scale. Plumb (1982: 310) notes that by 1780, toy shops were common in England and by 1820, the toy industry had grown large. This growth in the toy industry occurred in parallel with changing constructions of childhood. As Makman (1999: 119) suggests, in the nineteenth century, 'as "toy" came more frequently to denote a child's plaything, children themselves became toy-like, at least in the eyes of adults, who saw them increasingly as precious objects'. Of course, such judgements can be criticized as overgeneralizations, given that there were many, varied constructions of childhood in the nineteenth century, but the fact that so many historians have noted changes in relation to childhood in the nineteenth century does signal that this was a transformative era.

During this period, there was a growing concern for the health and well-being of children who worked, and this led to the de-labourization of children and their positioning as a member of the family who did not need to contribute economically (Zelizer 1985). As Freedgood (2012: 235) suggests, toys appeared more widely in the cultural lives of children and enabled them to play just at the point when they were no longer included in the workforce. In addition, children increasingly became the focus of parental desires to enhance their offsprings' minds and bodies through the use of instructional toys and books. An example of this phenomenon can be found in the emergence of what are commonly known as Georgian didactic stories in the late eighteenth and early nineteenth centuries. Located squarely within this genre is Maria Edgeworth's 1876 story, *The Purple Jar*. The story outlines how 7-year-old Rosamond, walking with her mother in London, looked at various goods in shops and tried to persuade her mother to buy them, but her mother noted that she did not need the goods. Although Rosamond's shoes hurt her, and she had the opportunity to buy a pair of shoes when entering into a shoemaker's shop, Rosamond insisted instead on buying a purple jar that she spotted in a chemist's window. However, when she returned home, she found that the jar was filled with black liquid. Rosamond poured this out, only to find that the jar was transparent. In the meantime, the condition of her shoes continued to deteriorate. She was subsequently very upset about her purchase and wished that she had bought the shoes instead. Edgeworth is considered to be the first classical writer for children and her work has engendered numerous discussions of *The Purple Jar*, with varying interpretations. Denisoff (2008) contends that the work is an example of pre-nineteenth-century attempts to construct children as consuming subjects, in this case as one that should purchase items based on needs and not desires. Myers, however, argues that *The Purple Jar* challenges cultural stereotypes of females as passive victims of 'undisciplined emotions by granting girlhood the potentiality for rational agency and self-command' (1989: 55) and Myers highlights how, by positioning the mother as enabling Rosamond to learn by experience rather than telling her what she should purchase, Edgeworth challenges traditional models of rote instruction.

In one sense, Edgeworth's book was expressive of the middle-class anxieties in that period about the move from open-air markets to closed shops with their tempting window displays, anxieties which found their way into picture books for children. Trumpener reviews a number of books which reflected these concerns and she suggests that toy shops in nineteenth-century children's books 'fill children with particularly acute consumer anxiety, and provoke unseemly behaviour' (2002: 355). She documents changes in attitudes towards consumption in children's books over the nineteenth century. For example, Taylor and Taylor's *City Scenes: Or a Peep into London for Good Children* (1809) points to social inequalities when it describes a woman about to purchase a morning dress in a shop for five guineas, not because she needs it, but because it is attractive and cheap. However, the narrator reminds its child readers:

> Five guineas would make a poor perishing family happy. And how many poor perishing families are there in this crowded city! Old lady! Do not squander such a sum upon useless finery, while there is *one* starving fellow creature within your reach.
>
> (1809: 23)

In contrast, just over a hundred years later, books such as *Kensington Rhymes* (Mackenzie 1912) portray well-off 'child flaneurs' (Trumpener 2002: 371) who roam about London, relishing their freedom to shop. In Lucas's (1902) *The Visit to London*, an illustration appears of two unkempt girls, pressing their noses against the window of a toy shop. Trumpener suggests that:

> Half a century earlier, the image of the ragged child in front of the shop window, dreaming over inaccessible dolls and toys, seemed intensely tragic, dramatising the unbridgeable social divide between rich and poor, while suggesting their commonality of desires. Now the treatment of the gamine is jocular, the image of the shop window cheerful, the sight of consumer goods a simple source of pleasure.
>
> (2002: 371)

The eighteenth and nineteenth centuries can thus be characterized as eras in which products for children increased and shopping for them became a more widespread and acceptable practice, at least for children in middle- and upper-class families. However, the advertising of goods for children was aimed primarily at adults. It was in the early twentieth century that advertisers began to target children directly in a more concerted manner. Daniel Cook (2004) has charted this process in relation to the marketing of children's clothing in the US. He describes how as early as the 1910s, but certainly over the 1920s and 1930s, children's clothing retailers organized their stores and products to appeal directly to children. Clothing began to be grouped by age categories and, eventually, children's departments were opened in department stores. Cook suggests that this process within the clothing industry was replicated across a range of other areas and demonstrates the way in which 'the child' became increasingly central to the economic lives of families in the twentieth century. Cook suggests that childhood, through this process, is commodified and 'acquires exchangeable values in that the very transitions between life stages create perpetual and market-necessary forms of scarcity' (2010: 165). Instead of seeing childhood and commercial culture as separate, therefore, Cook argues that they are co-constitutive (2008, 2010).

Child as consumer: 1950s–2010s

In the 1950s, children became the focus for intensified commercial practices when television became more widely adopted in households. In general, the older respondents were not able to remember advertisements specific to children in the early to mid-fifties, but they recalled adverts for household goods, such as washing powder (e.g. Omo and Persil). As is inevitable, given children's creativity in relation to the texts they encounter, some of the adults remembered rhymes based on adverts. Beryl was able to recall rhymes based on adverts for products such as Andrews Liver Salts and Pepsodent toothpaste:

Beryl: *And I'll tell you another chant we had . . . Do you remember Andrews Liver Salts?*

Julia: *Yes.*

Beryl: *Skipping to this: 'Andrews, Andrews, Andrews for inner cleanliness. What a blessing Andrews, effervescent Andrews, Andrews. Andrews, Andrews for inner cleanliness'.*

Julia: *So did you sing that?*

Beryl: *You're actually skipping about going to the lavatory. Yeah.*

Julia: *But that came off the wireless then or the TV?*

Beryl: *I think that came off the wireless, I can't swear to it. But it also appeared on TV that. And also an advert for Pepsodent, do you remember Pepsodent? . . . And I remember, I don't know whether we skipped to it but I remember us singing it, 'You wonder where the yellow went when you brush your teeth with Pepsodent.'*

As indicated in Beryl's report, some of the rhymes adopted from adverts served as skipping rhymes (cf. Opie and Opie 1997: 212–14) or, in the case of the following, a double ball rhyme, recalled by Beryl, based on the Wrigley PK chewing gum:

PK penny a packet
First you chew it
Then you crack it
Then you stick it to your jacket
PK penny a packet.

The Opies note that this rhyme was widespread throughout the country for two-balls, and occasionally for skipping or clapping, the words suggesting the actions to be done (Opie and Opie 1997: 156). As advertising to children grew on ITV, its impact could be traced in some of the interviews in terms of the toys they acquired. Marion recognized the influence of adverts for branded toys:

I mean I think going back to them days, because there was only effectively one commercial channel, being what is now ITV1, during the children's programmes you would always get . . . they'd obviously do a lot of marketing there, and that's when you got the children's adverts on for the certain games. And I remember you could . . . you know, there was things I think for LEGO and stuff like that. And I think a lot of them were sort of aimed at, perhaps, more the girls, because you'd get things sort of . . . oh, I don't know what sort of dolls they were, I don't know if Barbie was out in them days but, you know, Sindy or something like that. So there was quite a lot of adverts on television into that sort of, the 4 to 6 o'clock bracket before the evening news started, and then obviously it got a bit more TV for the adults at 6 o'clock in the evening. But, you know, there was a lot of toy adverts on. And Chad Valley was another one wasn't it, Chad Valley had a lot of games, and I think they're still going to this day. I can't remember what they do now but they used to have more sort of I think plastic type things, you know, shapes and that. I had a gun called Johnny 7, I remember that . . . Basically, it was a gun which had seven different uses, I think that's why it was called Johnny 7. But it was like a big machine gun, and then you could fire rockets with it and you could fire bullets with it, and then you pulled another button and it made a sort of a shooting noise, and then it had a couple of other bits, attachments, to it. And then you could detach one part, which then became a hand gun. That was quite good. And then you could throw yourself on the ground and it had a . . . you could pull two legs down and it became a sort of tripod effect and then you could pretend you were shooting from the bushes and that. So that was quite big.

The 1964 television advert for Johnny Seven OMA[101] (one-man army) toy gun indeed emphasized its versatility, having seven shooting options in one. Due to the success of the advertising campaign, it was the best-selling boys' toy of 1964 and, like toy guns at that time, looked quite realistic in terms of its colour, size and shape. Toy gun design has changed since then and most toy guns for children today are bright in colour (to avoid being mistaken for the real thing) and are often linked to fantasy themes such as sci-fi, rather than linked to traditional war play, although there are still toy guns produced for that purpose. This move reflects both changing perceptions of replica gun play, particularly in the light of mass shootings such as those that took place at Dunblane and Columbine schools, but also signals interest in some of the weaponry used in science fiction films, such as the light sabres of *Star Wars*.

Machin and Van Leeuwen (2009) suggest that key developments in this field relate to global politics, in that the war toys played with by past generations were generally toy soldiers that represented World War II troops. From the 1960s onwards, however, the dominance of US war toys became apparent globally, as the US expanded its economic and political influence around the world. In addition, they note that whilst war toys in the early to mid-twentieth century 'represented first massive passive anonymous armies, and then active heroic large armies that symbolized society as a whole, contemporary war toys suggest individualism, the small flexible team able to operate swiftly' (2009: 62).

Further, it is clear that contemporary war play has also taken on the 'war on terror' discourse, particularly noticeable in the numerous computer games that enable users to take on the persona of a military hero seeking out terrorists, such as *Call of Duty: Modern Warfare* and *Medal of Honour*. At Monteney Primary School, children who engaged in war play in the playground did so using such computer games as their source material. Martin, for example, reported that he and his friends played games based on the computer game *Call of Duty* and that in order to play it, *'You'd be running round like this (runs around with imaginary gun) 'cos then you'd have an invisible gun and you'd be running round like that and then going prrrrrrt (makes shooting gesture) like that.'* In some ways, this description places Martin's imaginative play in a long-standing tradition of war play, in which children pretend to shoot each other with imaginary weapons. However, Burn (in press) suggests that there are new affordances of computer games for this sort of play as children can draw on both their representational content (e.g. characters, narratives), as they may do with other genres, such as war films, but they can also adapt the ludic structure (game rules) of computer games, such as incorporating the concept of levels in games into their playground play.

Returning to Marion's recollections, she mentioned other popular brand toys at that time, such as LEGO, Barbie, Sindy and Chad Valley toys. Additional brands recalled by participants in the study included Hornby trains, Meccano and Scalextric. Cross (1999), charting the rise of branded toys, notes that the educational toys beloved of parents in the early twentieth century were eclipsed in the post-war years by a burgeoning toy industry that focused on the promotion of fantasy. He argues that this created anxiety in parents, who became increasingly marginalized in the toy world as advertisers were able to speak directly to children due to the widespread adoption of television. In addition, television enabled toys to be linked to a multimedia network, a phenomenon that was exacerbated by technological developments over the next twenty years, particularly in relation to computer games, a process referred to by Kinder (1993) as 'transmedia intertextuality'. Brands, whilst having a history that reaches back to the eighteenth century, became positioned as a central aspect of social life in the 1980s, when they 'were spun into the social fabric as a ubiquitous medium in the construction of a common social world' (Arvidsson 2006: 3). At this point, it would be useful to trace the developments between the 1950s and contemporary society in terms of this intertextual process through a case study of one significant brand that was mentioned by the older participants and is still popular with children at Monteney Primary School – LEGO.

LEGO's origins lie in Denmark in the early twentieth century, where Ole Kirk Kristiansen began making wooden toys and, after variable success, named his company 'LEGO', an abbreviation of the Danish phrase 'leg godt', meaning 'play well' (LEGO Group 2012). When plastics became available after World War II, the company began to produce interlocking bricks that were embedded into systems, such as toy towns or train sets. An early advertiser on television, LEGO quickly gained popularity in the UK and expanded its range to include products for girls in 1971 (e.g. dolls' furniture) and large bricks for younger children in 1969, marketed as Duplo. In 1968 the company opened its first theme park, Legoland, in Billund. This, of course, was not novel. Disney was one of the first companies to link children's products with theme parks, with the opening of the first Disneyland in 1955. Theme parks enable the cross-promotion of goods for companies and, as Davis (1996) suggests:

> allow the close coordination of a new product promotion with family leisure time, recreation and vacations. In this sense, the theme park is a kind of physical eyes advertising, performative and kinetic space that makes the electronic or filmic product and its promotion literally material.
>
> (1996: 411)

In 1974, LEGO launched its first set of minifigures. Rather simple in design at first, these became more complicated over time and designed to hold a range of accessories. These have become hugely popular, with a company report suggesting that over four billion minifigures have been produced over the years (LEGO Group 2012: 16). Particularly successful were the mini-figures linked to licensed themes such as *Star Wars* and *Harry Potter*, an indication of the success of the interpenetration of toys with other aspects of the multimedia network. A further example of cross-media promotion took place in 1999 when LEGO linked their toys with McDonald's happy meals for children and this activity was marketed through TV and print media (Hollensen 1998: 550).

This use of toys to promote food, and vice versa, has been a long-standing strategy. Moira (born 1949), like many of the adult respondents, did not have access to many branded toys because of a lack of money, but was aware of the use of toys to promote cereals:

> *Everybody was in the same boat, unless you had a lot of money you didn't necessarily get the branded stuff. It wasn't until the '60s that I don't think my parents' finances improved enough to be buying stuff like that . . . but these cheap toys, they used to fall apart pretty quickly, but in general that's*

all they could afford, my parents, you know. Cars or . . . you know just nick-
nack things. I can remember one toy and it was a gyroscope . . . and stuff
like that. Or you used to get toys out of Kellogg's boxes and stuff like that
. . . I remember one was a submarine and you used to put baking powder in
it somehow and it used to make it go up and down in the water. And you'd
put baking powder in a little frogman or something and he used to swim
round. Various things like that. And making . . . I don't know what you'd
call them, but a disc and you had a string through it and you'd twist it and
pull it, keeping pulling it, and it makes a whirring sound . . . and stuff like
that. And ball in the cup thing, you know, ball on a string you know, that
old Victorian thing, we used to buy it. And a clicker one, you know? You
used to click it out and you used to catch it.

Many 'crazes' began or spread in this way, such as the more recent POGS phenomenon of the 1990s. This involved a Passion fruit–Orange–Guava drink whose bottle lids could be used in a flip-over game, as milk bottle tops had been previously (Opie and Opie 1997: 120–2). Moira's distinct memories of these toys, half a century or so later, attests to the attraction they held for children at that time. By the eighties and nineties, however, access to branded toys was more widespread and cross-promotion of toys and food extended beyond cereals to fast food, as indicated in the example of LEGO. This period of expansion in the cross-marketing of toys, television, film and other cultural artefacts has been the subject of extensive analysis (see, for example, Cross 1999, Fleming 1996 and Kline 1993). In this period, toy and media companies could be seen to be adopting the strategies identified by the political economist Eileen Meehan (2005) to increase cross-product synergy. She identified five behaviours that were indicative of this – recirculation, repackaging, re-versioning, recycling and redeployment. An example of recirculation is when a firm licences an artefact so that it can move from one venue/outlet/means of dissemination to another, e.g. a cinema-released film that is subsequently shown on a satellite/cable channel. Repackaging occurs when a text or artefact is placed on the market in a different form e.g. when a cinema-released film is launched as a DVD. Re-versioning takes place when multiple versions of the same artefact appear, e.g. a film along with directors' cuts. Recycling occurs when a part of an artefact is used to create another artefact. Meehan suggests that in the case of redeployment, 'the symbolic universe encapsulated in an artifact – whether a television series, film, novel, or other intellectual property – is moved to create a new TV series, film, novel, etc., that is both dependent on, but removed from, the original' (Meehan 2005: 125). Redeployment has been a key strategy for LEGO in the twenty-first century.

From 1998 to 2004, LEGO had to revise its business model following substantial losses, due primarily to over-growth and a lack of innovation in its core products, according to Mads Nipper, LEGO's Executive Vice-President

(Maclean 2009). However, it has recovered its position over the last few years, partly through its release of 'LEGO Friends', a version aimed at girls (criticized for its sexist nature, see Miller and Gray 2012), and the company's extension of its products to electronic gaming and other media. For example, LEGO videogames, 'LEGO Batman', 'LEGO Harry Potter' and 'LEGO Lord of the Rings' are widely available to play across a range of platforms, including Wiii and Xbox. The commercial partnership with Warner Brothers, which led to the development of the games, has involved LEGO's extension into 3D film with the release of 'LEGO Batman The Movie' (DC Superheroes Unite) in May 2013.

Hjarvard (2004) has suggested that the process of the mediatization of LEGO has involved three aspects: *imaginarization, narrativization* and *visualization*. In the process of *imaginarization*, LEGO managed to provide content for its bricks and artefacts linked to fantasy worlds through linking with other licensed media texts and characters. LEGO promoted *narrativization* through its extension into magazines and computer games, in which LEGO characters became engaged in storylines related to their thematic universes. The process of *visualization* occurred through the replication of LEGO's physical bricks on computer screens in the computer games it developed. In the years following Hjarvard's analysis, we would suggest that a further three aspects can be seen in the mediatization of LEGO: *participation, socialization* and *mobilization*. Screen-capture software and easily available video cameras now enable consumers to engage in production linked to their cultural passions, which fosters *participation* in a consumer society (see Jenkins *et al.* 2006). Users participate as producers in the LEGO universe as they create, for example, films of play with LEGO characters that they upload to YouTube. *Socialization* occurs as LEGO users discuss with each other aspects of their engagement. As Carrington and Dowdall (2013) point out, in an analysis of the popular LEGO minifigs, the LEGO brand has spawned flickr.com sites, online auction sites and blogs that all enable users to celebrate and share their use with others. *Mobilization* is possible through the use of apps for transportable iPhones/iPods which involve building using LEGO bricks, taking an image of the artefact and then uploading it to a website. Virtual bricks enable users to contribute to the LEGO universe without needing access to physical bricks. *LEGO Creationary* is an app that has adapted a board game for tablets and mobiles, so that players can guess what virtual artefacts are being built and earn points for correct guesses. This link between online and offline play is characteristic of contemporary culture (see Burke and Marsh in press; Marsh 2010a, 2011, in press, a and b) and is considered in Chapter 7 in relation to Disney products. Through the use of strategies outlined above, LEGO has sustained a brand that can measure its success through broad adoption across the world. Its 2012 report states that its products are on sale in more than 130 countries, eight LEGO sets are sold each second, on average each person on earth owns 80 LEGO bricks and the world's children spend 5 billion hours a year playing with LEGO bricks (LEGO Group 2012: 22).

Cross-media promotion, used widely by the LEGO Group, is not new, as many analysts have pointed out. Wasko (2001), for example, outlines how Disney was granted over 70 licences for tie-ins to *Snow White* before the film was released in 1937. Disney was also one of the first companies to engage in character merchandizing. Following the emergence of Mickey Mouse in the animation *Steamboat Willie*, in 1928, Disney agreed the licensing for a wide range of products, including books, toys and household artefacts. Nearly thirty years later, Disney undertook a similar campaign in relation to the character Davy Crockett, in advance of the release of the film *Davy Crockett, King of the Wild Frontier* in the UK in 1956. Crockett-related toys, dressing-up clothes, accessories and character toys flooded the market. The Opies note that as the campaign reached its climax in the month of the film's release, 'there was a defininte spasm of Crockett play. The *British Medical Journal* reported a significant increase in the number of children admitted to hospital with eye injuries. And the children began singing' (Opie and Opie 1959: 118). They did not just sing the official Davy Crockett ballad, however, but a host of parodic versions in which Crockett became, by turns, a spaceman, a Teddy boy, and a crockery washer, amongst other things (Opie and Opie 1959: 119). There were also Crockett jokes circulating, such as: ' "How many ears has Davy Crockett?" "Three. He's got a left ear, and a right ear, and a wild frontier" ' (Opie and Opie 1959: 120). According to the Opies, 'at the end of the summer Crockett play and costume disappeared as suddenly as it had arrived; only the Crockett songs continued, and still continue . . . in full throat' (1959: 120). Something analogous seems to have been the case with Mickey Mouse, about whom rhymes are still circulating eighty-five years after he was created (see Chapter 3 for a counting-out example from Monteney Primary School). It seems that there is strong relationship between character merchandizing and the process of 'onomastic allusion' (see Chapter 4) in children's rhymes.

Characters can, therefore, create consumer markets in the same way that brands do and indeed, the two can interact in dynamic ways through brands that incorporate a number of characters. For example, it can be argued that CBeebies itself is a brand that incorporates a number of characters that are merchandized both independently and in relation to the uber-brand, such as *Bob the Builder*, *Everything's Rosie* and the *Teletubbies*. Similarly, the Disney brand incorporates many characters that are merchandized independently, whilst strongly linked to the Disney brand. Whilst such patterns are well established, what is new in the current commercial landscape is the way in which children's playful engagement with brands crosses media, crosses physical and virtual boundaries and incorporates user engagement. This not just the case with childhood texts and artefacts, of course. Hardy, in an analysis of HBO's *True Blood*, notes that:

The commercial intertextuality of official merchandise is prominent across all the most popular 'independent' sites. Commodified intertextual flows thus extend into more 'autonomous' textual spaces, yet a counter flow is also discernible. Enabled by media corporations' efforts to encourage online participation is the space created within 'controlled' sites such as HBO's *True Blood* wiki (n.d.) for critical fan discussions, for instance on the show's double standards in regard to male and female nudity.

(2011: 13)

This 'transmedia intertextuality' (Kinder 1993), or, as Carrington (in press) has termed it, in a phrase which is, perhaps, more appropriate for the current era, 'new media assemblages', thus offers both children *and* adults creative spaces for play. It should also be noted that brands provide the framework for this play, but they do not limit it. Drawing on a theoretical tradition emerging from Latour (2005), Actor Network Theory (ANT), which emphasizes the agency of material objects, Woodyer (2010: 204) suggests that branded toys can be viewed as network objects that generate a network space through which they can move, spaces which are established and managed by the brands through their sharp policing of copyright. The materiality of branded objects offer a touchstone that can be returned to as users navigate the network space, but their actions are not constrained by this materiality. Woodyer offers the example of a girl she observed who played with Bratz dolls, but incorporated Barbie accessories into this play. As such, it is shown that brandscapes may have a core and periphery and, Woodyer (2010: 221) suggests, be characterized through the concept of 'fractionality', that suggests that different elements of the brand may play specific roles and have variable weightings.

In this complex commercial landscape, advertising to children has had to adapt over time. There is little need to rehearse the history of advertising to children here, given the extensive literature on the subject (see Buckingham 2011 for an overview). The adverts experienced by the adults in our study in their infant years were simple in structure, as in the case of the Johnny Seven gun. The 1964 advert for that toy consisted of a boy playing with the gun, whilst an adult voiceover invited child viewers to imagine themselves in the boy's shoes: 'Your squad is ready for you to lead them through . . .'. The gun's many features were pointed out, perhaps convincing parents, as well as children, of its value. This direct approach to the consumer was subsequently overtaken by more subtle forms of marketing in which products were placed in genres other than adverts. In the 1970s and 1980s, toy manufacturers began to commission animations that served to promote their products, key examples being *Transformers* and *Care Bears*, and there was no intention to address the adult audience. Buckingham (2011) outlines how subsequent product developments did not necessarily begin with the toy, but products were designed to be launched simultaneously through an integrated marketing strategy, as in the case of *Pokémon*. More recently, advertising strategies include peer-to-peer marketing, viral marketing using SMS texts and advergaming, all of which challenge traditional boundaries and raise issues of privacy and data management. Companies adopt popular cultural activities and incorporate them into their adverts in order to suggest that the goods they offer transcend the status of merchandise (Cova *et al.* 2007: 10), such as the recent advertisements for mobile networks that incorporate flash mobs. As Buckingham suggests, there has, therefore, been a significant shift in marketing techniques away from a focus on a mass audience to strategies that are 'more pervasive, more personalised and more participatory' and which, therefore, 'require us to move beyond the dichotomous thinking that so frequently characterises discussions of children's consumer culture' (Buckingham 2011: 102).

In an attempt to move beyond this dichotomous thinking which positions children as either media dupes or agentic individuals who are able to resist their positioning as consumers, Sparrman *et al.* (2012: 9) suggest that we consider the 'situated child consumer'. This may be represented, according to Gottzén (2012: 104) in terms of assemblages 'in complex relations to parents, money, commodities, and friends, as well as discourses on childhood'. What is of interest in the recent turn to Deleuzian theory to explain the complexity of children's engagement with media and/or commerce is that it signals a recognition of the way in which children's consumption is not straightforward and highlights how each consumptive act is a drawing together of various entities, organic and non-organic, that construct that act and its elements (including the child) in a specific way in the particular context in which it occurs. This does not mean, however, that we cannot draw out patterns across these consumptive acts, and in the next section we draw on data from our two projects to consider some of the experiences of the situated child consumer.

The situated child consumer

As we suggest above, the act of consumption is a complex process. Woolgar (2012) proposes three categories of consumption: (i) naive consumption, in which a straightforward relationship is assumed between the consumer and the consumed; (ii) consumption in context, in which the situation surrounding the act of consumption is taken into account and (iii) ontological enactment, that is in which the practices of consumption bring into being the entities involved in those practices. He gives the example of a child playing with a toy soldier and suggests that:

> the entity playing with the toy is constituted (enacted) as childlike at the same time as the toy is constituted as a thing with violent or

warlike properties. In this perspective, the existence, identity, and status of the entities involved, whether they be children or objects, emerge in the course of consumption rather than simply preceding consumption.

(2012: 39)

Viewing consumption as ontological enactment enables us to broaden the focus of consumption so that we can begin to trace other elements that are significant in this process, such as affect and emotion. Throughout the data from the 'Memories of Play Project' and the 'Playgrounds Project', there are many instances of children and adults expressing their joy and excitement when consuming toys and media texts and artefacts. The 'material turn' in cultural studies has highlighted the significant role that material culture plays in our lives. Miller (2009) notes the significance of 'stuff' for adults and this is no less the case for children. Marsh has written elsewhere about the important role that media-related toys and artefacts as material stuff play in children's lives, drawing both on Marx's notion of fetishized objects and Wolcott's analysis of transitional objects as offering children a means of transitioning from dependence on adults to independence (see Marsh 2005), and we would suggest that although the nature of the stuff itself has changed enormously over the last sixty years, the roles that such objects play in children's lives remain broadly the same.

This can be analysed in more detail through a focus on the practice of collecting. Throughout both sets of data, reflecting on the practices of children in the 1950s/1960s and the 2010s, collecting was a significant activity. The older participants remembered collecting a wide range of both natural (conkers, leaves, eggs) and manufactured objects, such as marbles, Airfix models, Dinky cars, stamps and cards given with products such as bubble gum, cigarettes and tea. A number of the women recalled collecting beads. Moira described how she and her friends collected beads:

Moira: *We collected beads. We had tins with beads in, just necklace beads, you know, if you'd got an old necklace you'd pull it to pieces . . . And we collected these beads, and you had a separate tin for diamonds. And you could swap say ten beads for one diamond, but if you had diamonds you were . . . ooh, you'd got something if you'd got, they were paste but, you know, they were diamonds to us. And we had that . . . oh years, I remember that going on for years and years, it went down the line . . .*

Jackie: *So what kind of tins, like cigarette, tobacco tins or . . .*

Moira: *Yeah, any, plaster tins, because plasters used to come in a tin and things, didn't they? So any tin we could get us hands on. And I can always remember this girl up at St Thomas Moores and she had the longest nails I've ever seen on anybody, really manicured they were, and her fingers*

never touched the beads or diamonds, she just picked them up with her
nails. And I always remember, she had more diamonds than anybody
else, you know. Oh, but if you saw an old necklace, 'Can we have this,
can we have this' and you'd pull it to pieces and . . . cadged off anybody,
neighbours, anybody, we used to cadge these. They used to give them
you, they'd heard, you know, 'Do you want this?', 'Oh yeah', you know.
So we loved that, we really loved that.

Jackie: *Swapping beads.*

Moira: *Yeah, because you'd got something if you'd a tin of beads, and especially*
if you'd a tin of diamonds, you know.

Jackie: *And did you do anything with the beads, did you play with them?*

Moira: *No, no, no just collected them, just . . . you know. That were your money*
sort of thing, that was, you know, that showed how high up you were,
you'd got this big tin of beads, you know . . . you just had them in this
tin and, you know, they used to say, 'We've got this diamond', and you
know, 'Oh I'll swap it you for ten of these beads', or twenty of these beads
depending on the size of the diamond, you know.

From Moira's account, it is clear that the beads offered a currency of sorts for the children (*'that were your money, sort of thing'*), which conveyed value (*'that showed how high up you were'*), with the paste gems being the most attractive and of highest value. Roud (2010: 232–43) discusses a range of similar examples involving everyday objects such as cherry stones, pins, buttons, and pieces of broken china, collected for use in certain games or for their intrinsic interest. As in Moira's case, 'these items often became the unofficial currency of childhood' (Roud 2010: 232), some items being more valuable than others, and some children proving to be particularly skilful 'wheeler dealers'. Evidence of the collecting and swapping of such 'commodities' dates from at least the mid-nineteenth century (Roud 2010: 236) and their use in games, such as those involving cherry stones, earlier still (2010: 237). The collecting of buttons and their use in throwing and flicking games was also very popular (Roud 2010: 239–41) and is mentioned in *London Street Games* (Douglas 1916), as noted in Chapter 2 in this volume. Such games illustrate the concept of children as bricoleurs, making do with whatever is to hand and this process continues to the present with children collecting, for example, pebbles from the beach. Commercially produced collectibles have also continued since the practice of toys being distributed in cereal packets proliferated in the mid-twentieth century, the main difference being that these items are now generally produced to be bought, rather than given away free with other products (Roud 2010: 235).

As with the older participants, the children at Monteney Primary School collected both natural and non-natural objects, although there was less extensive evidence of collections of traditional objects such as conkers and marbles in the contemporary playground and more evidence of the collection of purchased items that belonged to sets. As Moira's recollections indicate, some collectors' items are attributed greater value than others, and this is also the case in contemporary play. Value might change according to circumstances, however. Woodyer (2010: 169), in a review of one child's collection of cards, noted that 'value was shifting, performed differently according to how the card is configured in relation to webs of connection at any one time'.

Analysis of children's collecting has a well-established history. At the beginning of the twentieth century, Burk (1900) noted that most children have three or four collections and that collecting peaks between the ages of 8 and 11. Witty and Lehman (1930, 1931) and Durost (1932) identified that some children had as many as 11 or 12 collections. Collecting is a global phenomena that is culturally contextualized. For example, Danet and Katriel (1989) identified how ultra-orthodox Jewish children in Israel collected cards representing rabbis. Tobin's edited volume (2004) on *Pokémon* traces the adoption of that particular brand across the world and it is notable how this globalized commodity is localized in each of the contexts in which it is used. Whilst some scholars have denigrated collecting, suggesting that it demonstrates how children are obsessed with consumer culture (e.g. Hill 2011), it is important to note the significance that the practice has on a variety of levels. Danet and Katriel identified a number of metaphors that occur in discourse about collecting by collectors themselves and, as a result of this, contend that:

> Some cultural analysts might want to argue that collecting is nothing but a glorified form of consumerism, an excess brought on by bureaucratization and late capitalism. While we do not underestimate the power of commercialization to manipulate people, the metaphors used in discourse on collecting indicate that the collectors' objects and activities carry a rich set of meaning for them that have little to do with commercialization.
>
> (1994: 50)

These meanings included collecting as: play; a springboard to fantasy; a means to explore the dialectic between order and chaos; a means of offering structure; a form of both self-regulated energizing activity and relaxation; and a means of enjoying both 'meditative isolation and intense social engagements' (1994: 33). Whilst they are not focusing on children in this analysis, we would suggest that the same principles can be applied to child collectors.

A consistent trope throughout histories of society and culture is that practices are rarely new. Thus Stearns (2009: 62) notes that 'one of the world's first clear consumer fads' emerged in Holland during the middle of the seventeenth century, when the Dutch became passionate about tulips, to the point that they bought pictures of tulips when the flowers themselves were unavailable. In order to understand this persistent need to collect and engage in a collective consumer culture, Allison Pugh (2009) undertook ethnographies in three different schools in the US, focusing on children's and parents' consumer practices. Based on extensive fieldwork, she suggests that children's consumptive practices can be viewed as 'an economy of dignity' and that children 'collect or confer dignity among themselves according to their (shifting) consensus about what sort of objects and experiences are supposed to count for it' (2009: 6–7). The key motivation for engaging in these collective expressions of consumerism is, therefore, to seek a sense of belonging. Little has changed in that respect since the adult respondents swapped their cigarette cards and bartered their beads in the 1950s/1960s. What has changed is largely related to the material objects themselves, to which now can be added immaterial objects in the form of online currency and virtual artefacts, gained in children's virtual world play.

Conclusion

In this chapter, we have considered changes in consumer culture for children over the past sixty years and outlined the ways in which these changes have impacted on children's play. One of the areas we have not considered is the non-commercial play practices of children, that is, their play with home-made objects and toys. We review this issue in the next chapter, in which we examine play, media and commercial culture as they are embedded in family and school practices.

6 Play in the institutions of home and school

Homes and schools are significant spaces for children; they spend their formative years largely in one or the other and similar issues arise for them across both spaces in terms of the way in which power relationships with adults are at the core of their experiences in the sites. This chapter, therefore, considers both domains and reflects on the way in which play in homes and schools has changed since the mid-twentieth century. The chapter draws on data from the adult respondents in order to examine the nature of play in family life and schools in the mid-twentieth century. This is contrasted with research that has illuminated the way in which play is instantiated across homes and schools in contemporary society.

Play and family life in the mid-twentieth century

Underpinning our analysis is a notion of family that recognizes its complex nature, which is not fixed but, rather, consists of changing relationships and roles, is about process and might be characterized as 'doing the family' (Morgan 2011: 5). Indeed, such is the fluid nature of the concept of family that some have suggested that the term is too limiting (Roseneil and Budgeon 2004). Nevertheless, Edwards *et al.* (2012: 743) identify 'the analytic strengths of family in transcending a concern with individual actors and their identities and relationships, to identify collective fusions within and across generations'. We would also argue that the use of the term is helpful in signalling a focus on a particular set of institutional relationships that take place across a range of contexts, but have a particular intensity in home spaces.

In addition, there is a need to acknowledge that it is not an easy task to trace the changes in families over time. While some scholars identify how family structures have changed considerably in a post-industrial society in which individualization and privatization are key themes, others have emphasized the way in which families have always been diverse in nature (see Gillies

2003 for a review). Nevertheless, there were major social, cultural and political changes in the post-war period that inevitably had an impact on families. These include changes in women's employment patterns, greater use of contraception which limited family size, increases in the number of divorces, the rise of single-parent families and non-marital childbearing and developments in the welfare state, all of which had implications for children (Fass and Grossberg 2012). In the following discussion of family life in the mid-twentieth century, we will draw on the accounts of two of the respondents, one from Sheffield and one from London, in order to explore in depth the way in which play informed family life. Beryl was born in 1943 in Sheffield and Robert born in 1954 in London and we chose these two respondents to focus upon because they offer a contrasting picture in terms of the extent to which their parents were engaged in their play. This enables reflection on a number of issues pertinent to a social and cultural analysis of family life, including the impact of poverty, gender and the positioning of children within the family.

In the post-war period of the 1950s, there was much public debate about the way in which social life was becoming more inward-focused within families as people were, it was argued, becoming less engaged with their communities. Research has indicated, however, that people were more networked within their families and communities than was often assumed (Chambers 2012a). We should not be surprised at this dichotomy; as Gillis has argued, concerns about the disappearance of family life have been consistent over time:

> Looking back from the 1990s, and preoccupied with rising divorce and illegitimacy rates, we perceive the 1950s as a rock of stability. But that was a decade gripped by anxiety about family life, and especially about the threat posed by the new youth cultures. The 1950s version of the traditional family was an idealized image of the Depression family, which was imagined as holding on by holding tight to one another. But those who lived through the 1920s and 1930s would not have recognized themselves in the myths that later generations made of them, for these are the same people who saw themselves to be in the midst of the sexual revolution. The so-called Lost Generation felt wholly cut off from the past they imagine to have been as stable as their present was chaotic. For them, the Victorian family was tradition. But as we have seen the Victorians were by no means sure of themselves when it came to family matters. They were deeply anxious about the loss of community resulting from rapid urbanization and no more secure in their family life than we are.
>
> (1997: 5)

In the 1950s, housing expanded rapidly as bombed-out sites were cleared and new housing estates were built at the edges of towns and cities, which was the case for one of the communities featured in our studies, Parson Cross in Sheffield. In the post-war years, the estate, and its neighbour estate, Shiregreen, were viewed as healthy places to live, close as they were to the countryside surrounding the north of Sheffield. Indeed, families with members who suffered from tuberculosis were moved there for health reasons, as recalled in the story of Beryl and her family, who were moved to Shiregreen when she was 10 months old. Beryl was the middle child of the family, with a sister five years older than her and a sister 15 months younger than her. She recalled the family's relocation to the Shiregreen estate:

> *My dad was a steel works labourer. My mother couldn't work because she'd chronic ill health, she died when she was 53, she was chronic. She started to be poorly when in her 20s; she had tuberculosis which was a killer, you know, and as feared, tuberculosis was as feared as AIDS is today, absolutely as feared. People were petrified of TB, you know, they really were. And they'd been allocated that house because they were living in rooms, they were living in shared accommodation, which for somebody as ill as my mother was no use, so she'd got me and then she'd already got my elder sister, and certain houses on certain estates, which were considered to be in 'fresh air', even though there were over 3,000 smoking chimneys on Shiregreen alone, that were considered to be cleaner than living in rented accommodation and sharing bathrooms and things like that. And that house was allocated to them by the Chest Clinic in Sheffield.*

Life was not easy for Beryl and her siblings when her mother suffered serious bouts of illness:

> *And because when she'd gone to the sanatorium a big navy blue lorry used to come, a van, a big square box van with a Public Health insignia on the side, coat of arms, so everybody knew what it was. And two men used to come out of this van up the path in protective clothing and masks. And my little sister used to be terrified. She used to start crying and run away. And I can still smell that smell if I try. Everything in the house upstairs where my mum were had to be stoved, it were called stoving, and they saturated everything, and then they sealed the bottom of the door and we had to leave that. But it was so bad this smell that it used to start to permeate all in the house, and my dad used to go upstairs and open the landing window. Although they'd told us not to, it was so strong, so strong and unbearable this smell. And so everybody knew that we were back in another session of active tuberculosis, you know. And so people were scared. And then when my mother went in hospital to have a very, very serious operation – I don't even know if they do it now, it's quite brutalising and mutilating, breaking ribs and removing lungs and things . . . And we had to be farmed out, we*

had to be looked after. Because if you didn't go to work you didn't get paid, nobody paid your rent, there were no help. I mean there isn't a lot of help now but there were none then. If my dad didn't go to work he got 'sack. So because I had a persistent cough, which is what I had to have this operation for in the finish, it were never a problem who were going to have my eldest sister and my littlest sister, but there were always a little problem about who were going to have me, because they'd be scared. They would think I'd got what my mother had got . . . and sometimes we had to go to Fulwood Cottage Homes, because rather than have the three of us separate, because nobody could take three, because you'd got to take ration books and every-thing you know, we went to Fulwood Cottage Homes together.

Fulwood Cottage Home was a children's home, which housed the children when other accommodation could not be found for them. Beryl recalled the social isolation that she and her sisters suffered through her mother's bouts of illness, which impacted upon their play:

When she used to have to go into the sanatorium we were a little bit ostra-cised, as though people had said to their children, 'Keep away from them', or 'Keep away from there'. Because it was so frightening for everybody, you've got to think back.

Despite these challenges, Beryl remembered that in between her mother's bouts of illness, she played as others did:

We were just . . . we're like everybody else, in between those bad times and that, we were just like everybody else, you know, nobody had got anything and you played your own games and you went outside. And you never wanted to come in. You'd not got much to play with outside but you never wanted to come in; no, you wanted it to just last.

As will be discussed in further detail in Chapter 7, much of children's play took place on streets and neighbourhood areas, with little, or no, adult involve-ment. It was also the case that adults did not engage in play extensively in homes. Beryl stressed that there was little to do inside the house and that her parents were too busy to play with her:

And you see if you fell out with somebody you didn't stay fell out long because there were nothing else to do. You'd go in the house with face on and you'd find that when you got in the house there were now't to do anyway. Or your mother would say, 'What are you falling out for, there's now't to do in here', and you knew there weren't, it's perfectly true, there weren't owt to do in there. And your mothers were busy. And don't let's

> *forget, alright we'd gone from mangle to microwave so we fit more in, we have ridiculous amounts of work in a day, your mothers had got no labour-saving devices. And the work that they had to do – walk to the shops every day and get a meal on the table, it were phenomenal, the amount of work that they had to do were phenomenal.*

As Langhamer (2005) noted, ownership of labour-saving devices for housework was not widespread even at the end of the 1950s and, therefore, given the strains that were obviously apparent for Beryl's mum, it was not surprising that she did not engage in play with her:

Julia: *Was there any involvement with your parents in your play?*

Beryl: *None whatsoever. And my friend who died on Sunday morning said the same. 'None whatsoever Beryl, was there?' . . . We've said this before, me and my friends, we don't remember our parents being worried about whether we were going to be bored because it was the six weeks holidays or whatever, or not having enough to do, or not have any money to take us anywhere. Because . . . no, simply in a nutshell, no I don't, no they weren't.*

This was not the case for all respondents, as some reported that their parents did play card or board games occasionally with them, particularly during holiday periods, such as Christmas, and others noted that parents occasionally took them to local parks. Nevertheless, the engagement of parents was minimal in these reports and play appeared to be, in the main, a childhood activity.

Robert was born in Wanstead and lived in Manor Park as an only child. The family lived in a three-bedroom terraced house, which his grandmother bought in 1958. Robert's father was an upholsterer and his mother did bookkeeping. Robert defined himself as working-class:

> *I would always say working-class, you know, that would be how I would have viewed it . . . I think my mum always sort of liked to think we were sort of middle-class – but we weren't anything like that at all. My mum never had central heating in her house all the way through her life, we never had central heating. I don't think . . . they certainly didn't have a colour television whilst I lived there. I can't remember when colour TV came in but it was certainly a long time before they ever got a colour TV.*

Robert did enjoy a greater level of material comfort than Beryl and his family was able to buy him a range of toys, including train sets, Meccano and so on. Whilst Robert did not discuss his mother playing with him, he recalled that his father supported his play in a range of ways. For example, he stated that he and his dad played football in the garden:

> *My dad was always keen on football, so I mean it would have come from my dad and we would have . . . we sort of played in the . . . well we did play in the garden together. I don't know, it just seems like a natural thing.*

This reference to it seeming like 'a natural thing' indicates the way in which family habitus (Bourdieu 1990), established practices embedded within families, can influence each generation. Wheeler (2011), in a study of children with a propensity to play sport, identified that they were influenced by a strong family habitus in which sport was an important part of the family culture. There was evidence that Robert's family was very interested in football:

> *Because when you asked about how I'd got interested in football and I was trying to sort of relate it, but I mean I supported West Ham, my dad supported West Ham, and his dad did, and there's sort of quite a big sort of . . . you know, it's been quite a sort of family thing in recent times. Because in the First World War people joined up in the army, they sort of grouped them up in what they called Groups of Pals . . . in getting people to sign up, they'd get them to join up as groups, and my granddad joined the army as a group of pals, who all supported West Ham United. And about three or four years ago, West Ham commemorated this group and they put a plaque up on Remembrance Sunday. West Ham were playing at home and there was a sort of service when the plaque went up. And we were provided with free tickets . . . But it was such a nice thing, to actually have a reason to meet up really, you know, with family members that we hadn't seen for a very long time. And my granddad was actually mentioned in the programme. He was one of only a small number who actually survived out of the sort of regiment.*

Here we can note the interest of three generations of males in one family in football. Sports, and football in particular, are regularly cited as 'a major site for reinforcing hegemonic masculinity by creating and recreating what it means to be a man through masculine interaction' (Davis and Duncan 2006: 245). Thus, being a male in Robert's family was constructed across each generation in relation to football culture.

The other aspect of play in which fathers were frequently referred to throughout our data from the interviews with older respondents was that of the provision of home-made toys. Many of the adult respondents reported that their fathers made toys for them, which included forts, bicycles and go-karts. This may be as a result of woodwork and craft lessons in schools, which were timetabled for all children, rather than just those taking exams in the subjects, as is the case in secondary schools today. Using his skills as an upholsterer,

Robert's dad made a tent that his son could play with in the garden, in addition to a garage that Robert was able to leave out in the front room:

> *I mean I've been an only child as well, I sort of was quite used to sort of playing on my own as well. So I suppose we were pretty fortunate really because we had a front room which didn't tend to be used an awful lot, so I could lay out my toys in the front room and not be disturbed really . . . And, you know, I think I . . . well my dad made me little metal toys cars as well and my dad made me a garage once, so the garage would often be sort of where one group of soldiers would be hiding out. And then I also had a castle and that would be another area where different soldiers would be hiding out. As I say I was lucky because I did have that front room where I could lay things out.*

This spatial luxury, which was very unusual in the data, may have related to Robert's position as an only child in the family. This factor may also have afforded him greater opportunities to play with his parents. There is a distinct lack of data regarding the extent to which parents played with children at home in the 1950s and 1960s and only a limited number of studies on the subject in more recent decades (Mildon 2009). In an analysis of parental involvement in play of over 20,000 children who were part of the Millennium Cohort Study, children with no siblings were found to have more frequent opportunities to play with their parents than children with siblings (Mildon 2009). This study also identified that boys engaged more frequently in active play with their parents than girls, and that this play was more likely to take place with fathers rather than mothers.

Whilst the general pattern across the respondents' testimonies was that they reported that their parents rarely played with them, Robert's experience demonstrates that this was not the case for all families and reminds us that the relationship between play and family life is contingent upon a range of factors. Indeed, it may have been the case that the parents played more extensively with the respondents when they were infants, but they could not recall these first years of life. Nevertheless, there were normative expectations with regard to parenthood during those years, with it being deemed culturally inappropriate for fathers to be involved in caregiving, for example, as Josselyn (1956) noted. How far the situation has changed over the past sixty years is the focus for the next section of the chapter.

Play and family life in the 2010s

Large-scale time use surveys indicate that parents now spend more time with their children than was the case for previous generations. Using data obtained from national time-diary studies in the US, Bianchi *et al.* (2006: 3) state that 'parental time interacting with children has actually increased in the decades after 1965, when stay at home mothers with large families were far more prevalent in America than they are today'. Gauthier *et al.* (2004) analysed time use data across 16 different countries, including the UK, and found a similar trend, which was also identified in a study of time use surveys in the UK (Fisher *et al.* 1999). The rise in the increase in time spent with children is even more pronounced for fathers (Bianchi *et al.* 2006: 3). These data focus on time spent with children and not the amount of time spent playing, but it is reasonable to assume that there would be a related impact on the amount of time parents spend playing with their children. Maughan and Gardner (2012) suggest that a number of factors have led to these developments, including more widespread uptake of labour-saving household devices, which has reduced housework demands, smaller family sizes and changes in social and cultural expectations with regard to parenting practices.

The space of the home has changed considerably as a playspace for children in recent decades. As Karsten has argued, in a study of the history of play which focused on three streets in Amsterdam:

> The public space of the street used to be a child space, but in two of the three streets studied it has been transformed into an adult space. Conversely, private home space – traditionally the domain of adults – has become a child space.
>
> (2005: 275)

This is partly due to changing discourses with regard to parenting. Parenting as a socially constructed discourse has dominated the political agenda over recent years and the term, as Faircloth and Lee (2010) suggest, represents a focus on child rearing as the acquisition and implementation of a set of skills that is informed by the latest policy and research. Government-commissioned reports that present a series of recommendations regarding parenting have proliferated during this period, such as the Byron Review (Byron 2008) or Bailey Review (Bailey 2011), and there are deemed to be particular practices that need to be adopted in a more widespread manner if children are to be brought up appropriately. The pedagogization of parenting has led to an increased focus on the home as a site for early education and this has influenced the kinds of play parents foster and support, with a move to the purchasing of toys that are purported to support learning (Buckingham and Scanlon 2003). Play has thus become part of the project of parenting in a post-industrial society and has become increasingly organized and planned into many families' schedules, rather than allowed to emerge organically. As Gillies (2003: 150) notes, 'Time spent with children today is far more organized, far more ritualized.' Playgroups, after-school clubs that involve playful activities, planned trips to play centres and theme parks, all are mobilized in an attempt to deliver the perfect childhood. There are cultural differences in relation to parenting and play (Roopnarine 2012), however, and the material context of parenting needs to be taken account of in any analysis of child-rearing practices (Braun *et al.* 2010).

A further difference in the play that takes place in contemporary homes, in contrast to those of the 1950s and 1960s, is that technology now plays a central role. This is particularly the case in relation to computer games and there has been a deliberate strategy in recent decades by companies that develop hardware for games to ensure that they develop family-friendly equipment. The Nintendo Wii, Microsoft Xbox and Sony PlayStation all now enable multiple players and a range of games have been developed that encourage family play. Drawing on Flynn (2003) and Mitchell (1997), Voida and Greenberg (2010) reflect on the 'digital hearth', a metaphor which replaces the traditional fireplace and mantelpiece in the living room with the console player and screen as the key focus for the family. However, whilst the hearth metaphor might conjure up a warm and rosy picture, Voida and Greenberg point to the way in which there may be competing interests and thus arguments about the use of the console player and screen. In their study of the domestic use of games, they found that some families organize their gaming around meals, with family members taking it in turns to play games and prepare dinner, thus emphasizing the way in which such practices have become woven into the daily fabric of family life. Indeed, as Enevold argues (2012: 4), in her analysis of the way that game playing has become an everyday practice in homes, 'Play is in the process domesticated in the double sense of the word – brought into the home, but also subordinated and subjected to the norms of the family and the home.' Chambers (2012b) makes the point that this collaborative game play takes place mainly between younger children and parents, as adolescents enjoy playing on their own.

In addition to playing with console games, there is also growing evidence of family play in online virtual spaces, such as Massive Multiplayer Online Games (MMOGs) and virtual worlds. In Monteney Primary School, some pupils reported playing with their parents on the virtual worlds *Club Penguin* and *Farmville* and given that approximately a third of the 5- to 11-year-old pupils who completed the online media survey suggested that they had a *Facebook* page, which, from follow-up semi-structured interviews it seemed were apparently mediated by parents, it may be the case that the driver for this use was collaborative play with families on *Farmville*. One of the key factors in this growth of intergenerational play within families is, we would argue, the de-infantilization of play. In recent decades, it has become more acceptable for adults to engage in play that is adult-focused. For example, games such as paintballing have become popular, in addition to location-based gaming in which adults run around specific areas using GPS technology. Technological advances have been a key driver of these changes and there are now a number of advocates for the recognition of the need for adults to engage in playful activities (e.g. Kane 2004).

In this review of the changes in family life and play between the 1950s and 2010s, there are general patterns that can be discerned, as outlined above. It should be pointed out, however, that research in this area is very limited and the conclusions to be drawn can only be tentative in nature. There needs to be more extensive research undertaken of the ways in which play is instantiated in family lives in the future if we are to develop a fuller understanding of the motives and practices of parents and carers and the impact they have on the way that family members play together.

Play in schools in the 1950s

As we move on to consider the nature of play in the institution of school, the accounts of another two members of the older respondent group are drawn upon in order to explore some of the issues in depth. These data are compared with the experiences of pupils at Monteney Primary School and the wider literature on schooling today.

Caroline was born in Sheffield in 1942 and was the oldest of three children. She had a sister who was ten years younger than her and a brother who was 14 years younger than her. Caroline's mother was a cleaner and her father worked in industry. Caroline identified her primary school as having strong discipline:

> *You had to do as you were told. I remember having to line up in the yard when you first got there before you went into school, they used to blow a whistle, line up and you had to line . . . really line up in a straight line before you could move.*

Lining up in this way is still a common feature in schools and indeed was used in the two schools in the 'Playgrounds Project'. Richards (2012: 387), in reflecting on the lining up procedures in Christopher Hatton primary school, suggests that lining up serves as a liminal space between the playground and the classroom and offers a means of transitioning emotionally and mentally from one space to the other.

Between the 1950s and the 1980s, corporal punishment was widely used in schools as a means of disciplining pupils (Parker-Jenkins 1991). Caroline recalled an incident in which she had to stay in during playtime in order to complete a mathematics task, which stirred up memories of corporal punishment practices within the school:

We had one or two teachers who were very strict indeed, and the Maths teacher, I do remember this very clearly but this would be at Junior school, and she had a little green cane, only about that long . . . Maths wasn't my subject by any stretch of the imagination, and I struggled with this long multiplication, and I couldn't get it right. And she kept me in over playtime, and I still couldn't get it right, and because I'd done it about four times she'd cane me, she rapped my knuckles with this little green cane. I mean I think girls got off more lightly than boys in general, because boys are generally more mischievous aren't they, and I do remember there being quite a bit of slip-pering and caning. That was the only time I got any sort of corporal punish-ment, but the boys were often whisked away – well, caned in front of the class. And I do remember as well, teachers throwing . . . you know, there used to be rubbers for the . . . well we used to call them blackboards, they call them chalk boards now don't they, and they were wooden. They were about that long and quite . . . and they used to hurl those at pupils from time to time.

The teachers appeared to keep their distance when supervising at playtimes:

Jackie: *What about hopscotch, did you play hopscotch?*
Caroline: *Yes that's down, oh loved hopscotch, played that for hours. But you had to . . . now they have them in the yard don't they, painted on? Well we used to have to draw it.*
Jackie: *And how would you draw it?*
Caroline: *Just with chalk, yeah. Not . . . often, one of the teachers would draw you a hopscotch, yeah, so I think they encouraged you to play these games because . . . well I think people were very active then weren't they, a lot more than nowadays.*
Jackie: *And did the teachers ever lead the games or . . .?*
Caroline: *No, not at playtime. In fact I don't even remember them . . . I think there must have been somebody on yard duty. I don't even remember teachers like supervising at playtime, but they must have done because I know sometimes, particularly the boys, they'd get like shouted at, they'd blow the whistle and say, 'Stop doing that' you know, because they used to get rough. So there must have been somebody on duty. But I think it would only be one, one person to supervise a lot of chil-dren, because I think there were round about 40 in our class. They were big classes, I'm sure there were. So 40 in a class.*
Jackie: *Mmm, big class isn't it?*
Caroline: *I think there were about three classes in a year. So it's a lot of chil-dren, yeah. But they did blow whistles a lot.*

It appeared that the playground supervision undertaken by adults was minimal enough to allow children to play in areas that were not sanctioned:

But at the back of the playground, away from the school towards the main road, which is Harris Road, there was a grass area, it was banked up. And there were the air raid shelters on there. And we were warned we mustn't go near them. But I don't think they were blocked off properly, and the boys sometimes used to go down there. We didn't want to go down there because they smelt horrible. I don't know whether they used to go down there and have a wee because it smelt disgusting, so the girls tended to stay away. But I suppose they were quite dangerous, really, if you think about it now.

Caroline recalled that children were allowed to take their own toys to school and a particularly popular toy was the whip and top:

And we used to be allowed to take a whip and top, which was a wooden stick type with a . . . well it was probably a leather whip part to it, and a proper little wooden . . . I remember they were wooden tops shaped just like a little mushroom. And at the bottom they'd got, well it was like a nail, but it was a metal bit at the bottom, and you were either very good at doing them or a bit rubbish. And you used to wrap the thing round and then put your knee on it, it used to go under your knee, and then you used to pull, you used to kneel down, pull the thing and that used to send it off, 'Shhh', like that. And if you were lucky it would . . . and then you could whip it to keep it going.

Interestingly, the Opies include a quotation from one of their child contributors which characterizes this as 'the girls' way' of setting a whipping top spinning (Opie and Opie 1997: 309). Around the turn of the nineteenth century, some adults regarded playing with tops as 'a hoydenish thing for a girl to do' but later the convention seems to have been 'peg tops for boys, whip tops for girls' (Opie and Opie 1997: 310, 311).

The school experiences of the older respondents were similar across the group, as is indicated in the following vignette. Joseph was born in 1953 in London, the second eldest of four brothers and a younger sister. His dad was a factory worker and his mum worked at the General Post Office exchange. Joseph described his family as working-class, and he felt that the school discriminated against its working-class pupils:

Joseph: *And back in the school in them days, if you [were] blue collar, from a blue collar family, you never got an opportunity to go into the music lessons and that, it was all taboo. It was all . . . it was bang out of order. But that's the way it was, you know, so when I went into the music class, you'd all line up and there would be the music teacher sitting there by a piano and she would bang a note on the piano saying, 'What note's that?', you wouldn't have a clue, and she'd go, 'Next', you know. But the kids that came from, you know, upper classes, normally were more au*

>   *fait with music lessons because their mummies and daddies wanted*
>   *them to play a musical instrument, you know.*
> Jackie: *And you never had the chance.*
> Joseph: *So there was a lot of unfairness in the school back then, very much so.*

As was the case with Caroline, Joseph recalled the teachers doling out corporal punishment:

> Joseph: *It was fairly strict. Well the headmaster was Mr Brazen, he was a*
>   *boring old bastard, he was, I'll tell you . . . He used to get a lot from*
>   *giving me the cane I think, that was one of his main ambitions in life.*
>   *I'm not joking.*

Corporal punishment was eventually banned in British state schools in 1987, prompted by the action of two Scottish mothers in 1982, whose appeal to the European Court of Human Rights to support their rights as parents to object to corporal punishment was upheld. The introduction of the law was controversial, with numerous Conservative backbenchers objecting and sections of the media prophesying out-of-control schools. The law was, however, overdue. In 1985, there were 4.7 recorded beatings per 100 pupils in secondary schools and one beating per 100 primary pupils (Gould 2007).

In an account of Scottish schoolchildren's play contemporary with the Opies' research, James Ritchie (see Chapter 2) describes teachers' long-standing use of the 'tawse', a leather strap divided into thongs at one end, and the defiant attitude of children towards it:

> Scottish bairns have always put up a cheerful and good-natured front
> to this undignified and degrading form of violence, whether in plain
> strokes or in the form of 'doublers' or 'cross-handers' or 'blackboard
> blindies'. Like Walter Scott they're determined never ever to be the
> better of it.
>
> (Ritchie n.d.)[102]

The Opies document terms current among children for corporal punishment and a variety of practices said to mitigate the pain inflicted (Opie and Opie 1959: 374–5). These include the widespread belief that a hair placed on the palm would cause the teacher's cane to split and possibly inflict pain on the teacher instead (Opie and Opie 1959: 375). The harshness of school punishment regimes, and in some cases parental ones too, is reflected in the 'retributions', 'ordeals' and 'tortures' visited by children on each other, reported by the Opies (1959) and Ritchie (n.d.). These include 'ducking', sometimes done in the toilet, 'sending to Coventry', which was a form of ostracization, 'running the gauntlet', which involved repeated and increasingly harsh types of hitting, and the 'barley sugar' in which the victim's arm was twisted up her or his back (Opie and Opie 1959: 198–203). As Warner, writing in 2001, comments, 'Now that corporal punishment has at least been banned in schools in the UK, children's own tribunals and penalties no longer reflect adult discipline and punishment, and are consequently no longer tolerated but treated instead as bullying behaviour' (Warner 2001: xv).

As was the case with Caroline, the lack of close supervision by adults at Joseph's school meant that the children could escape the adult gaze together:

Joseph: *The playground, it was all tarmac. There was two. There was a back playground then a forward playground, because we used to get round all sorts of nonsense round the back playground because nobody could see us.*

Jackie: *What, teachers never went round there?*

Joseph: *Well they would because they'd realize that half the school wasn't in the playground, they were all round the back, and we were playing like 'Penny up the Wall' or something like that, you know.*

Playing 'Penny up the Wall', as the game appears to have been known in London (cf. Opie and Opie 1997: 91), or 'Pitch and Toss', involved throwing pennies and the person throwing the penny nearest to the wall won all of the pennies thrown.[103] The game was a form of gambling and thus needed to be played away from the prying eyes of teachers. The clandestine nature of this kind of play at school is also implied in the testimony of one of the Opies' child contributors who said, 'I often see the game played behind the shelter in the playground' (Opie and Opie 1997: 91).

Joseph remembered a range of other playground games including football, hop, skip and jump and tag. He also recalled fighting:

Joseph: *Yeah, we were always fighting. In fact the headmaster used to always say to my mother, you know, 'Your son spends most of the time in a big bundle on the floor' you know. Only friendly fighting but, you know, just . . . we used to like to do that.*

Jackie: *When you say, 'friendly fighting' what do you mean by friendly fighting?*

Joseph: *Messing about, really, with each other quite often. We were only young remember, weren't we?*

Jackie: *You deliberately tried not to hurt anybody then when you did that?*

Joseph: *Oh yeah, yeah, it was all in good fun.*

Jackie: *Yeah. And did it ever escalate into a sort of real fight?*

Joseph: *Yeah, yeah got out of hand occasionally.*

The Opies describe what appear to have been more serious conflicts by means of which the 'pecking order' among boys was tested. These could clearly take place at school, where they might be brought to an end by the arrival of a master or prefect, or sometimes in the playground after school. They often attracted an audience who cheered their favoured fighter on (Opie and Opie 1959: 196). In Joseph's case, it appeared that the headmaster had a fairly relaxed attitude to this rough-and-tumble play. In contemporary playgrounds, however, the issue of play fighting is contentious, with some schools not tolerating it at all (Holland 2003). Richards (2013) notes that, when engaging in pretend fighting, boys he observed were controlling its emotional intensity, making snap judgements about the meanings and intentions of the physical actions of others and their responses to them. Children were able to make subtle judgements about the point at which fighting moved from pretend to not pretend. He argues that attempts to ban such play may reduce opportunities for children to learn and practise the kind of modality judgements that are required for their normal social interactions.

The accounts of Caroline and Joseph both indicate the way in which playground life for the adult respondents was organized and managed very differently to the playgrounds in the 'Playgrounds Project'. The nature of play in playgrounds in the twenty-first century is considered next.

Play in schools in the 2010s

At Monteney Primary School, discipline in the playground was a fairly relaxed matter. This was partly due to the numbers of adults who supervised play. The school employed play workers, who worked alongside teachers to ensure that playtime ran as smoothly as possible. In addition, the school ran a system of buddying, which meant that pupils were given the task of looking out for, and supporting, other pupils when necessary. Blatchford and Sharp, writing in 1994, note that playgrounds were a much better managed space than they were when they were conducting research in playgrounds five years previously. They identified that there was a growing awareness of the value of playtime, an understanding of the significance of design and more effective supervision (1994: 1). Since then, there have been a number of initiatives that have focused on improving responses to bullying (Smith 2013), involving children in the design of playgrounds (Dudek 2005) and using play workers to support and extend play (Patte and Brown 2011).

Despite these advances, there have been sustained concerns about playground provision and management across Britain in recent decades. For example, in the follow-up to a national survey of school breaktimes conducted in 1995, Blatchford and Baines (2006) report that the length of breaktimes (morning, lunchtime and afternoon) had been reduced during the years 1990–95. By 2006, there were further reductions. Whilst half of primary schools in 1995 had an afternoon break for Key Stage 2 pupils, only 26 per cent of schools did so by 2006 and in secondary schools, the afternoon break no longer existed. Pupils reported that they felt that there were limited opportunities for fun activities and disliked restrictions on the time taken for eating. Beresin (2010), in her study of recess in a Philadelpia schoolyard, reports much the same picture in the US and makes an impassioned plea for the crucial importance of play in the face of policy which removes recess altogether from the school day in favour of supposedly more 'edifying' activities. There are also worries that, as the number of adults in playgrounds has increased over the years, they may be over-supervising play (Patte and Brown 2011), expressing an overly protective concern for health and safety issues (Gleave and Cole-Hamilton 2012).

There are certainly restrictions which relate to the ability of children to bring items from home into the playground because of health and safety concerns. Caroline reported how she and her peers were able to bring whip and tops to school, which no doubt would be frowned upon by many schools today. Jones *et al.* (2012), for example, report on a study conducted across four primary schools in the North of England. They itemize the range of objects that were confiscated by teachers, which generally related to children's popular cultural interests e.g. a small plastic *Winnie the Pooh* model, a *Top Trumps* pack, a replica *Star Wars* sabre and superhero figures such as *Spiderman*. Whilst we did not encounter this level of restriction in Monteney Primary School, the banning of objects such as this is reported more broadly (e.g. Holland 2003). Indeed, in Monteney Primary School, children's popular culture appeared to be welcomed in the playground. For example, a large CD player was provided in the playgrounds, next to which children listened and danced to pop music. Children showed us objects they had brought to school, such as *Top Trump* football collecting cards. Children were not restricted in terms of the media texts they drew on in their play, even when this included programmes that were controversial in nature, such as the *Jeremy Kyle Show*.

Conclusion

The institutions of home and school are significant places for children's play. In both arenas, issues of children's agency are writ large, and there have been some major developments over the last sixty years in this regard. We would argue that children today have increased agency in homes and schools, in comparison with the older respondents, in certain contexts. For example, numerous schools now have School Councils in which children can voice their concerns. Many parents today allow children to have input into key family decisions, such as holidays and major purchases (Lindsay and Maher 2013). Nevertheless, the picture is complex. In recent decades, we have seen the increased institutionalization of the child, through standardized approaches to education and the extension of the welfare state into previously marginal areas of childcare and health. In some ways, children today are subject to much closer surveillance and supervision in homes and schools than were the adult respondents, with a range of professionals having greater access to both spaces. Further, there have been recent arguments regarding the way in which children lack agency in terms of accessing spaces outside either school or home (Gill 2007), which is the focus for analysis in the next chapter.

7   Space and play

The 'spatial turn' in sociological and cultural theory has enabled an understanding to be developed of the way in which space is not an independent, neutral entity but is socially constructed and in a constant state of being made and remade (Massey 2005). The material aspects of space have the potential to impact on context and, therefore, it might be useful to 'think of space as comprised of an irrefutable capacity for material agency that was perpetually *in process*' (Allen 2013: 62, author's italics). In this chapter, the relationship between space and play is considered, drawing on theories of space that reflect its contingent nature. It is recognized that a distinction between space and place can be made, in that there is a particularity with regard to place that does not apply to space, but it is also acknowledged that the two are very much linked (Agnew 2005; Allen 2013).

In the chapter, the similarities and differences in the data from the older participants and the children from Monteney Primary School are reviewed when reflecting on the relationship between space and play in the childhoods of the mid–twentieth century and early twenty-first century. The first part of the chapter considers space and play in school playgrounds, before moving on to examine out-of-school play, primarily in homes and neighbourhoods. This leads on to a discussion of the contrast between previous decades and the spaces of out-of-school play in contemporary society, considering in particular the increasingly fluid boundaries between online and offline play.

Space, play and schools

As Pearce and Bailey observe (2011: 1363), 'there is evidence that memories of play times remain in children's minds after much of the formal school experiences have faded away'. The adult respondents retained vivid memories of their playground activities and were able to describe the spaces in which they played. Playgrounds of the nineteenth and early/mid-twentieth centuries were, in the main, rather barren spaces that served merely as a means of enclosing children during breaks in the school day. The respondents describe playgrounds that were largely bereft of specifically demarcated play spaces, apart from occasional markings on the ground or walls, whilst the contemporary playgrounds we studied did contain adult-constructed spaces that were intended to promote particular types of play, such as covered areas, and landscape features such as log trails and playground markings, including a large snakes and ladders game (see Figures 7.1 and 7.2).

These changes have arisen largely through initiatives which have aimed to enhance the quality of playtimes (Ross and Ryan 1994) and improve the playground space so that it offers more child-centred features (Thomson 2005). Similarly, contemporary playgrounds are constructed with a concern for health and safety issues, whilst the older respondents remembered aspects of their playground which would certainly not be tolerated today. For example, Robert remembered the air-raid shelter in his playground, which was played upon, reported in Chapter 6, and Marion recalled a game which involved sitting on hot pipes:

> We used to have these enormous external heating pipes, I mean I'm talking a foot in diameter, and one of the games . . . and that was where we had our lunch as well, our school lunch, in the little school hall. And one of the games which the boys used to come in and play as well was how long you could sit on the pipes! And I am talking about a boiling hot pipe. And when we went round the school, my friend and I went round as I said with the current Head, and we all remembered these enormous pipes. And of course in the winter we used to sit on it because it was warm, on our bums, but then the game was how long you could sit on the pipe before you basically burnt yourself! And we all remembered, including the Head, you know we were all laughing. And then, you know, today that would be . . . I mean the pipes had gone obviously and it was properly plumbed, but it was Angela my friend that said, 'Oh God, do you remember when we used to play on the pipes?' and I said, 'Oh God!' you know.

Despite the differences in the way in which the playgrounds were constructed, the patterns of use of the spaces were similar in many ways across the decades. In Chapter 8, the gendered use of the playground space will be reviewed and the point made that little has changed between the sixty years spanning the studies in that boys and girls tended to locate themselves in different playground spaces. Similarly, across both studies, children appeared to remain largely in same-age groups when playing in the playground, which was partly due to the physical separation of infant/Key Stage 1 pupils from

Figure 7.1 Covered area in Monteney Primary School playground.

junior/Key Stage 2 pupils, but also a result of the construction of class groupings with strict age boundaries.

Also similar across the two studies was the way in which the respondents shaped spaces of playground to suit their particular play needs. Marc Armitage's (2001) work has demonstrated clearly how children find particular spaces in school playgrounds and create imaginative play related to them, such as using metal bars on windows at ground level to create jails, or viewing holes in the ground as witches' cauldrons. As Factor (2004: 145) notes, children have always had the 'capacity to utilize materials at hand and the available space (including areas not intended for play) for their own inventive and imaginative purposes'. The adult respondents in our study also described specific places in the play-ground that afforded particular types of play. Graham (born 1961) recalled the place where marbles were played:

> *Within the Juniors' playground there were like areas that you knew this area was for football. But over near to where the bins were, believe it or not, there is like a different kind of tarmac and you could make, like, a little indentation in the tarmac and that was where the ball bearings or the marbles had to go into as, like, a home base, if you know what I mean.*

Figure 7.2   Snakes and ladders game painted on Monteney Primary School playground.

Marion remembered a place that provided a means of girls hiding their play-related materials from the boys:

> *There was a brick missing from the building and we used to hide things in . . . well it wasn't missing, it was loose, so we used to hide things like the slate and the bit of chalk and things like that from . . . you know, that's where we had that. And that was in the girls' playground. And, you know, the big thing was to make sure the boys didn't discover where we hid our little bits and pieces because they would have taken them.*

At Monteney Primary School, we invited members of the children's panel to annotate maps of the playground in order to mark out particularly salient spaces for play. We then interviewed the children about their maps. There were some general trends that could be discerned from this exercise. First, it was clear that children were very specific about what they played and where, pointing out particular areas, nooks and crannies in which certain activities took place. Second, there was not necessarily always a relationship between the type of environment and the type of play that took place there, although this was the case for some activities – for example, children recorded performing handstands on a grass bank, which offered them a soft landing. Third, the children sometimes drew on particular affordances of the play materials available to them in their environment. For example, Anton in Year 4 recorded how Tiggy was played under the canopy and children could make themselves safe by hiding behind a pole if they were wearing that colour (see Chapter 3 for a description of related games played in the same space).

Finally, the gendered patterns of play that are discussed further in Chapter 8 were discernible in the data. For example, many of the boys documented playing ball games on the large open spaces, whilst girls noted spaces around the edges of the playground (as noted in other studies, e.g. Thorne 1992; Armitage 2001). Emma, in Year 6, did document the space for football, but it was the space around the edges of the playground that she enjoyed using. For example, Emma noted the presence of benches, where she and her friends went to share secrets and chat (see Figure 7.3):

Emma: *Yeah, well, say if we just want to, like, relax at breaks, we go to the benches, and you tell like . . . Yeah, we play dares there and we tell jokes and secrets and stories. Then that's a place where you can sit sit down and just not do nothing.*

Julia: *. . . and you said you tell stories there and I wasn't quite sure what sort of thing you meant by that.*

Emma: *Like, say . . . It's not like stories as in like* Snow White *and stuff like that.*

Julia: *No, not fairy stories.*

Emma: *No. It's, say, if something's happened. We just tell each other stuff.*

Julia: *Do you talk about your own lives, that sort of thing?*

Emma: *Yeah, it's just like, say, if we're going on holiday, we just tell our friends about that. It's not really stories as in what we can tell what's, like, really exciting. Sometimes it is. But it's usually just talking.*

The children also reported that there were some areas of the school, including the toilets, that gave rise to ghost stories. This is a common aspect of primary school life, as suggested in Chapter 3. Armitage (2001) noted that in a group of 120 primary schools in which he conducted play audits, there was a toilet ghost story in more than 65 per cent. He also notes that this is a global, not a UK, phenomenon, and could serve the purpose of allowing children to confront fears, although there are differences in children's reports on the purpose of such play. Sutton-Smith suggests that adults who study play tend 'to overemphasize the creative and innovative aspects of their play at the expense of both the contraries, the phantasmagorical and the ritualistic' (1997: 171) and thus the role and nature of phantasmagorical play that focuses on

Figure 7.3 Emma's annotated map of the playground.

ghosts and spooks deserves further investigation (see Wilson 1997, for a discussion of teenagers' ghost stories).

Whilst there are a number of continuities that can be discerned across the decades with regard to play in school playgrounds, this is not the case to the same extent in relation to play in out-of-school contexts. In the next section of the chapter, play in streets and neighbourhoods is considered prior to a discussion of children's more recent experiences of virtual spaces.

The great outdoors

There has been concern in recent years about the way in which children in contemporary society do not play freely in outdoor spaces. Gleave and Cole-Hamilton (2012), in a literature review developed for Play England on the current state of play, report that 'children's presence in public space seems to have declined dramatically in recent decades' (2012: 15). There are multiple reasons for this, although the main worry for parents is the fear of child abduction by paedophiles, despite evidence that children are much more likely to be a victim of sexual abuse by adults in the home environment (Valentine 2004). Concerns about the restrictions adults impose on the spaces of children's play are not new, however. A reviewer of *London Street Games* (Douglas 1916) commented on the 'stupidity of the social reformer who desires to close to the children the world of adventure, to take from them their birthright of the streets, and coop them up in well-regulated and uninspiring playgrounds where, under the supervision of teachers, their imagination will decline, their originality wither' (Douglas 1931: xi). These sentiments were echoed fifty years later by the Opies. Puzzled by the prevalence of games involving cruelty and domination in the school playground compared to the street and wasteland (Opie and Opie 1969: 13), they concluded that the places made by adults for children's play were restrictive environments, hedged around with rules and designed to allow adult surveillance (Opie and Opie 1969: 12), and encouraging aggressive play. In their view,

> something is lacking in our understanding of the child community . . . and . . . in our continual search for efficient units of educational administration we have overlooked that the most precious gift we can give the young is social space: the necessary space – or privacy – in which to become human beings.
>
> (Opie and Opie 1969: 14)

Speaking of the 1950s and 1960s, the Opies observed that children found the street in front of their home 'more theirs sometimes than the family living-room; and of more significance to them, very often, than any amenity provided by the local council' (Opie and Opie 1969: 10). This may have changed for children playing in the late 1960s and 1970s, as Moss's study indicates (2011). Moss interviewed 17 people about their memories of childhood and many of the respondents were slightly older than the people we interviewed. Moss's study includes one chapter on play and, in it, she reports that 'play involved children in weaving indoor and outdoor spaces' (2011: 188). For the respondents in the 'Memories of Play Project', there was little recall of indoor play and yet there were very strong memories of play in public spaces. All of the adult respondents remembered that the majority of their leisure time was spent playing outdoors, in streets, wasteland and parks. The street was often a safe place because of the limited traffic, as remembered by Bobby (born in 1941):

> You needed to find a fairly flat stretch of the street and you'd play on the gutter . . . play on the pavement. But, you see on our street, you know if a car came down once in a month . . . I mean, the milk came on a horse and cart in those days. So there wasn't a lot of traffic disturbance on the street.

Robert reported more traffic, but it was easily dealt with:

> You know, in those days we could play football across the street with the front garden walls being the goals, and you could . . . you know, you could be sort of playing for quite some period of time before someone would shout, 'There's a car' and you'd sort of move out of the way to let the car go through. But one or two cars might be parked, sort of dotted down the street, but generally speaking it was . . . you could just play right across the road, the street.

Adults reported a range of games in the street, including skipping, football, chasing games and imaginative play. Nevertheless, the streets were not always free of traffic or other dangers and the Opies note that children's street play has perennially been the subject of adult complaint due to conflict with adults' uses of the same space (Opie and Opie 1969: 10–11). Some games took advantage of this, such as games of risk like 'Last Across', which involved children running in front of vehicles on the road (Opie and Opie 1969: 269–70). The hills of Sheffield also provided play opportunities, as Enid (born 1941) recalled:

> And of course in the winter you'd get your sledge and you'd be tobogganing down, no cars, not so many cars then. So from Penton Street right down to Carlisle Street, which is like passing at least two streets, maybe three streets, you could sledge all the way down, you know.

Garden play was not as extensive as street play and for those respondents who lived in flats it was impossible, but there were aspects of gardens that lent themselves to play, such as bushes, which provided spaces for escaping robbers and other baddies in imaginative play, or steps, which became stages, as in Beryl's case:

> In the home, because at my mother's house you'd two steps, part way down the path we'd two steps, and what went to my mother's front door were a tiny little bit elevated, and we had it as a stage. We used it as a stage. And because the garden were like a little embankment then there, and then the

flat bit. And down this embankment here there were always a load of that white stuff – I think they call it Snow in Summer or something, like a white rock plant, droves of it. So it were like a separation between the grass and this white stuff, and then this elevated bit that you walked on up to . . . and then two more steps to the front. And we had that as a stage. And we used to come on from round the side of the house. Hide round the side of the house and then come on and do your little bit on this elevated part, and then go and sit on the step near the front door. Because there were two steps up to my mother's front door, quite deep, and when you'd done your stint you sat on that step till the next person come on.

The majority of the respondents did not have play equipment in gardens, with only the wealthier families being able to afford a swing. Of course, garden play equipment has become big business in the twenty-first century with sales of swings, slides, climbing frames, ball pools, trampolines, amongst many other outdoor play items, increasing by 12 per cent in the UK in 2011, in comparison with an overall growth figure for the toy industry of 3 per cent (Carter 2012).

Beyond the immediate vicinity of gardens and streets, there were many other opportunities to play in local neighbourhoods during the decades of the mid-twentieth century. In the 1950s, the Parson Cross social housing estate, on which many of our Sheffield interviewees lived, was developed in a rural area, close to Ecclesfield woods. The woods were central to children's play, as Bobby recalled:

Well I mean, locally we had just across the road from us there was a kind of field that was ready to be developed. But it wasn't developed for about two years and that was nice and flat, it made a great football pitch, cricket pitch, anything we wanted to do on it. So we got a kind of built-in play area just across the street from where our houses were. We used to go down into Ecclesfield. There was a great fishing pond down there by the Working Men's Club where I used to go fishing. There was Keppel's Column, which was a kind of mile or so walk away which we used to go to and we used to make parachutes out of handkerchiefs with little toy figures on the end and climb up all the steps to the top of Keppel's Column and throw them over the top and then run back down and pick them up and then run back up and throw them down again. And there was Shroggs Woods. We used to spend hours and hours in Shroggs Woods. That's in Ecclesfield, just down by Ecclesfield, making dens and swinging off ropes from trees and, you know, building dams.

The Opies drew attention to the appeal of 'disused and overgrown and silent' places, such as woods, rubbish tips, the least maintained parts of parks and, following the Second World War, bombsites (Opie and Opie 1969: 15). Inevitably, children's relative freedom to play in such spaces led to risky play,

much of it conducted without the knowledge of parents, as Joseph recalls in
his memories of play in East London:

Joseph: *Well we used to . . . you know, we couldn't wait to get out of school and*
          get over the bombsites and that, you know, the stuff that was all left
          over, and the old . . . the factory sites that were abandoned.
Jackie: *Yeah, and what did you do there, then, when you got to those sites?*
Joseph: *We'd explore, you know, we'd go down in the cellars and . . . God, we'd*
          go down them places now that our mothers would go mad if they knew
          where we were at the time. We'd shoot rats, go rat shooting.
Jackie: *What did you shoot the rats with?*
Joseph: *Air guns.*
Jackie: *Oh right, you had air guns?*
Joseph: *Yeah, air guns. You know, your mum and dad didn't know.*
Jackie: *Where did you get them from, then?*
Joseph: *We bought them from a shop, or got them from our older brothers or . . .*
          yeah, there were ways and means, we'd get hold of them.

Access to air guns for children today would not be so easy. In 2011, a law was
introduced which made it an offence to fail to take reasonable precautions to
prevent unauthorized access to air guns by children and young people under
the age of 18, following concerns about the number of serious accidents, and
sometimes death, through the use of the weapons.

Given the risks taken by the adults in our study during their childhood
play, it was not surprising that accidents were reported, as in the following
incident, recalled by Samuel (born in 1942):

> *Well, I was born in Sheffield at the bottom of The Moor in a place which*
> *got quite severely bombed in the Blitz but our house survived, but all around*
> *it was bombed flat. So I can remember as a young child playing on the*
> *bombsites, as a little child, and I got hit in the head, somebody threw a*
> *piece of shrapnel at me – a bit of a bomb splinter – which gashed right*
> *across my forehead and the next thing I knew I woke up in Sheffield*
> *Children's Hospital wondering what the hell had happened.*

Some of the activities undertaken outdoors were influenced by the
domestic sphere in that they involved building dens. Dens in the urban environment were built using discarded building materials, such as bricks and
planks, whilst dens in rural settings were constructed using resources to hand.
Caroline recalled making dens in her garden using a wooden clothes horse:

> *I mean we used to kind of do dens with, you know, if it wasn't a washing*
> *day the clothes horse was available, you know, the old wooden kind of*

> *frame that you used to put the clothes on. So you'd get a sheet or a blanket or something like that and you'd build a den within the corner of the yard, you know, at the back of the yard there used to be an angle of a wall, you know, where you could build something in so you could have dens. I remember we'd have one gang's den in one yard and another gang's den in another yard. You know, you'd be kind of having a pretend war across, from one den to the other.*

Such play fulfils basic needs to create safe, quasi-home settings in which children can play away from the adult gaze. In contemporary society, dens have become a site for commercial activity, with a wide range of merchandised dens, which include replica houses, castles, rockets and even inflatable Volkswagen camper vans.

Dens enable invisibility from adults, but the older respondents also reported games which involved jeopardizing this invisibility deliberately for fun. For example, many people discussed playing 'Knock and Run', which involved knocking on someone's front door and then running away, leaving adults rather exasperated. Beryl described a game which disrupted adults on election days:

> *We used to hide behind the hedge and we don't know why, whether it were just a fallacy, but it always seemed to be nice when it were polling time. And they'd come along, the men and women walking in their cardigans and their little jumpers or whatever the men, and we used to have a big stash of all these heads that we'd pulled off the grass – you know them heads that look like blades of corn but they're not, they look like wheat or something, and there were all this unkempt grass in this boy's garden, into all his garden. And we used to . . . somebody's would be tasked with having little lumps of paper, me, anybody, and with a pencil – I don't think there were any biros, we had a pencil and we used to write 'Vote Labour' on this piece of paper and we use to roll it round these stones. And then just as they were coming past we used to roll it from under the hedge.*

Heightened concerns regarding interaction with strangers that are prevalent in contemporary societies may have led to a reduction in these types of play, and there is also evidence of adults becoming increasingly intolerant of groups of children playing together in public spaces, finding large groups threatening, despite children feeling safer when playing in groups (Gleave and Cole-Hamilton (2012).

The demarcation of public space as adult- or child-orientated has thus become more distinct in recent decades and, inevitably, increasingly shaped by commercial concerns. In more recent years, the trend has been towards privatization of play, with the development of play spaces that provide a range of play equipment and experiences and which require an entry fee. McKendrick *et al.* (2000) suggest that the rise of commercial adventure playgrounds is due to three specific sets of circumstances. First, commercial providers have noted the success of play areas developed by non-sector organizations. Second, developments in urban planning mean that there have been opportunities to build playgrounds on empty industrial units, or exploit opportunities due to changes of land use or change of function (e.g. the development of family-friendly pubs). Third, there has been a growing focus on childhood as a commercial market. This last point has also led to a rise in what has been termed 'toddler tourism', that is, the development of theme parks linked to popular television programmes, or the marketing of specific places linked to media, such as Tobermory in the Isle of Mull, which featured in the BBC programme *Balamory* (Connell 2005). Indeed, such is the trend for the development of child-specific public spaces that Gillis (2003:15) has bemoaned the fact that children's play spaces are increasingly 'islanded, separated from one another and from the adult world at large'.

This is a trend to which the Opies drew attention sixty years ago. In particular, they lamented the attempts of local authorities to colonize and prettify wild spaces in the name of 'improving' them for children to play in (Opie and Opie 1969: 15). They draw attention to the circularity of the argument that children's games are in decline, which is used to justify such developments:

> Nothing extinguishes self-organized play more effectively than does action to promote it. It is not only natural but beneficial that there should be a gulf between the generations in their choice of recreation. Those people are happiest who can most rely on their own resources . . . If children's games are tamed and made part of school curricula, if wastelands are turned into playing-fields for the benefit of those who conform and ape their elders, if children are given the idea that they cannot enjoy themselves without being provided with the 'proper' equipment, we need blame only ourselves when we produce a generation who have lost their dignity, who are ever dissatisfied, and who descend for their sport to the easy excitement of rioting, or pilfering, or vandalism.
>
> (Opie and Opie 1969: 16)

A further impact of the move away from self-directed outdoor play is that children in contemporary society have fewer opportunities to play in cross-age groups. The respondents in the 'Memories of Play Project' reported playing with children in their neighbourhoods across the primary, middle years and secondary span, with even babies being included in the groups, as May recalled:

Well I mean everybody had these right . . . well big prams, they were like [unclear] prams weren't they, two big wheels at back and two small wheels at front. And they were like a carriage pram with a big . . . old things. And I can remember we always had a baby strapped in with . . . I think they called them reins. And they'd clip them in and your mum would bring the baby out and say, 'Watch our so and so, I'm just getting tea on.' And the baby would sit there quite happy, and if it started crying we'd just run up and down the street with it and the baby used to laugh and . . . I mean our Charles, I think he grew up as a girl, because he was the first boy in my family, do you know what I mean, and we always had him. You was never allowed off street, so little kids would play. I mean there always seemed to be a baby there, do you know what I mean, somebody's baby that you played with. And they used to say, 'Don't get in the pram because you'll break it', because another little kid would come and you'd think, 'Do you want a ride in the pram' and they'd be about five or six and you'd put them at that side and you shouldn't have . . . do you know what I mean, you just did it. And I mean there just always seemed to be a baby.

Whilst play across age groups is less possible in some contexts today because of the changing patterns in the use of outdoor space, other opportunities are developing for play that enable children to move beyond their immediate peer groups. In the final section of the chapter, the growing relationship between online and offline spaces in children's play is considered and the implications for friendship groups reviewed.

The relationship between online and offline spaces of play

The children in Monteney Primary School had access to a multitude of play spaces that were not available to the adult respondents, which were constituted as online play spaces. As discussed in Chapter 4, children completed a survey which required them to record the frequency with which they accessed the internet. Forty-five per cent of children reported that they used it every day, 16 per cent two or three times a week and 9 per cent once a week. Twenty-three per cent of children suggested that they used the internet less than once a month and 13 per cent stated that they never used it. Of the 70 per cent of the children completing the survey who said that they used internet at least once a week, a wide range of websites were noted as the most frequently used including games sites (e.g. Miniclip, Stardoll), virtual worlds (e.g. *Club Penguin, Moshi Monsters, Farmville*) and Massive Multiplayer Online Games (MMOGs) (e.g. *Age of War* 2; *Runescape*). All of these sites can be viewed as embodying some element of game play within them, although virtual worlds and MMOGs also enable extensive social interaction. Whilst this represents only a sample of children within one primary school, it is fairly representative of the extent of children's engagement with internet play spaces in the UK, with 91 per cent of the nation's children stating that they use the internet from a range of places including homes and schools to access games and other sites, such as YouTube, Facebook, music sites and sites related to their wider popular cultural interests (Ofcom 2012a).

There have been numerous conceptualizations of online space. Gibson (1984) first introduced the term 'cyberspace' and described it as: 'the graphical representation of data abstracted from banks of every computer in the human system' (1984: 51). Early conceptualizations focused on cyberspace as an entirely separate and distinct space from the material world but in recent years, more nuanced understandings of the relationship between the material and the online have been developed (see Graham 2012, for a review). It is not possible to view online and offline as totally separate spaces, given that humans are located materially in offline spaces as they engage in online activities.

Posthumanist philosophy, which seeks to de-privilege human-centric ways of perceiving the world and acknowledges non-human agency, enables a fuller understanding of issues such as embodiment and presence when playing in online space. As Czaja suggests, if an understanding is developed that the body is 'the original prosthesis we all learn to manipulate, so that extending or replacing the body with other prostheses become a continuation of a process that began before we were born' (Hayles 1999: 3), then 'being there in mediated space and time might be as psychologically natural as non-mediated experience' (Czaja 2011: 3). One might argue that the physical body plays a more significant role than simply acting as a cipher for the mind; nevertheless, posthuman theory does enable the dialectic often posited between online and offline experiences to be challenged. What is clear from this and related work is that technology has profoundly impacted upon our experience of embodied space and time, to the extent that 'technology does not simply organise the spaces in which humans live in different ways, but shapes how space itself is perceived and experienced by humans' (Ash 2010: 414–15). Ash develops the concept of 'teleplasty' to describe the way in which technologies pre-shape the possibilities for human activities and sensory experiences. In particular, he argues, whilst all technology is teleplastic to some extent, technologies that involve a close relationship between gesture and interface are more intensely teleplastic. Describing 'cardinal orientation' as 'the spatial orientation given by the structure of human bodies, rather than in relation to external points in space' (2010: 416), Ash analyses cardinal orientation in relation to videogame play, arguing that:

Whilst the user's body is still corporeally 'present', located and placed in front of the screen, the user's sense of perception of presence is spread and distributed into the environment on screen. In other words, through the creation of a disinhibiting ring (the limits and potentials for movement and action in the game), videogame environments operate teleplastically to reorganise users' cardinal orientation.

(2010: 427)

Acknowledging teleplasty means attending to the way in which technology impacts on children's play experiences and recognizing that online and offline environments are constructed as a continuum and not separate spaces. Marsh has argued elsewhere that, for example, children's engagement in online virtual worlds should be examined across both online and offline contexts, given that economic, cultural and social capital operate across both spaces (Marsh 2011) and that forms of play are transferred across these boundaries, with games played in playgrounds being played in online spaces and vice versa (Marsh 2010a, in press, a and in press, b).

At Monteney Primary School, children played with each other in the school playground and also in online spaces after school. Children were given a list that contained the names of all the children in their class inside individual circles. They were then asked to draw a black line to a circle that contained the name of a friend they played with in the playground and a red line to a circle that contained the name of a friend that they played with online. One hundred and forty-five children in Years 1–6 (aged 5 to 11) completed the diagrams. The data were then analysed at a whole-class level for six classes, as not all children in the other five classes completed the diagrams. An example of a sociograph of online and offline friendships developed from the data from children in one class can be found in Figures 7.4 and 7.5.

Twelve children across the three year groups in Key Stage 2 (Year 3, 7- and 8-year-olds; Year 4, 8- and 9-year-olds and Year 6, 10- and 11-year-olds) were then interviewed in order to explore the friendship patterns further. A girl and a boy in each of the year groups who, according to the sociographs had few (three or less) or no online friends, and a girl and a boy in each of these year groups who had reported having lots of online friends (ten or more) were interviewed regarding their online and offline friendships. A full discussion of the findings from these interviews can be found in Marsh (in press, a), but here key patterns can be identified. First, it was found that older children were more likely to play online with people they did not know offline than younger children. Second, children who had few or no online friends did not appear to experience any negative effects of this in the playground, that is, they were not more likely to experience social exclusion than children who had

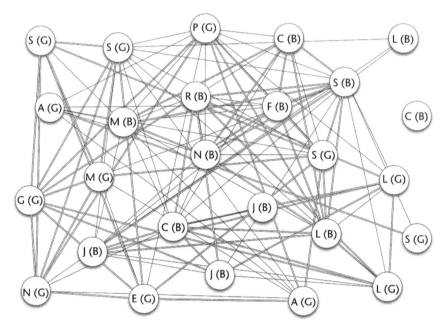

Figure 7.4 Sociograph of offline friendships in Class Y6b.

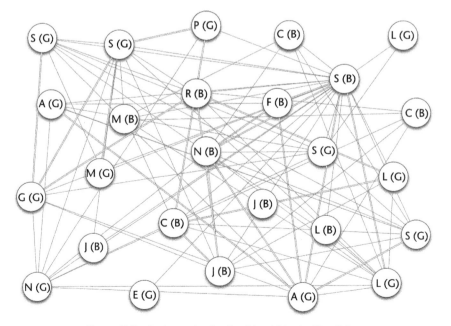

Figure 7.5 Sociograph of online friendships in Class Y6b.

many online friends. This is illustrated in the following exchange with Carl, aged 7:

Jackie:	*So all of these children you've played with online, yeah?* [Pointing to Carl's sociograph]
Carl:	*Mmm.*
Jackie:	*And then all of these children that you've played with in the playground.* [Pointing to Carl's sociograph] *So did you choose children to play with in the playground that you played with online, or not?*
Carl:	*No 'cos . . . I played with John, I didn't play with him online.*
Jackie:	*Oh right OK. So why didn't you play with him online – John?*
Carl:	*Because he didn't have an account.*
Jackie:	*Oh right OK, he didn't have an account. And did it make any difference to how you felt about him playing in the playground?*
Carl:	*No.*
Jackie:	*No, OK. And do you think he felt any different?*
Carl:	*No, 'cos we played a lot in the playground.*

Whilst the absence of online presence did not appear to have a negative impact on playground friendships, however, offline behaviour did appear to influence children's decision-making about who they would play with online, as illustrated in the interview with David in Year 6:

Jackie:	*Is there anybody that you wouldn't play with online?*
David:	*Charlie.*
Jackie:	*Why?*
David:	*Because he gets too violent and things and he swears and stuff, so . . .*
Jackie:	*He gets violent in the playground or online?*
David:	*Well he does it in a bit . . . well I think he would do it online because he just sort of does it in the playground.*
Jackie:	*And what are you worried about, then, if you play with him online?*
David:	*That he'll start talking about violence and it's not really my . . . I don't really like talking about it.*

For children at Monteney, therefore, there existed complicated patterns between online and offline friendships and experiences and the two spaces could not be easily separated.

Toy manufacturers have become increasingly aware of children's movement across online and offline spaces and, in recent years, have developed a range of online spaces that interact with material toys and artefacts. Chapter 5 outlined how LEGO, for example, had enjoyed commercial success through the extension of their product onto technological platforms. This leads to play that moves fluidly across a range of boundaries, as illustrated in Giddings'

(2007) account of his own sons' play with a LEGO video game and their LEGO blocks. He found that, through experiencing the LEGO video game, the children changed the way in which they played with their blocks, operating their constructed LEGO cars in ways which replicated the on-screen car activities. He notes that:

> Not only were the images and actions of the computer game being played out with real toys, but *the ways* the boys played with their actual LEGO blocks was now quite different from how it had been before the experience of the computer game. The boys were not only continuing the game of racing LEGO cars begun on the computer screen (its characters, scenarios and dramas), they were also playing with actual LEGO as if it were a videogame. They were, on one level, *playing at playing a video game.*
>
> (Giddings 2007, author's italics)

Eventually, the boys drew Giddings himself into the play episode, asking him to manipulate the keyboard whilst the children replicated the kinds of activities that would have been represented on a computer screen. At one point, Giddings suggested that one of his sons could pretend to be the one logging in to play the virtual game but his son told him, 'I am the one who makes the LEGO Racers go!', suggesting that he was playing at being the video game itself. This illustrates the complex modalities at work in these liminal play spaces that involve both online and offline contexts. Whilst this may be considered as a process of blending or merging the geographical spaces of play, it remains the case that there are ontological differences between playing on- and off-screen, as there are inhibitors and disinhibitors, to draw further on Ash's (2010) concept of teleplasty, that are specific to both environments. Thus the differences between children playing imaginative role-play games in the offline world, which involves an escape to a (virtual) cognitive world, and children playing an imaginative game in the online virtual world through the use of an avatar (Burn, in press; Marsh, in press, a) can be teased out.

There are also differences in experiences across these dimensions, which can be characterized as being linked to the way in which they offer possibilities for immersion. Ryan (2003) distinguishes between the act of fictional re-centring and immersion. Re-centring involves people transporting themselves in their imagination into a fictive world that is represented as if it were actual, which can take place through reading a fictional text. Immersion involves being fully immersed in the fictional world through the way in which the text operates, although Ryan does make the point that immersion is not restricted to fictional texts. Some novels resist immersion, making their fictional construction clear to the reader, whilst others actively promote the immersive experience. Similarly, in play, some experiences are more immersive than others, creating a more profound sense of 'flow' (Csikszentmihalyi 1990). The factors which enhance the possibilities for immersion can be different in online and offline spaces, with quality of narrative, characterization, graphics and sound being salient in online games and the quality of relationships between children being key in offline play (Dunn 2009). Dunn and O'Toole also suggest that:

> The greatest area of difference between these two worlds lies, however, in the way in which the fictional context is built, for within the virtual world, the play is treated to an environment that has been envisaged for them (at least partially) and where the imagination is only required to accept these prepared or self developed images as 'real'. In the dramatic world, however, the individual participants must work much harder to create in their minds an 'illusion of realness' (Griffin 1984: 88) and then, throughout the action, conserve that illusion.
>
> (Dunn and O'Toole 2009: 26–7)

The relationship between online and offline play is set to become even more intense in future years as toy developers embrace developments in technology. It is no surprise, given the extent to which Disney has always been at the forefront of the provision of media-related play opportunities for children, that they are one of the market leaders in this area. Disney went early into the virtual world market through its acquisition in 2005 of *Club Penguin* from the independent Canadian company that developed it. It has been a phenomenal success, with an estimated user base of over 30 million across several countries, including Canada, France, Germany, Spain, the US and the UK. Disney has produced a range of toys and artefacts that relate to *Club Penguin*, including stuffed toys, play figures, a magazine, books, collecting cards and tins, lunch boxes, backpacks, clothing, bedding, jigsaws and games. There are also *Club Penguin* games for console platforms, such as Nintendo and Xbox, which enable players to accrue virtual coins that can be transferred to users' online accounts. Children at Monteney Primary School reported enjoying these because they could be played away from the home environment if there was no online access. Portability is also a key theme in the development of apps for tablets, and the *Club Penguin* app enables children to play the game from wherever they are based.

The development of apps is also leading to increased opportunities for augmented reality play. Disney have introduced *DreamPlay*, which enables children to buy physical toy instruments, such as a drum and a keyboard, then download an app that links to the toy and which presents a virtual character that interacts with the instrument, attempting to teach the user to play a song, for example. In a further indication of their understanding of the relationship between online and offline in children's worlds, Disney has also started to use QR codes to promote their goods to children, posting QR codes on a cinema wall to relate its toys to a screening of *Cinderella* (*Inside Retail*, 15 March 2013). These developments offer an indication of the way in which the toys and games industry will be exploiting the developing dynamic between online and offline play in the years ahead.

Conclusion

From the analysis developed in this chapter, it can be seen that whilst there are a number of continuities in the experiences of participants across all of the studies in relationship to space and play, there are key differences. These changes are closely related to technological developments in recent decades, which enable play to take place across virtual spaces. In these contexts, children can play both with children they know and with unknown others, and they can adopt different identities that might or might not contrast with their offline identities. Further, technology enables children to pause play. Through the switch of a button, they can store their play to date and then return to the same game at an entirely different time, picking it up exactly where they left it. They can also engage in play which is either synchronous, taking place in 'real' time, or asynchronous, taking place over extended time, which means all players do not have to be simultaneously present, which was not generally the case for previous generations. Technology offers a range of rich and exciting environments for play, which can foster the imagination, creativity and agency (see Marsh 2010b, for a review of relevant research). Unfortunately, this is an area that leads to numerous misconceptions. For example, Frost, in a book which argues for the need for children to engage in outdoor play in natural environments, a worthy project, unfortunately demonizes technology at the same time, stating that, because of it:

> Already children are denied opportunities for hands-on manipulation and exploration of real objects, forget how to play in imaginative games, fail to learn through kinesthetic experience, and rarely engage in face-to-face social play with their peers.
>
> (Frost 2010: 259)

These assertions are not supported with reference to evidence and indeed, we would suggest that there is evidence to support alternative readings of the relationship between technology and play (Willett *et al.*, 2013). Bishop (in press), for example, examines closely the relationship between children's offline engagement in clapping games and their use of YouTube and argues that hands-on play (in the case of clapping) has a symbiotic relationship with online examples which support acquisition of new repertoire and variation. We would contend that children should have access to a range of play spaces in both material and virtual worlds and that the criteria that should be used to judge the quality of such play spaces need to attend to questions relating to how far they foster innovation, imagination, independence and social engagement, amongst other aspects. 'Real'/virtual, material/immaterial, outdoor/indoor play spaces would all benefit from attention to these qualities, moving away from an obsession with the technologies of play to focus on the opportunities the various contexts for play offer for fostering the creative agency of childhood.

In this chapter, the gendered nature of children's spatial engagement in play has been considered briefly and in the following chapter, the discussion of this issue is extended further in order to examine how far the gendered patterns of play have changed over the past sixty years.

8 Gender, sexuality and play

Gender and play intersect in a number of significant ways. In this chapter, the nature of the way in which gender shapes play choices and orientation to particular toys and artefacts of play is explored, with key trends over the past sixty years highlighted. First, however, the theoretical framework for the conceptualization of gender utilized in the studies is outlined, given the diversity of positions the field generates.

Gender is, as many scholars have pointed out, a contested and complex matter (Renold 2005; Paechter 2007; Francis 2010). Butler suggests that gender identity is 'performatively constituted by the very "expressions" that are said to be its results' (1990: 34). Thus, differences in gender are normalized and appear to be fixed in nature. These differences self-perpetuate through 'gender regimes', or the working of habitus (Bourdieu 1990). In the 1980s and 1990s, Connell (1987, 1995) developed the concepts of 'hegemonic masculinity' and 'emphasised femininity' to describe the way in which subjects adopt normative gendered positions in which masculinity is linked to power, patriarchy and dominance, whilst femininity accepts this subordinate positioning. In the 2010s, more nuanced conceptualizations of gender have been developed, building on this significant early work of Connell. Recent research has emphasized the complex nature of gender construction and has challenged the assumption that gender can be linked directly to the body (Francis 2010), thereby equating masculinity with the male sex and femininity with female sex. Certainly, in an attempt to move beyond this binary, notions of 'female masculinities' (Halberstam 1998) and 'male femininities' have been developed in order to account for those instances in which gender identity and sex do not align with normative conceptualizations of this relationship. However, Francis (2010) suggests that Bakhtin's notions of monoglossia and heteroglossia can be drawn upon in the analysis of how gender is performed in order to move away from measuring masculinity and femininity only in relation to each other.

Monoglossia (Bakhtin 1986) is a term used to refer to language which reflects the power status and interests of dominant groups in societies.

Heteroglossia, in contrast, emphasizes the way in which language draws upon many different voices. In utterances, we always speak through, with or against other voices, and this communication is dialogic, in contrast to monologism. Francis (2010) contends that the construction of gender as a binary is a monoglossic act in which masculinity is constructed as strong and rational and femininity as emotional and weak. Alongside this, the concept of heteroglossia allows for a close analysis of those instances in which individuals might perform constructions of gender which challenge monologic understandings. Francis suggests that this analysis addresses the challenges and tensions borne by the need to understand both the micro-practices of gender construction at an individual level and gender discrimination at a macro level:

> The conceptual tools of gender monoglossia and heteroglossia facili-
> tate a marrying of these two positions: we may see patterns of
> gendered behaviours and inequalities as expressive of monoglossic
> gender practice, but within this be attuned to the complexity and
> contradiction at play (heteroglossia), both in the diversity of gender
> production, and in our categorisation of it. It is this attunedness to
> heteroglossia that offers potential for disruption and the avoidance of
> reification of gender norms, and the exposure of gender as discur-
> sively produced rather than inherent.
>
> (Francis 2010: 488)

This enables a fluid account of the construction of gender to be made and allows for a movement beyond the notion of 'female masculinities' or 'male femininities' when attempting to describe constructions of gender that transgress norms. Haywood and Mac an Ghaill (2012), in a review of recent theoretical developments relating to masculinities, suggest that this use of Bakhtin demonstrates promise and that further research might usefully extend the analysis to incorporate Bakhtin's notion of 'polyglossia', which refers to multiple and conflicting voices being present simultaneously in a text.

In the studies reported in this book, theories of gender construction are drawn upon that point to its relative, contingent, complex and fluid nature (Paechter 2007; Francis 2010; Renold and Ringrose 2011a). In the first part of the chapter, the nature of gendered play as instantiated in the datasets is considered. In reviewing the similarities and differences in the datasets in more detail, we focus on two specific gendered activities – football and 'paper' doll play – and discuss developments in these play activities due to technological changes. The chapter moves on to consider the phenomenon of border crossing (Thorne 1993) in order to explore some of the complexities of gendered play. In the final section of the chapter, the debates concerning sexualization are examined and the continuities and discontinuities in the datasets in relation to these issues are discussed.

Gender and play 1950s–2010s

All of the older respondents recalled the way in which the play of boys and girls in their childhoods was very separate. For some, this was the result of having discrete school playgrounds for boys and girls, but for others it was a marker of the way in which gender impacts on play. Barrie Thorne, on reviewing the data in her longitudinal ethnography of school playgrounds in the US in the 1990s, suggested that 'sex segregation is so common in elementary schools that it is meaningful to speak of separate girls' and boys' worlds' (Thorne 1992: 117). Thorne summarizes the key differences in friendship and play thus: boys interact in larger groups and engage in more physical, rough-and-tumble play, using contests as a means of interacting. Girls' play is more co-operative, friendships are private and they interact in smaller groups or pairs. Friendship is intense and secrets and exclusivity are common features. But, as Thorne notes, these are generalized observations that cannot account for all groups of children. Aydt and Corsaro (2003), for example, suggest that whilst gender segregation appears to be a universal feature of children's play, children in some cultures do not enforce gender boundaries in the way that others do and they offer the example of children in an Italian pre-school they observed, who appeared not to construct distinct gender boundaries in the way that the white, middle-class American children they studied did. Munroe and Romney (2006), however, argue that there are no consistent patterns in gender segregation within cultural groups. Drawing on a study of four countries, Belize, Kenya, Nepal and Samoa, they suggest that there are variations in the patterns of gender and play *within* cultural groups. Further, they propose using the term 'aggregation' rather than 'segregation', given that they did not identify fully exclusionary play in all of the play episodes they observed.

Nevertheless, there were distinct gendered patterns across the datasets considered in this book in terms of the types of play in which boys and girls engaged. The older male respondents reported their interest in football, war play and play with toys such as train sets and construction toys, whilst the women remembered their play with dolls and skipping ropes. From the extended observations of Monteney playground, in addition to a survey in which children reported on their play, it was clear that ball games such as football and basketball, in addition to play fighting, were predominantly played by boys, whilst girls enjoyed clapping games and playing with hula hoops, thus the dominant gendered patterns appeared to have persisted across time. This is also the case in relation to fantasy play. The women who were interviewed recalled playing fantasy games based on domestic themes such as homes and weddings, in which they would use net curtains or their mothers' dresses as dressing-up clothes, whereas boys enjoyed war play, as recalled by May:

I can remember boys played with . . . they always wanted to be fighter pilots didn't they? They used to run round the streets with their arms and 'de-de-de . . .' pretending to shoot people down. And I suppose that was because, you know, because it was related to the war and things like that. I know they used to get into trouble for taking the pegs, because they were wooden pegs, and they'd get one peg and then connect two to it and use them for guns and make noises. But I can't ever remember playing games like that with boys . . .

As noted in Chapter 5, war play has been a consistent interest of boys throughout centuries and, therefore, it was no surprise that examples of this play were found in Monteney School playground, although the war play was largely based on computer games rather than the Second World War or Cowboys and Indian films enjoyed by the older participants, and the hastily assembled guns consisted of plastic LEGO bricks rather than wooden pegs.

Football was also a consistent theme across the datasets. Whilst some girls liked to play football, they were in the minority and it was very much a boys' game in both the 1950s and 2010s. This appears to have been a growing trend since the late nineteenth century. Sutton-Smith and Rosenberg (1961) undertook a review of historical changes in the game preferences of American children over the first half of the twentieth century and they found that by 1959, even though girls had adopted more traditionally masculine pursuits, such as 'Leap Frog' and 'Tag', football was very much a boys' game. Indeed, they suggest that:

> masculine rough play (Football, Boxing, Wrestling) and masculine-like intrusiveness (Horseshoes, Throwing snowballs, Marbles and Darts) have become the residual and central facets of the male sex role.
>
> (Sutton-Smith and Rosenberg 1961: 31)

One of the older respondents, Robert, recalled how the boys dominated the playground space whilst they played football, although there was an age hierarchy at play:

Well, I mean I do remember . . . I remember a game that again sort of dominates my mind really is football, and I've a vague feeling that when we were younger we'd play across the width of the playground, whilst . . . I mean there would be a number of football games and all sorts of other activities all going on at the same time. So, you know, I remember when we were younger we would be playing across the width, and the older kids would be the ones that sort of tended to play from one end of the playground to the other, well one end of the playground, the sort of boundary, to the actual school building.

Thorne (1992: 124) points out that boys control as much as ten times more space than girls in the playground and this was also the case at Monteney, in which ball games took up a large section of the Key Stage 2 playground.

Swain (2000) notes the relationship between football and the construction and performance of hegemonic masculinity, based on his observations of three primary playgrounds. He argues that:

> Football was a major component of successful (heterosexual) masculinity, and establishing oneself as a good footballer went a long way in helping to establish one as a 'real' boy. The game personifies the acme of masculinity, and communicates ideals of fitness, strength, competition, power and domination; and through playing the game, and simulating their adult heroes, the boys were seen tending to perform their skills on a public stage, and practising to be a man.
>
> (Swain 2000: 107)

Little has changed in that respect since the 1950s. What has been transformed is the way in which football can now permeate all aspects of young boys' lives, given the way in which new media assemblages (Carrington in press) operate, as discussed in Chapter 4. Therefore, boys can transfer their interest in football on the playground to virtual environments as they play football games on their Wii, Xbox or Playstation and they can follow the season's results on their mobile phone or tablet apps. Boys have always emulated their favourite sports star on the playground or in the street, but now they can actually adopt a David Beckham avatar and immerse themselves in the character's style and persona as they become him on screen. There are computer games that enable users to build and manage football teams, facilitating the trading of virtual team members across an online community. For example, the advert for the computer game *FIFA 13* encourages users to use the EA SPORTS Football Club iPhone app to 'manage your squad, search live auctions and bid to win new players'.[104] Similarly, there are aspects of girls' play that demonstrate such continuities and discontinuities across time. One of these activities is focused upon in order to illustrate developments – paper doll play.

Many of the older women who were interviewed recalled playing with paper dolls. The practice was popular of dressing and undressing paper dolls, which were often placed in comics. As May recalled, of the paper dolls printed in the comic *Bunty*, produced from 1958, *'You'd cut them out and then they'd have little tabs and you could fold them over and change the outfits on them'* (see Figure 8.1).

Figure 8.1 Paper doll cut-out in *Bunty* ©DC Thomson & Co. Ltd. Used by kind permission.

Paper dolls have a history as long as paper itself, but it was in the eighteenth century that they began to be mass-produced in Europe. In their combination of doll play with a focus on fashion, they are part of a broad range of dolls that serve to construct girls' identities in relation to clothes, accessories and beauty, a tradition that was continued with the introduction of Barbie dolls in the 1950s and Bratz dolls in the 1980s. Inevitably, technological transformations have radically changed the nature of paper doll play. Girls at Monteney Primary School mentioned using the site Stardoll,[105] a website which enables users to dress virtual dolls – 'MeDolls' (see Figure 8.2).

The affordances of this site are very different from the paper dolls of the 1950s and 1960s that the older respondents in the 'Memories of Play Project' played with. Users are able to dress their MeDolls using readily available virtual clothes and they can buy the latest fashions using virtual cash – 'Stardollars'. Users can also choose celebrity personas, such as Katy Perry and Cheryl Cole, for these dolls and they can become virtual fashion designers. Burke (in press), in an analysis of two Canadian children's use of the site, notes that, 'options for imaginary play on the site include designing and selling fashions they create or decorating user suites, which offer homage to consumerism but also

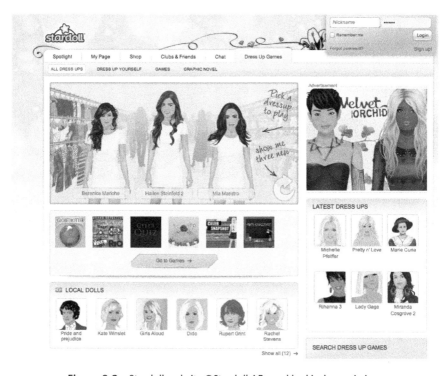

Figure 8.2   Stardoll website ©Stardoll AB used by kind permission.

a real avenue for young players to share their creative expression.' A smartphone app ensures that this online experience is transportable and the provision of chat forums provides opportunities for the children to interact with other users. Hosts of blogs set up by users of Stardolls enable fans to share information and there are countless videos on YouTube which provide peer-to-peer guidance on using aspects of the site, such as how to create particular make-up and hair styles.

Whilst the opportunities to extend doll-focused play communities are much greater than was the case for previous generations, there are sedimented practices across time, such as the social construction of girlhood. Formanek-Brunell (2012: 4) points to the wide range of research on the 'role of mass-produced and mass-marketed dolls in the socialization, sexualization, commodification, exoticization, commercialization, racialization, and essentialization of girlhood in the twenty first century' and there is certainly much evidence that these artefacts present normative and limited constructs of gender. However, as Formanek-Brunell (1993) has noted previously through her historical review of American girl play, girls do not acquiesce to the restrictions that producers of these dolls attempt to place on them. For example, Esfahani studied the use of Barbie and Bratz dolls by girls from immigrant Iranian families living in Australia and found that some of the girls did not subscribe to the intentionality (Verbeek 2006) of the producers in that girls consistently resisted dressing the dolls, ascribed female dolls with a male gender in play and also drew on the dolls.

Both of these examples of gendered play, football and paper/online dolls, have illustrated the way in which the play of contemporary childhoods intersects with celebrity culture. The adults interviewed did engage in celebrity-imitation play, primarily in relation to pop singers and film stars, but it was clearly the case that children in the 2010s engaged much more broadly with fame and celebrity in their play as they replayed talent shows, such as *Britain's Got Talent* and *X Factor*, taking on the personas of celebrities such as Cheryl Cole and Simon Cowell, and imitated their favourite celebrities as they played football or when dancing and singing. Numerous commentators have criticized this aspect of contemporary society, using terms such as 'fame addiction' (Ju Choi and Berger 2009) to describe the attraction for celebrity. Allen and Mendick (2013), however, suggest that this dismissal is shortsighted. Instead, they argue that celebrity is a discursive device that structures young people's cultural worlds within neoliberalism and can operate to both reproduce and resist dominant discourses about fame, ambition and morality. Social class is at the heart of this discursive construction of celebrity. Reality TV stars, or 'celebrity chavs', that is working-class celebrities such as Rylan Clark, the 2012 X-Factor contestant who later won *Celebrity Big Brother*, are positioned as undeserving of fame because it is construed as being achieved through means other than hard work. Inevitably, gender inflects this discourse, as the focus on

WAGs and female reality TV stars frequently points to the use of sexuality to achieve fame. Drawing on three research projects which examined young people's career aspirations, Allen and Mendick point to the way in which the young people they interviewed held alternative readings of celebrity culture, challenging the reductive assertions frequently made about working-class women such as Jade Goody. Allen and Mendick suggest that for those who face disadvantage in education and employment through gender, class or ethnicity, then 'celebrity culture offers important sites of fantasy and investment for young people, representing the possibility of visibility, symbolic capital and self-betterment' (2013: 87). At the same time, the authors recognize the way in which celebrity culture reproduces normative gendered identities, such as hyper-heterosexual femininities. The arguments made by Allen and Mendick point to the way in which quick and simple judgements cannot be made about children's relationship to celebrities and the way that they mobilize related tropes in their play.

In the consideration of continuity and change in the relationship between gender and play, concepts such as borderwork (Thorne 1993) are also pertinent: those instances when children deliberately activate the boundaries between males and females in order to reify the distinctions. Thorne identified three types of borderwork: contests, chases and invasions. Normally initiated by boys to assert their dominance over girls, these practices provide further opportunities to perform gendered identities. May recalled play in the 1960s:

> *There were another song, but I can't remember, and you used to stand and you'd get your toe and you'd cross your legs and kick up in the air and clap your hands and turn round. And I can remember the boys used to sit there laughing, do you know what I mean, and giggling and things like that because you were doing stuff, you know, that they thought were funny.*

This type of borderwork was also prevalent in the data from the more recent study. For example, boys were observed attempting to subvert girls' clapping games by standing behind girls, making faces and mocking actions, or running through groups in an effort to disrupt them. As Thorne (1993) noted, girls are adept at ignoring or working through these frequent disruptions. Not all boys engage in this behaviour and in the data from Monteney playground it seemed to us that this kind of disruption was a plaintive attempt to join in the play by those boys who did not feel confident to transgress gendered boundaries. It has been noted in previous studies that girls are more willing to challenge gender boundaries than boys through the adoption of male characters in play, or through playing with toys traditionally aimed at males (Thorne 1993). Partly this is due to the gender stereotyping prevalent in many media texts, which means that in order to undertake the role that has any agency, girls have little option but to adopt male personas. As Emily recalled:

Emily: *But isn't it strange I didn't want to be the posh Lady Penelope.*

Julia: *Yes, again it's interesting isn't it? Were any of you Lady Penelope in your group who played with you?*

Emily: *Nobody really wanted to be Lady Penelope, or Parker like I said, or people . . . it's really weird. And as I say it didn't strike me until I was thinking, why did we want to be the males?*

Julia: *Yes. Do you think also those roles, there was more to do as part of those roles?*

Emily: *Possibly yeah, because remember, Lady Penelope, she was kind of the spy person I think but she only really looked pretty, so it wouldn't have been . . . there wouldn't have been much action, would there, I suppose when you think about it.*

There are also girls who take up play practices that are normally sequestered to boys; for example, there were a few girls in the Monteney playground who enjoyed playing football. Such girls are frequently identified as 'tomboys' who aim to adopt masculine practices, but Renold and Ringrose challenge the notion that these girls are mimicking boys:

> Rather than understand girls' attempts to take up masculinity as mere mimicry of the phallus, as has been promoted in recent feminist theorizing, we suggest . . . that many of these girls' practices indicate radical disruptions and displacements of phallocentric power.
>
> (Renold and Ringrose 2011b: 48)

Girls, in the act of taking up masculinized practices, may do so in ways which reject the discourses of male power embedded within those practices. Such identity work is complex and subject positionings fluid in attempts to resist or challenge established notions of gender and sexuality. In the final section of this chapter, issues relating to sexualization and the complex work involved in mobilizing non-stereotypical identities are considered.

Childhood, play and sexualization

One of the 'moral panic' discourses that has circulated with regard to children and media in recent decades is that of the sexualization of childhood. An independent review for the government undertaken by Reg Bailey, reporting in June 2011, suggested that sexualized imagery is now part of the 'wallpaper' of children's everyday lives (Bailey 2011). The report points to advertising in the street, magazines and newspapers, and content on television and the internet as the major culprits, along with developments in the fashion industry for children. The report oversimplifies the pertinent issues and fails to attend to the range of research which has pointed to the complexities of this area. For example, Buckingham *et al.* (2010: 5), in a report on children and sexualization for the Scottish government, state that there are actually few 'sexualized' goods available to children and that children might buy items 'in contexts surrounded by sexual imagery and products, but such products are not necessarily aimed at them'.

If there is a lack of empirical evidence for the way that children are now influenced by sexualized commercial cultures, this is not the case with regard to children's socialization into sexualized identities, which appears to have remained fairly consistent over decades. There are many ways in which the accounts of the adults who were interviewed and the data from the more recent ethnography overlapped in terms of sexualized play. Drawing from queer theory, which 'inverts the relationship between margin and mainstream, putting mainstream values and norms under examination rather than those which "deviate" from it in whatever ways' (Wells *et al.* 2012: 110), the sedimented practice of heteronormative play (Blaise 2005), which serves to privilege heterosexuality, can be seen across both datasets. Debbie Epstein (1996), in a study of primary schools in England, identified that heterosexuality is privileged across primary playgrounds and classrooms and she identified that it is represented in: (1) imagined futures; (2) traditional games and rhymes; (3) versions of games involving running and catching; (4) sexist/ sexual harassment; (5) assays into the world of 'going out'; and (6) gossip networks. Running and catching games include 'Kiss Catch', or 'Kiss Chase', as Dora (born in 1953) recalled:

> *I can remember playing 'Kiss Chase' and pretending that you don't want the boys to chase you, saying, 'Oh no, no, no', but you're looking round to see who is running after you, I can distinctly remember doing that.*

Traditional rhymes and games are also replete with heteronormative references. May recalled a skipping rhyme that she and her friends sang:

> *'Sally in the kitchen, doing a little bit of knitting, in came a bogeyman and chased Sally out', so you'd jump out and then the next person would jump in. 'I'm a little girl guide dressed in blue, these are the actions I must do. Salute to the king and bow to the queen, turn your back to the reading machine. The boys throw the kisses, the girls show their knickers, I'm a little girl guide dressed in blue.'*

These patterns were also prevalent throughout the data from Monteney Primary School. For example, in the following field notes, a group of 6- and 7-year-old boys and girls engage in teasing play:

A group of Y2s accost me to tell me their song. Two of the girls are particularly vocal about it, Laura and Amy. They can barely get through the first time due to giggling and amusement:

> Lee and Carys
> Snogging in a tree
> K-I-S-S-I-N-G
> First comes (the) love [one says 'the' and the other one doesn't]
> Then comes marriage
> Then comes the baby with the baby's carriage.

They ask if I want to hear another one. I enthuse, thinking I'm going to get another song altogether, but this brings forth version after version of the above but with different children's names substituted. Boys get involved and some object vigorously to having their names put in, leading to some restraining and chasing. There are quick conversations, such as 'You fancy Jake.' 'No, we just go together.' 'I've got another' – at which point the boy who thinks he's going to be included in the song attempts to stop them singing it. By the end of this episode there are eight children involved in this activity, of which five are boys.

(JB fieldnotes, 23.6.09)

Nevertheless, in the 'Playgrounds Project', there was evidence that children had multiple discourses to draw on in their construction of sexualized identities. In the musical play observed in Monteney playground, there were numerous examples of girls adopting what on the surface could be labelled as hyper-feminized and heterosexual identities, but which on closer analysis defied simple categorization. For example, an extended episode in which children were singing and dancing to their favourite songs was videoed. They were able to play songs on a CD player that had been brought into the playground and which was used frequently by the Year 5 and Year 6 groups. In one of the episodes, a Year 5 girl led a line of other girls as they sang to Justin Bieber's song 'One Time'. She adopted some of the gestures used by Bieber in the video of the song, but added particular gestures which are more attributable to female dancers, which emphasize specific parts of the female body, e.g. hips. These gestures were copied by other girls in the line. However, it was clear that this dance was not intended for the male gaze. Avidly watching the Year 5 children was a group of Year 6 girls who looked on intently throughout the whole performance and the younger girls frequently watched to see if they had the approval of their older counterparts. Whilst a few boys appeared on the periphery of this episode, and one in particular attempted to disrupt the play through mimicry, they were ignored and thus the point was made that the purpose of this event was girl-performer to girl-audience musical play. In one sense, this episode might be an example of 'how the heterosexual regulation of the self and other girls forms the fabric of girls' attachments' (Renold and Ringrose 2008: 325) in that the older girls' presence may have encouraged the younger girls to conform to hyper-feminine performances, but on the other hand, it could be viewed as an example of the resistance of the 'heterosexual matrix' (Butler 1990) in that the male gaze is actively ignored. The Opies document a similar use of singing games in past decades to thicken female friendships:

> The girls who play the games in the present day enjoy them for reasons unconnected with the choosing of sweethearts. They enjoy (though they may not be able to say so) the gaiety, warmth, sociability, excitement; the chance to thump their friends on the back or tangle with them in helpless laughter; and the chance to star (most singing games provide two opportunities for the ego to shine: once when the soloist plays her part in the centre of the ring, and once when she chooses her successor). Girls, too, seem to like games that are rhythmic and repetitive, formal and enigmatic. They accept them uncritically, not worry that the words make little sense; in fact the stranger the words are, the greater is the liberation into fantasy. Singing games are now played almost exclusively by seven to nine-year-olds, with older and younger girls joining in on occasion.
>
> (1985: 26)

They do note, however, that such activities are also used by girls to distance themselves from childish pleasures, and 'ten-year-olds who are happily playing singing games at one end of a playground may be despised by girls of the same age group at the other end, who say scornfully, "We never play them sort of games, they're boring", and go back to their netball' (1985: 26).

In addition to those instances in which it appeared that girls were resisting normative categorizations in relation to sexualities, there were also events in which girls deliberately downplayed hypersexual elements of source texts in their play. For example, Willett (2011), in an analysis of girls' musical play in the London school that was also part of the 'Playgrounds Project', reflects on a play episode in which a group of girls in Key Stage 1 performed Beyoncé's hit song 'Single Ladies'. She notes that the girls adapted the performance to play down the sexual gestures that are part of the Beyoncé/Destiny's Child video. The girls also draw on a performance of the song by Alvin and the Chipmunks, which repositions their play within a more age-appropriate set of references:

> Importantly, in the girls' performances of songs from Beyoncé, JLS and Mamma Mia, through their adaptations of lyrics, gestures and

contexts, the girls appropriate an innocent child discourse, at least in the context of the playground. For example, rather than referring to Beyoncé to explain the performance of 'Single Ladies', Anna refers to Alvin and the Chipmunks to explain the actions and the meaning of the song (in Anna's words, 'the boys sing "all the single ladies", [the girls] have to put their hands up . . . the girls have to do what the boys are saying').

(Willett 2011: 352)

This could have been a strategy to allay any perceived fears the children felt the adult researcher may have had in relation to the Beyoncé/Destiny's Child version of the song, but it does point to the multiple resources available to children which they can draw on to position themselves in discussions relating to sexualization.

Conclusion

In this chapter, the way in which gender and play intersected in the accounts of the older respondents who were interviewed and in the ethnographic data from the more recent study has been considered. From this analysis, two main overarching points about changes in relation to gender, play, media and commercial culture from the 1950s to the present day can be made. First, whilst the texts, artefacts and images available to contemporary children portray a much more diverse picture of gendered subjectivities, which includes counter-stereotypical subjectivities, than was available for previous generations, it is also the case that this portfolio contains more intensely configured constructions of hyper-heterosexual, hyper-feminine and hyper-masculine identities than encountered previously. This inevitably suggests, as Renold and Ringrose (2008) point out, that 'schizoid subjectivity is a contemporary norm', although they also make it clear that such an understanding can be held 'without pathologising the condition of contradiction' (2008:318). Constructions of gendered subjectivities is a much more complex process for the younger respondents than the older people who were interviewed, with implications for how this complexity is instantiated in play. Further, whilst it has been suggested that gender shapes the way in which children take up particular aspects of play, or orientate themselves to specific toys, in fact the process is rather more two-way than this suggests. Gender and play are co-constitutive in that the adoption of particular practices reinforces gendered subjectivities.

Second, it has been suggested that the context for play has changed considerably over the past sixty years in terms of the mobilization of gendered discourses in toys and media texts and artefacts. Whist sedimented practices have been traced in this chapter in terms of football and dolls, it is also the case that the digital landscapes of contemporary childhoods have changed the way in which gendered play may be taken up and embodied. Online extensions of offline texts and artefacts enable different kinds of gendered immersions and extend the opportunities to play with gendered subjectivities. In pre-digital generations, for example, boys who wished to adopt feminine subjectivities through dressing-up play risked being mocked and derided if caught; now they can engage in such play through the use of online avatars in screen windows that can be minimized at a stroke. Girls can immerse themselves in hyper-masculine discourses if they so wish through the adoption of a fighter in a first person shooter game, which provides an experience of a different order than pointing a wooden peg gun in the playground. At the same time, gender discourses are constrained in new forms of toys that have emerged in recent decades. Plastic replicas of smart phones, laptops and tablets are made to appeal to gender-specific audiences, so that girls are targeted with an array of 'pink technologies' (Marsh 2010c). This provides a continuation with the past, in that some toys have always been marketed to gender-specific audiences, but it also signals a newer trend of exaggerating the use of colour in marking gendered otherness.

This chapter, therefore, offers a similar analysis of the relationship between gender and play to that of other areas of study in previous chapters in that, inevitably, there are both continuities and discontinuities to be discerned over time. In the final chapter of the book, this dynamic is focused upon in depth in an attempt to distil the key features of change and sedimentation that permeate the datasets engaged with throughout this book.

9　Conclusion

Throughout this book, the discussion of the data from the 'Memories of Play Project', the 'Playgrounds Project' and the Opies' surveys has identified the way in which there are both continuities and discontinuities in relation to play, media and commercial culture between the 1950s/1960s and the 2010s. In the concluding chapter, this issue is revisited in order to draw out some of the key themes that have emerged in this analysis. The continuities in play are first considered before the chapter moves on to examine some of the major changes that have occurred over the past sixty years.

Continuities in the relationship between play, media and commercial markets

This discussion begins with a recognition that, in fact, nothing ever stays the same. It is the nature of human life that 'everything changes, all of the time' (Giddens 2009: 121). Indeed, one may go further and agree with Pieterse (2001: 221) who proposes, rather than accepting that contemporary society is different from the past, adopting, 'a more radical and penetrating angle that suggests not only that things are no longer the way they used to be, but were never really the way they used to be, or used to be viewed'. Nevertheless, we would suggest that there can be discerned persistent, or sedimented, aspects of play over time, whilst recognizing that these patterns are differently articulated in diverse contexts and accepting that they are coterminous with changing patterns of play. As Bishop and Curtis have argued, it is possible to identify within children's play practices 'continuity *and* change, stability *and* variation, dynamism *and* conservatism' (2001: 10, our italics). Here, it is contended that the key continuities can be represented by the themes of *functions*, *framings* and *forms*.

Functions

Without subscribing to an account of play which suggests that its purposes are narrow or can be easily discerned, it can be argued that there are functions of play that remain persistent over time. One of the most prevalent purposes discussed by children is play for amusement, for fun or to relieve boredom. In one of the sound recordings at the British Library, Iona can be heard asking a group of girls if they are playing clapping games because there is a craze for them. One girl responds, 'If you're bored, you just do that, you know.'[106] As van Tilburg and Igou (2012: 193) suggest, boredom is 'an experience that relates to central human needs for meaningful and challenging activities'. When asked why they enjoyed playing with each other, children at Monteney Primary School responded with similar expressions of the need to engage in challenging and meaningful experiences with others through play. Play has an important affective role, which is timeless in its appeal and value to humankind.

A further function of play is to explore and respond to the social and cultural contexts that surround players. Through their games, rhymes and playground rituals, children examine cultural and social values and practices, seeking to reinforce normative discourses but also to question them. In their carnivalesque play (Bakhtin 1984) culture becomes a subject of parody as well as a site for imitation (Willett 2013: 159–60). Across all of the datasets, the research participants could be seen engaging in a critical dialogue with the society that surrounded them.

Play also functions as social glue. Through play, children construct, deconstruct, reconstruct and perform friendships (Corsaro 1997; Pellegrini and Blatchford 2000). This was as true for the older respondents as it was for the children in Monteney Primary School playground. Further, play provides space for identity construction and performance, allowing children to adopt a variety of identity positions and experiment with them (Wohlwend 2009). Play also enables children to explore and extend the parameters of their lifeworlds. Drawing on a Habermasian notion of lifeworld, which signals the significance of interpersonal communication in the construction of a public sphere (Habermas 1987), it can be seen that play enables children to examine the nature of social engagement itself – and, indeed, disengagement.

Not intended as an exhaustive list, the functions of play outlined above persist through generations and thus serve to illustrate the way in which the sedimented practices and meanings of play are deeply embedded in social and cultural life. This is also the case for 'framings' of play, discussed below.

Framings

Bateson (1972) suggested that play frames shape children's play activities. Play frames signal a move into imaginative territory and are communicated through a range of signals, which can be verbal or non-verbal, thus the 'actions of "play" are related to, or denote, other actions of "not play"' (1972: 181). Through metacommunication (or what Bateson terms 'metamessages' (1972: 188)), children signal that the behavior, speech and actions that exist inside the play frame are pretend. Goffman (1974) also used a notion of framing in relation to everyday interaction. He argued that individuals interacted within a 'participation framework', a set of codified rules of conduct that are, in 'normal' contexts, intuitively understood and employed in order to construct and maintain an interaction order (Goffman 1983).

Drawing on both of these conceptualizations of framing, it is suggested that little has changed over time in relation to the way in which children construct play frames; the same 'metamessages' are apparent in play today that were prevalent in earlier decades and enable children to manage modalities in play. Of course, play in online environments raises additional challenges with regard to how the 'metamessages' required to signal play frames can be communicated as different modes and spatial dimensions are experienced. Nevertheless, children do manage to signal play frames in virtual spaces using a range of semiotic cues; for example, Marsh (2011), drawing on Goffman's concepts, illustrates how children established an interaction order in the virtual world *Club Penguin*.

Forms

There are many continuities in relation to forms of play that can be distinguished over time. Table 1.1 in Chapter 1 outlined the classification system employed in the 'Playgrounds Project' and, drawing on this, Chapter 3 examined how the majority of activities undertaken in Monteney Primary School playground could be traced back to the Opies' corpus and beyond. Nevertheless, whilst the form of a particular game may remain, its purpose can change, as identified by Iona Opie:

> The structure of a game changes over the years to suit the social climate. Nubile maidens played ring or line singing games in the fifteenth century as part of the process of wooing a young man; in the twentieth century, younger girls played those games for their entertainment value, especially when, as in 'The Dukes a-Riding', they were given a chance to be rude about their friends. The words, too, change over time; it is a long evolutionary process, which incidentally obviates many of the so-called 'historical origins'.
>
> (Opie 2001: xii)

Therefore, simply because continuity in forms across the datasets was identified does not suggest that these were identical in nature or purpose.

Whilst this reflection on functions, framings and forms signals that persistent patterns over time are discernible, what is less clear is *how* these patterns remain embedded within culture. As identified in Chapter 6 in the discussion of the place of football in Robert's family history, the impact of habitus (Bourdieu 1990) can certainly be discerned in that 'systems of durable, transposable dispositions, structured structures predisposed to function as structuring structures' (1990: 53) are present in the histories and practices of play. In Willett *et al.* (2013), we draw on Raymond Williams (1977, 1981) to reflect on ways in which sedimented aspects of play are present in residual, dominant and emergent cultural forms. Bourdieu and Williams focused on macro-level operations of cultural reproduction. At a micro-level, we would also like to suggest that important in the endurance of aspects of play over time is the concept of 'chronotopic lamination' (Bakhtin 1981; Prior and Shipka 2003). Prior and Shipka, drawing on Bakhtin, suggest that chronotopic lamination refers to the 'dispersed and fluid chains of places, times, people, and artifacts that are tied together in trajectories of literate action along with the ways multiple activity footings are held and managed' (2003: 181) and, by 'literate action', they argue that Bakhtin meant 'representational practices, complex, multifarious chains of transformations in and across representational state of media' (2003: 181–2). Whilst Prior and Shipka focus on demonstrating the way in which the process of writing involves drawing on a range of experiences across time and space that are layered in the text and practice of writing, we would suggest that a similar process of chronotopic lamination occurs in children's representational practices through play. Thus, play activities take place across time and space and layers of a play activity are linked to the past, present and future. The persistent patterns over time discussed above, however, need also to be juxtaposed alongside the disjunctures and fissures that emerge in any analysis of social and cultural change. In the following section, some of the key changes in play that have occurred over the past sixty years are considered.

Discontinuities in the relationship between play, media and commercial markets

Whilst it is recognized that sedimented aspects of play have been persistent across decades, indeed centuries, there have also been substantial changes, which are discussed below in relation to four over-arching themes: *contexts, texts, practices* and *processes*.

Contexts

Inevitably, there have been significant shifts in the political, economic, social and cultural landscape over the past sixty years, which have impacted upon the experiences of the participants in the research studies considered in this book. If just one area is focused upon in depth, the economics of family life, and the changes that have taken place are considered, it is clear that the social context for play is markedly different for contemporary children than for the respondents in the 'Memories of Play Project'. One of the factors impacting on economic changes in families is family size. Average household sizes have decreased since the 1950s. In 1950, the average household size was 3.2 people per household (Kuijsten 1995: 67) and in 2011 this average had fallen 25 per cent to a figure of 2.4 (Macrory 2012). Despite the decreasing size of the household, family expenditure has increased, with an attendant impact on standards of living. As the authors of a report for the Social Issues Research Centre note:

> Nostalgic visions of family life before the rise of 'consumer society' often revolve around the notion of a 'safer' society, where community spirit prevailed and one did not have to lock one's door. If this was indeed the case it was probably because there was not a great deal to be lost from leaving the door unlatched.
>
> (SIRC 2008: 24–5)

As was the case in the studies considered in this book, children in the 2010s had access to a greater range of material goods related to their play activities than the older respondents and they were able more readily to obtain access to purchased play resources (such as theme parks and adventure play areas) outside the home. Children in contemporary society, however, are more likely to witness disparity across social groups than children in the 1950s. Whilst family income has increased since the 1950s, there is a more uneven distribution of wealth than in previous decades. Therefore, whilst families in the 2010s are able to spend more on leisure activities and children's play than families in the 1950s and 1960s, the disparities between families are marked, with many single-parent families and families with unemployed parents and carers frequently unable to afford what are now considered to be necessities, such as an annual family holiday (Conolly and Kerr 2008). Institutional racism also impacts upon economic life, as black and minority ethnic people are more likely to be unemployed than white people, with an unemployment rate of 12.4 per cent in Asian communities and 13.4 per cent in Afro-Caribbean communities in 2012, compared with 7.9 per cent for the UK as a whole (Office for National Statistics 2013). In terms of impact on the relationship between play, media and commercial markets, these social changes are significant. Whilst there were certainly differences in terms of what families could afford in the 1950s, as expressed by the participants, these differences were not as marked. Given the costs of hardware and software that facilitate play, the gaps between what different families can afford are greater in contemporary society than in the 1950s and, therefore, social exclusion in relation to digital play is a key area of concern. For example, Common Sense Media (2011) report an 'app gap' with regard to American children, in that 47 per cent of children from middle-class families have access to tablets that enable children to access apps, but only 17 per cent of children from working-class families have access to the same technology. As play becomes increasingly shaped by technological advances, these patterns are concerning. The changes in the economic landscape, therefore, have impacted in important ways upon play over the past sixty years and this is also the case in relation to other elements of post-industrial, neo-liberal societies. Over a decade ago now, Giddens (2002), in a discussion of the 'Runaway World', noted a series of major trends such as globalization, risk, detraditionalization, individualization and cosmopolitanism, all of which he noted would have a profound impact upon society. Many of the consequences of these trends are still being played out today and are as relevant to issues of childhood play as other areas of social life. Future likely trends, such as global fiscal uncertainties, issues relating to food and water security and the impact of ageing demographics, will also have a concomitant impact on childhoods and it will remain important to trace the consequences of these trends in order to attend sufficiently well to the structures which frame children's play.

Texts

If a text can be defined as 'any instance of communication in any mode or any combination of modes' (Kress 2003: 48), then the texts that children produce in their play are broad and include songs, rhymes, games, play scripts in fantasy play, and so on. Bishop (2010) has identified continuity in children's play texts across time in her analysis of the rhyme 'Eeny Meeny Dessameeny', encountered in Monteney Primary School in 2009, which she relates to a group of counting out rhymes that can be traced back to the mid-nineteenth century. There are also differences, however, in terms of the texts produced in play in the 2010s and the 1950s/1960s. First, we would argue that children's play texts are now more intensely shaped by media and popular culture than they were sixty years ago, as discussed in Chapter 4. This may be because children's play texts are always shaped by their experiences, and children's experiences are now more squarely located within a media-inflected and technological landscape than in previous generations. Second, there are new kinds of texts encountered in today's playgrounds, as identified in Chapter 3, such as rap-influenced song and dance routines, which also reflect the increasing interest in street dance over recent decades. These may have taken the place of other kinds of texts less prevalent today, such as entertainment rhymes. Finally, the intertextual referencing frequently embedded in play texts, which includes postural intertextuality (Taylor 2012), has become even more fluid in contemporary society, as such intertextual practices are now established practices in everyday life as the authority of the text is questioned in an online world in which texts can be easily mixed and mashed-up (Kress 2010). It should be said, however, that children have never subscribed to a model in which the authority of the source text is paramount in play, but it is certainly the case that children today are accustomed to a social context in which intertextual referencing is used to signal cultural allegiances, pop cultural savviness and technical prowess.

Practices

Reckwitz argues that:

> A 'practice' (Praktik) is a routinised type of behaviour which consists of several elements, interconnected to one another: forms of bodily activities, forms of mental activities, 'things' and their use, a background knowledge in the form of understanding, know-how, states of emotion and motivational knowledge.
>
> (Reckwitz 2002: 249)

From the work of scholars in New Literacy Studies on literacy as a social practice, we have learned that routinized meaning-making behaviour is shaped by social and cultural understandings (Street 1995; Gee 1999). Similarly, play practices are informed by the social structures of which they are a part and thus the key changes that can be traced in this regard in the last decade relate to media, technology and commercial culture. Thompson suggested that if:

> 'man [sic] is an animal suspended in webs of significance he himself has spun,' as Geertz once remarked, then communication media are spinning wheels in the modern world and, in using these media, human beings are fabricating webs of significance for themselves.
>
> (Thompson 1995: 11)

Play practices are inexorably shaped by habitus (Bourdieu 1990) and forms of capital (Bourdieu 1986), at the same time as constituting generative spaces that enable children as social agents to perform transformational acts. In the twenty-first century, developments in posthumanist theory mean there is enhanced understanding of the way in which practices are shaped by both human and non-human elements (e.g. Thrift 2007), although Schatzki (2001: 2) notes that whilst there is general agreement that 'activity is embodied and that nexuses of practices are mediated by artefacts, hybrids and natural objects', the extent of the impact of these various elements is contested. Play practices today are embedded in a range of material and technological objects that actively shape the play episodes. This has led to criticisms that contemporary electronic toys have tightly defined play scripts that limit children's play (Levin and Rosenquest 2001 – although see Marsh (2002) for a rejoinder to this piece). Instead, we would argue that opportunities for imaginative play are extended in some of the artefacts available to children today, such as physical toys that interact with apps, for example, in ways which are productive rather than limiting, as they enable play across online and offline domains, as discussed in Chapter 7.

Processes

In using the term 'processes', we refer to the ways in which play texts and practices are transmitted and shared across contexts. In identifying the nature of change here, we refer back to Chapter 3, which considered the way in which online forums, such as YouTube, now enable the rapid transmission of play. In understanding processes of play in contemporary society, it might be fruitful to draw from Deleuze and Guattari's concept of the 'rhizome' (1987), which has become widely used across a range of disciplines. Indeed, Wallin (2010: 83) refers to a current 'romance with the rhizome' and cautions against a superficial engagement with the concept. In the context of our studies, rhizomatic analysis is helpful in understanding the way in which new play texts and practices are generated. The rhizome is an 'image of thought' (Deleuze 1994) that has multiple and non-hierarchical points of contact, exit and entry. It is contrasted to 'aborescent' modes of thought, which Deleuze and Guattari (1987) define as dualistic in nature, based on totalizing principles, and which can be characterized through the image of a tree, in which branches split as it grows on a vertical plane. The process of the creation of this structure seems to embed 'infinitely reproducible principles of TRACING' (Deleuze and Guattari 1987:13, author capitals), whereas 'the rhizome is altogether different, a *map and not a tracing*' (1987: 13). Buchanan (2007) summarizes Deleuze and Guattari's six principles of a rhizome to suggest that: (i) any point in the rhizome can connect to any other point; (ii) the rhizome is composed of dimensions and cannot be reduced to One or multiple, thus if any point in the rhizome is changed, then the whole is altered; (iii) the rhizome does not reproduce itself but extends by variation, expansion, offshoots (lines of flight); (iv) the rhizome has multiple entrances and exit points; (v) the rhizome does not have a centre; (vi) the rhizome is not amenable to any structural or generative model (Buchanan 2007: n.p.).

In relation to children's play, a rhizomatic analysis recognizes the way in which a particular text or practice cannot be traced back to a single origin, but instead texts and practices extend themselves by variation, by exploding into multiple lines of flight. Wallin argues that the rhizome 'is a practical matter of creation' (2010: 86) and, in children's playful creativity, texts and practices emerge that connect to multiple modes and codes and relate to both the material and immaterial, the organic and non-organic:

> Not every trait in a rhizome is necessarily linked to a linguistic feature: semiotic chains of every nature are connected to very diverse modes of coding (biological, political, economic, etc.) that bring into play not only different regimes of signs but also states of things of differing status.
>
> (Deleuze and Guattari 1987: 7)

A play text can be viewed as assemblage, which is 'a kind of chaotic network of habitual and non-habitual connections, always in flux, always reassembling in different ways' (Potts 2004: 19) and which, as Deleuze and Guattari suggest, is both content and expression, consisting of a machinic assemblage of bodies, of actions and passions, and a 'collective assemblage of enunciation' (1987: 88–9). Assemblages are created, not randomly pulled together:

> Assemblages are necessary in order for the unity of composition enveloped in a stratum, the relations between a given stratum and the others, and the relation between the strata and the [virtual] plane of consistency to be organised rather than random.
>
> (Deleuze and Guattari 1987: 79)

In viewing assemblages as 'the key entities in conjoining interactions of a rhizome' (Harvey and Chrisman 2004: 69), it can be seen that play texts are, thus, composed of elements of different types that converge momentarily and create specific meanings in context, and some of those elements may then emerge in future texts in ways that cannot be explained through a linear and hierarchical process.

A further aspect of the play text as assemblage that is of note here is that such a concept relates well to the notion of bricolage, which is also a valuable way of considering the nature of children's playful constructions (discussed further in Willett *et al.* 2013). Lévi-Strauss's (1966) concept of bricolage was developed to characterize a construction of knowledge in which the constructor, the bricoleur, draws on whatever is to hand in order to create. Lévi-Strauss suggests that bricolage is characteristic of mythological thought. This is in contrast to the scientist, the engineer, who uses tools that are specifically created for the purpose of construction. Derrida argues that it is a mistake for Lévi-Strauss to distinguish between the scientist and the bricoleur, given that all construction of knowledge is bricolage: 'If one calls *bricolage* the necessity of borrowing one's concept from the text of a heritage which is more or less coherent or ruined, it must be said that every discourse is *bricoleur*' (Derrida 1989: 920, author's italics). In the same essay, Derrida points to the absence of a privileged centre in bricolage as being the most significant aspect of this work:

> What does Lévi-Strauss say of his 'mythologicals'? It is here that we rediscover the mythopoetical virtue (power) of *bricolage*. In effect, what appears most fascinating in this critical search for a new status of the discourse is the stated abandonment of all reference to a *center*, to a *subject*, to a privileged *reference*, to an origin, or to an absolute *arche*.
>
> (Derrida 1989: 920–1, author's italics)

This, then, relates the notion of bricolage to that of the rhizome and reinforces the argument that textual play does not involve a privileging of an original source. Chapter 3 highlighted how the notion of bricolage has a long heritage in childlore. If this is the case, then what are we suggesting that is new? We would propose that the process of bricolage in contemporary children's play is different than in the childhoods of the adults interviewed for the 'Memories of Play Project' and the work of Pieterse (2001) is drawn upon in formulating this analysis. Pieterse, in considering the notion of hybridity in relation to cultural syncretism, the mixing of people from diverse cultures, suggests that 'A distinctive feature of contemporary times is that they are times of *accelerated mixing*. Thus, it is not mixing that is new but the scope and speed of mixing' (2001: 231, author's italics). Likewise, we would like to propose that, in relation to children's play, in the twenty-first century there can be discerned a process of *intensified bricolage*. This is preferable to a notion of acceleration, as that denotes a time-based analysis, a speeding up of bricolage, which certainly may be taking place due to technologies but is not the sole characteristic of the changes. Instead, *intensified bricolage* points to the way in which *some* play texts, in *some* contexts, are now more laminated, that is multi-layered, due to the complexities of the textual landscapes of contemporary childhood. Localized practices are now conflated with the global in ways that were not possible in previous generations because of the way in which digital technologies accelerate and extend the 'glocalization' (Robertson 1995) process.

To summarize, therefore, it has been suggested that the key continuities in the relationship between play, media and commercial markets over the past sixty years can be clustered under the themes *forms*, *framings* and *functions* and the discontinuities characterized by the themes of *contexts*, *texts*, *practices* and *processes*. This appears, on the surface, to offer a set of firm and robust conclusions to what has been a complex enterprise, the study of change in play over time. Inevitably, the process of arriving at such summative judgements can oversimplify and may ignore particular lines of flight. This is not our intention. Rather, the proposals are offered as a series of contentions that are presented in order to be considered, resisted and, indeed, contradicted in future work in this field.

It is also recognized that there are a number of aspects of the studies discussed in the book which mean that to arrive at any generalized notion of change is problematic. First, the studies discussed in this book have focused primarily on white, working-class communities. Whilst the London school in the 'Playgrounds Project' was multicultural, Monteney Primary School serves a largely monocultural community, and it is this school on which has been focused much of the discussion of play in the twenty-first century. The adults who were traced in the 'Memories of Play Project' were all white and all defined themselves as working-class. This does not mean that the aspects of play that have been discussed take place only in such communities. Many elements of play are universal and global (Roopnarine 2012). Nevertheless, it may be the case that continuity and change may be differently played out in specific cultural contexts due to the different rates at which social and cultural changes take place at the macro level of societies. In addition, there is a need to view the self-reports of the adults in the 'Memories of Play Project' with some caution, given that memories are reconstructed through present subjectivities, meaning that some events may be foregrounded or reported in ways that do not necessarily represent past events, whilst other relevant activities are forgotten. This is why, throughout the book, we have been careful to consider these data in the light of other work, including that of the Opies and more recent folklorists such as Steve Roud (2010). Having said this, we do not think it is the case that drawing on oral narratives is a problematic exercise. As Wright and McLeod (2012: 18) argue, 'working with personal narratives and memories of schooling offers important ways to understand the cultural meanings and effects of education, ones that complicate and enrich documentary or institutionally-focussed approaches to educational history'.

What we hope to have achieved in this volume is to have made a contribution to a consideration of developments in the relationship between play, media and commercial markets in the UK since the middle of the twentieth century, at which point, we have argued, there was an intensification of the dynamic between these elements. There is much more research to be undertaken in this field in future years in order to extend our understanding. We would suggest that there are three key potential lines of inquiry to be pursued. First, the way in which technological developments continue to push the ontological boundaries of play is of great interest. Virtual, blended, augmented realities – all deserve further consideration in relation to both the play texts and practices that emerge across these domains. Second, further consideration needs to be given to the relationship between mobile and immobile and global and local, given the processes of migration, immigration and cultural hybridization and the way in which space and place are no longer constrained to the specific geographical context in which play takes place. Finally, it is likely that recent developments in relation to intergenerational play will accelerate in future years due to continued technological advancements. As computer games, for example, become easier to play because of simplified interfaces, which promote embodiment and fluidity across online and offline domains, the involvement of children and adults of all ages and abilities in such play becomes more possible. It would be useful to examine the impact of this upon family and community relationships. Such work is important if play is to be properly recognized as a central aspect of childhood cultures. Further, offering the last word on the matter to Iona Opie, which appears to us to be entirely fitting, this ongoing project would be a significant tool in continued and important attempts to discount:

> that long-lived and lusty meme, nowadays fuelled by newspaper articles in the tabloid press, 'children don't play their own games any more' (or even, 'children don't know how to play any more').
>
> (Opie 2001: xiii–xiv)

Notes

Chapter 2

1. The Opies' focus was on children's folklore, which includes all cultural traditions of children including language, narrative, custom, belief and material culture, as well as play.
2. The term 'folklore' was only coined in 1846 and the Folklore Society founded in 1878 (as discussed in Bishop and Curtis 2001: 3–4).
3. The Golspie children's essays done for Nicholson are held at the Bodleian Libraries, MS. Eng. Misc. c. 58.
4. James Madison Carpenter Collection Online Catalogue (2008), Available at: http://www.hrionline.ac.uk/carpenter/. The Carpenter collection, which is held by the Library of Congress (AFC1972/001), was unknown to the Opies at the time of their research into singing games.
5. Further information is available at the University College Dublin National Folklore Collection website pages, http://digital.ucd.ie/view/ivrla:7613 and http://www.ucd.ie/irishfolklore/-/schoolsfolklorescheme1937–38/.
6. Further information about Mass Observation and its history is available on its website, http://www.massobs.org.uk/index.htm.
7. Ritchie's third and final book, originally entitled *The Bumbee Bell*, presenting play and verbal wit in the school playground, has been edited for publication by Bishop.
8. Apart from assisting the American folksong collector, Alan Lomax, to make a few recordings of Norton Park pupils involved in the film.
9. For further information about Webb, see *Playtimes: A Century of Children's Games and Rhymes*, http://www.bl.uk/playtimes.
10. Webb's British recordings are now deposited with the British Library Sound Archive (C1431) and have recently been digitized. His papers and photographs are held by the Pitt Rivers Museum, Oxford, and digital copies of the photographs can be accessed via the Pitt Rivers website at http://www.prm.ox.ac.uk/photocollection.html.

11. The following account is drawn from Avery (2012), Opie (1988) and Opie (1989), unless otherwise indicated.
12. Further information about the Survey of English Dialects is available on the Leeds Archive of Vernacular Culture website, http://www.leeds.ac.uk/library/spcoll/lavc/.
13. Letter to Julia Bishop from Iona Opie, 8 March 2013.
14. The Skylon was a futuristic sculpture built for the Festival of Britain in 1951.
15. Letter from Iona Opie, 8 March 2013.
16. Further information about the Opies and a copy of the Finding Aid to their papers at the Bodleian Libraries are available at the University of Sheffield's Childhoods and Play website, http://www.opieproject.group.shef.ac.uk/.
17. This collection was deposited by Iona Opie with the British Library Sound Archive in 1998 and is now entitled 'The Opie Collection of Children's Games and Songs' (BL shelfmark: C898).
18. The quoted sections are from Paulin (1990).
19. Kathryn Marsh contests this view, arguing that 'children . . . use deliberate processes of innovation to vary game material for a range of different social and aesthetic purposes, in some cases creating entirely new compositions' (2008: 199).

Chapter 3

20. Wikipedia, *Teenage Mutant Ninja Turtles*, available at http://en.wikipedia.org/wiki/Teenage_Mutant_Ninja_Turtles_%281987_TV_series%29 (accessed 24 February 2013).
21. See MPJB2010-05-26v01558 and MPJB2010-05-26v01559.
22. See MPJB2009-10-01at00089.
23. MPJB2009-10-01at00089.
24. CHRW2010-01-12v00060.
25. MPJB2009-10-01v00242 ('Banana Split') and JB fieldnotes, 4.6.09 ('Coconut Crack').
26. MPJB2009-11-26v01104.
27. MPJB2009-11-26v01102.
28. MPJB2009-11-26v01102.
29. MPJB2010-05-20v01528; CHRW2010-01-11v00055.
30. The exception is 'Ip dip do, The cat's got flu', which seems to derive from a singing game of recent origin (see Roud 2010: 288–9).
31. MPJM2010-06-24v01621.
32. MPJB2010-07-21at00143.
33. MPJB2009-11-26v01102.
34. JB fieldnotes, 4.6.09.
35. JB fieldnotes, 23.6.09.

36. MPJB2010-11-23v01654.
37. JB fieldnotes, 16.6.09.
38. Roud regards this game as having declined in popularity (2010: 14–15).
39. MPJB2010-05-24v01545.
40. A midday supervisor at the school who attended Monteney when she was a child recalls the same game as 'Tiggy on the Corners' (JB fieldnotes, 23.11.10).
41. JB fieldnotes, 4.6.09.
42. MPJB2010-07-21v01601.
43. MPJB2010-01-21v01387.
44. MPJB2009-10-01at00089.
45. MPJB2009-06-11v00012.
46. MPJB2010-05-11v01515.
47. MPJB2010-07-15v01574, MPJB2010-07-15v01575.
48. These are individually cited in the Wikipedia entry *Thumb War*, available at http://en.wikipedia.org/wiki/Thumb_war#cite_note-10 (accessed 26 February 2013).
49. MPJB2010-05-11v01515.
50. We gratefully acknowledge the contribution of Jonathan Robinson, lead curator in Sociolinguistics and Education at the British Library, for this information and the phonetic transcriptions.
51. MPJB2009-10-01at00089.
52. MPCC2009-09-16v00572, MPCC2009-09-16v00583, MPJB2010-10-21v01639.
53. JB fieldnotes, 26.06.09.
54. MPJB2009-07-01v00021, MPJB2009-07-09v00032.
55. MPJB2010-05-25v01551.
56. See http://www.youtube.com/watch?v=edHLDTA2B5E.
57. This information derives from the Wikipedia entry, *DJ Q and MC Bonez*, available at http://en.wikipedia.org/wiki/DJ_Q, accessed 24 February 2013.
58. MPJB2009-11-05v01044.
59. MPJB2010-03-11v01438.
60. MPJB2009-10-01v00232.
61. MPJB2010-05-11v01519, MPJB2010-05-11v01520.
62. JB fieldnotes, 1.10.09.
63. MPJB2010-03-11v01446.
64. MPCB2009-09-29v00672.
65. MPJB2009-07-09v00038.
66. Nevertheless, some children responded to our questionnaire that they played with marbles.
67. JB fieldnotes, 4.6.09.
68. These are not discussed in the Opies' book (1997) but there are notes on some of them, such as football, in the archival collection at the Bodleian Libraries.
69. MPCB2009-11-02v01347, MPCB2009-11-02v01360.
70. MPJB2010-01-28v01396, MPJB2010-01-28v01398.

71. MPJB2010-03-04v01425, MPJB2010-03-11v01442.
72. MPJB2010-03-11v01447, MPJB2010-03-16v01461.
73. MPJM2010-03-30v01473.
74. MPJM2010-03-30v01480, MPJM2010-03-30v01481.
75. JB fieldnotes, 11.11.10.
76. JB fieldnotes, 18.6.09.
77. MPJB2010-06-17v01562.
78. MPJB2009-10-08v00255.
79. JB fieldnotes, 13.10.09.
80. JB fieldnotes, 18.6.09.
81. JB fieldnotes, 18.6.09.
82. MPJB2010-03-04v01427.
83. MPJM2010-05-20v01607.
84. MPJB2010-07-20v01592.
85. Clapping survey, response by three Year 6 girls.
86. JB fieldnotes, 4.3.10, Year 6 boy response.
87. MPJB2009-06-11v00010. This game is not described by the Opies but it is now very widespread (Roud 2010: 96–7) and does have similarities to variants of 'Film Stars', as described by the Opies (1969: 276).

Chapter 4

88. http://www.youtube.com/watch?v=H5KfHEoZDKI.
89. A number of variants are quoted by the Opies in their discussion of skipping rhymes (1997: 270–2).
90. MPJB2009-07-01v00021.
91. MPJB2009-10-01at00088.
92. MPJB2010-05-11at00131.
93. MPJB2010-05-11at00131.
94. See http://www.youtube.com/watch?v=cCVI06qmKA8 and MPJB2010-05-11v 01517.
95. MPJB2009-07-16v00056.
96. See, for example, MPJB2009-06-11v00003.
97. MPJB2009-10-08v00256.
98. MPJB2009-10-08v00252.
99. The origin of dap greetings is not certain although they are regarded as American and have been popularized through television and film, such as in the remake of *The Parent Trap* (1998). For more information, see Powell (2012).
100. MPJB2010-07-21at00143.

Chapter 5

101. Can be viewed on YouTube at http://www.youtube.com/watch?v=GPhZsaulu
XM.

Chapter 6

102. This is a reference to *Redgauntlet*, a novel by Walter Scott (1824), in which one
of the characters writes of learning to 'endure my pawmies without wincing,
like one that is determined not to be the better for them'.
103. The Opies describe a further refinement to the game in which the winner
threw all the pennies and was allowed to keep all those which came down
'heads' up. The player who had come second then did likewise with the
remaining coins and so on until the coins ran out (1997: 91).

Chapter 8

104. http://www.ea.com/uk/football/fifa/ps3.
105. http://www.stardoll.com/en/.

Chapter 9

106. C898/63; available at http://sounds.bl.uk/Oral-history/Opie-collection-of-
children-s-games-and-songs-/021M-C0898X0063XX-0100V0.

References

Abrahams, R.D. (ed.) (1969) *Jump-Rope Rhymes: A Dictionary*. Austin, TX: University of Texas Press.

Abrahams, R.D. and Rankin, L. (eds) (1980) *Counting-Out Rhymes: A Dictionary*. Austin, TX: University of Texas Press.

Agnew, J. (2005) Space: place, in P. Cloke and R. Johnston (eds) *Space of Geographical Thought: Deconstructing Human Geography's Binaries* (pp. 81–96). London: Sage Publications.

Allen, K. and Mendick, H. (2013) Young people's uses of celebrity: class, gender and 'improper' celebrity, *Discourse: Studies in the Cultural Politics of Education*, 34(1): 77–93.

Allen, L. (2013) Behind the bike sheds: sexual geographies of schooling, *British Journal of Sociology of Education*, 34(1): 56–75.

Appadurai, A. (1996) *Modernity at Large: Cultural Dimensions of Globalization*. Minneapolis, MN: University of Minnesota Press.

Arleo, A. (1991) Strategy in counting out in Saint-Nazaire, France, *Children's Folklore Review*, 14(1): 25–9.

Armitage, M. (2001) The ins and outs of school playground play: children's use of 'play spaces', in J.C. Bishop and M. Curtis (eds) *Play Today in the Primary School Playground: Life, Learning and Creativity* (pp. 37–57). Buckingham: Open University Press.

Armitage, M. (2006) 'All about Mary': children's use of the toilet ghost story as a mechanism for dealing with fear, but fear of what? *Contemporary Legend* (new series), 9: 1–27.

Arvidsson, A. (2006) *Brands: Meaning and Value in Media Culture*. New York: Routledge.

Ash, J. (2010) Teleplastic technologies: charting practices of orientation and navigation in videogaming, *Transactions of the Institute of British Geographers*, 35: 414–30.

Avery, G. (2012) Opie, Peter Mason (1918–1982), *Oxford Dictionary of National Biography*, Oxford University Press. Available at http://www.oxforddnb.com/view/article/31517 [Accessed 5 April 2013].

Aydt, H. and Corsaro, W.A. (2003) Differences in children's construction of gender across culture: an interpretive approach, *American Behavioural Scientist*, 46: 1306–25.

Bailey, R. (2011) *Letting Children be Children: Report of an Independent Review of the Commercialisation and Sexualisation of Childhood*. London: Department for Education.

Bakhtin, M.M. (1981) *The Dialogic Imagination* (translated by C. Emerson and M. Holquist, edited by M. Holquist). Austin, TX: University of Texas Press.

Bakhtin, M.M. (1984) *Rabelais and his World* (translated by H. Iswolsky). Bloomington, IN: Indiana University Press.

Bakhtin, M.M. (1986) *Speech Genres and Other Late Essays* (translated by V.W. McGee, edited by C. Emerson and M. Holquist). Austin, TX: University of Texas Press.

Barnier, A.J., Sutton, J., Harris, C.B. and Wilson, R.A. (2008) A conceptual and empirical framework for the social distribution of cognition: the case of memory, *Cognitive Systems Research*, 9: 33–51.

Bateson, G. (1972) *Steps to an Ecology of Mind.* New York: Ballantine Books.

Beresin, A.R. (2010) *Recess Battles: Playing, Fighting, and Storytelling.* Jackson, MS: University Press of Mississippi.

Bianchi, S.M., Robinson, J.P. and Milkie, M.A. (2006) *Changing Rhythms of American Family Life.* New York: Russell Sage Foundation.

Bickford, T. (2012) The new 'tween' music industry: the Disney Channel, Kidz Bop and an emerging childhood counterpublic, *Popular Music*, 31(3): 417–36.

Bishop, J. (2010) 'Eeny Meeny Dessameeny': continuity and change in the 'back-story' of a children's playground rhyme, AHRC Beyond Text, Available at: http://projects.beyondtext.ac.uk/research_workshops.php?i=35&p=Children's Playground Games and Songs in the New Media Age [Accessed 2 April 2013].

Bishop, J. and Burn, A. (2013) Reasons for rhythm: multimodal perspectives on musical play, in R. Willett, C. Richards, J. Marsh, J.C. Bishop and A. Burn, *Children, Media and Playground Cultures: Ethnographic Studies of School Playtimes* (pp. 89–119). Basingstoke: Palgrave Macmillan.

Bishop, J.C. (2011) 'Docky' Ritchie and 'The Bumbee Bell': James T. R. Ritchie as a collector of children's folklore. Paper presented to the Folklore Society AGM Conference on 'Childlore and the Folklore of Childhood', University of Worcester, 15–17 April.

Bishop, J.C. (in press) 'That's how the whole hand-clap thing passes on': online/offline transmission and multimodal variation in a children's clapping game, in A. Burn, and C. Richards (eds) *Children's Games in the New Media Age: Childlore, Media and the Playground.* London: Ashgate Press.

Bishop, J.C. and Curtis, M. (eds) (2001) *Play Today in the Primary School Playground: Life, Learning and Creativity.* Buckingham: Open University Press.

Bishop, J.C. and Curtis, M. with Woolley, H., Armitage, M. and Ginsborg, J. (2006) Creative engagements: children's uses of media elements in peer play at school. Paper presented at the Folklore Society Conference, *Folklore, Film and Television: Convergences in Traditional Cultures and Popular Media*, London, 31 March–1 April.

Blaise, M. (2005) *Playing It Straight.* London: Routledge.

Blatchford, P. and Baines, E. (2006) A follow-up national survey of breaktimes in primary and secondary schools: report to the Nuffield Foundation. Available at www.breaktime.org.uk/NuffieldBreakTimeReport-WEBVersion.pdf [Accessed 28 March 2013].

Blatchford, P. and Sharp, S. (1994) Introduction: why understand and why change school breaktime behavior?, in P. Blatchford and S. Sharp (eds) *Breaktime and the School: Understanding and Changing Playground Behavior* (pp.1–10). London: Routledge.

Bock, S.R. ([1993]2010) Guide to the Norman Douglas Collection GEN MSS 88. Yale University Library Beinecke Rare Book and Manuscript Library. Available at http://drs.library.yale.edu:8083/fedora/get/beinecke:douglas2/PDF [Accessed 5 April 2013].

Bolton, H.C. (1888) *The Counting-Out Rhymes of Children*. London: E. Stock.

Bourdieu, P. (1986) The forms of capital, in J. Richardson (ed.) *Handbook of Theory and Research for the Sociology of Education* (pp. 241–58). New York: Greenwood.

Bourdieu, P. (1990) *The Logic of Practice* (translated by R. Nice). Cambridge: Polity Press (original work published in 1980).

Boyes, G. (1990) Alice Bertha Gomme (1852–1938): a reassessment of the work of a folklorist, *Folklore*, 101: 198–208.

Boyes, G. (1995) The legacy of the work of Iona and Peter Opie: the lore and language of today's schoolchildren, in R. Beard (ed.) *Rhyme, Reading and Writing* (pp.131–46). London: Hodder & Stoughton Educational.

Boyes, G. (2001) 'A proper limitation': stereotypes of Alice Gomme, *Musical Traditions*. Available at http://www.mustrad.org.uk/articles/gomme.htm [Accessed 5 April 2013].

Braun, A., Vincent, C. and Ball, S. (2010) Working-class fathers and childcare: the economic and family contexts of fathering in the UK, *Community, Work and Family*, 14(1): 19–37.

Braun, V. and Clarke, V. (2006) Using thematic analysis in psychology, *Qualitative Research in Psychology*, 3(2): 77–101.

Brumfield, S. (2011) Father Damian Webb: a song of childhood. Paper presented to the Folklore Society AGM Conference on 'Childlore and the Folklore of Childhood', University of Worcester, 15–17 April.

Bruns, A. (2006) Towards produsage: futures for user-led content production, in F. Sudweeks, H. Hrachovec and C. Ess (eds), *Proceedings: Cultural Attitudes towards Communication and Technology 2006*. Perth: Murdoch University. Available at http://snurb.info/files/12132812018_towards_produsage_0.pdf [Accessed 23 January 2013].

Buchanan, I. (2007) Deleuze and the internet, *Australian Humanities Review*, Issue 43, December. Available at http://www.australianhumanitiesreview.org/archive/Issue-December–2007/Buchanan.html [Accessed 2 April 2013].

Buckingham, D. (2000) *After the Death of Childhood: Growing up in the Age of Electronic Media*. Cambridge: Polity.

Buckingham, D. (2011) *The Material Child: Growing up in Consumer Culture*. Cambridge: Polity.

Buckingham, D. and Scanlon, M. (2003) *Education, Entertainment and Learning in the Home*. Milton Keynes: Open University Press.

Buckingham, D., Willett, R., Bragg, S. and Russell, R. (2010) *Sexualized Goods Aimed at Children. Report for the Scottish Parliament Equal Opportunities Committee*. The Scottish Parliament. Available at http://archive.scottish.parliament.uk/s3/committees/equal/reports–10/eor1002.htm. [Accessed 4 March 2013].

Burk, C.F. (1900) The collecting instinct, *Pedagogical Seminary*, 7: 179–207.

Burke, A. (in press) Stardolls and the virtual playground: how identity construction works in the new digital frontier, in A. Burke and J. Marsh (eds) *Children's Virtual Play Worlds: Culture, Learning and Participation*. New York: Peter Lang.

Burke, A. and Marsh, J. (eds) (in press) *Children's Virtual Play Worlds: Culture, Learning and Participation*. New York: Peter Lang.

Burn, A. (2013) Computer games on the playground: ludic systems, dramatized narrative and virtual embodiment, in R. Willett, C. Richards, J. Marsh, A. Burn and J.C. Bishop, *Children, Media and Playground Cultures: Ethnographic Studies of School Playtimes* (pp 120–43). Basingstoke: Palgrave Macmillan.

Burn, A. and Richards, C. (eds) (in press) *Children's Games in the New Media Age: Childlore, Media and the Playground*. London: Ashgate Press.

Burn, A., Bishop J., Jopson, L., Marsh, J., Mitchell, G., Richards, C. *et al.* (2011) Children's playground games and songs in the new media age: final report. Available at http://projects.beyondtext.ac.uk/playgroundgames/uploads/end_of_project_report.pdf [Accessed 3 March 2013].

Butler, J. (1990) *Gender Trouble*. New York: Routledge.

Byron, T. (2008) *Safer Children in a Digital World*. Nottingham: DCSF Publications.

Carrington, V. (in press) An argument for assemblage theory: integrated spaces, mobility and polycentricity, in A. Burke and J. Marsh (eds) *Children's Virtual Play Worlds: Culture, Learning and Participation*. New York: Peter Lang.

Carrington, V. and Dowdall, C. (2013) The stuff of literacies: constructing an object ethnography of global media cultures and young people's everyday lives, in C. Hall, T. Cremin, B. Comber and L. Moll (eds) *International Handbook of Research in Children's Literacy, Learning and Culture* (pp 96–107). London: Routledge.

Carter, L. (2012) Toy fair daily: UK toy industry grows three per cent in 2011, remains largest in Europe, *Toy News*, 24 January, 2012. Available at http://www.toynews-online.biz/news/35339/TOY-FAIR-DAILY-UK-toy-industry-grows-three-per-cent-in-2011-remains-largest-in-Europe [Accessed 21 March 2013].

Chambers, D. (2012a) *A Sociology of Family Life: Change and Diversity in Intimate Relations*. Cambridge: Polity Press.

Chambers, D. (2012b) 'Wii play as a family': the rise in family-centred video gaming, *Leisure Studies*, 31(1): 69–82.

Chambers, R. (1826) *Popular Rhymes of Scotland*. Edinburgh: Duncan/London: Hunter.

Common Sense Media (2011) *Zero to Eight: Children's Media Use in America*. Available at http://www.commonsensemedia.org/research/zero-eight-childrens-media-use-america [Accessed 2 April 2013].

Connell, J. (2005) Toddlers, tourism and Tobermory: destination marketing issues and television-induced tourism, *Tourism Management*, 26: 763–76.

Connell, R. (1987) *Gender and Power*. Cambridge: Polity Press.

Connell, R. (1995) *Masculinities*. Berkeley, CA: University of California Press.

Conolly, A. and Kerr, J. (2008) Families with children in Britain: findings from the 2006 Families and Children Study (FACS). Department for Work and Pensions Research Report No. 486. Available at http://research.dwp.gov.uk/asd/asd5/rports2007–2008/rrep486.pdf [Accessed 2 April 2013].

Cook, D.T. (2001) Exchange value as pedagogy in children's leisure: moral panics in children's culture at century's end, *Leisure Sciences: An Interdisciplinary Journal*, 23(2): 81–98.

Cook, D.T. (2004) *The Commodification of Childhood: The Children's Clothing Industry and the Rise of the Child Consumer*. Durham, NC: Duke University Press.

Cook, D.T. (2008) The missing child in consumption theory, *Journal of Consumer Culture*, 8: 219–43.

Cook, D.T. (2010) Commercial enculturation: moving beyond consumer socialization, in D. Buckingham and V. Tingstad (eds) *Childhood and Consumer Culture* (pp. 63–79). Basingstoke: Palgrave Macmillan.

Corsaro, W.A. (1997) *The Sociology of Childhood*. Thousand Oaks, CA: Pine Forge Press.

Cova, B., Kozinets, R.V. and Shankar, A. (2007) Tribes, Inc.: the new world of tribalism, in B. Cova, R.V. Kozinets and A. Shankar (eds) *Consumer Tribes* (pp. 3–26). Oxford: Elsevier.

Cox, J.C. (1903) Preface, in J. Strutt, *The Sports and Pastimes of the People of England*, rev. edn. London: Methuen.

Cross, G. (1999) *Kids' Stuff: Toys and the Changing World of American Childhood*. Cambridge, MA: Harvard University Press.

Csikszentmihalyi, M. (1990) *Flow*. New York: Harper & Row.

Curtis, M. (2001) Counting in and counting out: who knows what in the playground, in J.C. Bishop and M. Curtis (eds) *Play Today in the Primary School Playground: Life, Learning and Creativity* (pp. 62–79). Buckingham: Open University Press.

Czaja, J. (2011) The cyborg habitus: presence, posthumanism and mobile technology. Paper presented at the International Society for Presence Research Annual Conference, 26–28 October 2011. Available at http://www.temple.edu/ispr/prev_conferences/proceedings/2011/Czaja.pdf [Accessed 2 April 2013].

Danet, B. and Katriel, T. (1989) No two alike: the aesthetics of collecting, *Play and Culture*, 2(3): 255–71.

Danet, B. and Katriel, T. (1994) Glorious obsessions, passionate lovers, and hidden treasures: collecting, metaphor, and the romantic ethic, in S.H. Riggings (ed.) *The Socialness of Things: Essays on the Socio-Semiotics of Objects* (pp. 23–61). Berlin: Mouton De Gruyter.

Davis, N.W. and Duncan, M.C. (2006) Sports knowledge is power: reinforcing masculine privilege through fantasy sport league participation, *Journal of Sport and Social Issues*, 30: 244–64.

Davis, S.G. (1996) The theme park: global industry and cultural form, *Media, Culture, Society*, 18: 339–422.

Deleuze, G. (1994) *Difference and Repetition*, translated by P. Patton. New York: Columbia University Press.

Deleuze, G. and Guattari, F. (1987) *A Thousand Plateaus: Capitalism and Schizophrenia*. London: Continuum.

Denisoff, D. (2008) Small change: the consumerist designs of the nineteenth-century child, in D. Denisoff (ed.) *The Nineteenth-Century Child and Consumer Culture* (pp.1–26). Aldershot: Ashgate.

Derrida, J. (1989) Structure, sign and play in the discourse of human sciences, in D.H. Richter (ed.) *Classic Texts and Contemporary Trends* (pp. 914–26). New York: St Martin's Press.

Douglas, N. (1916) *London Street Games*. London: St Catherine Press.

Douglas, N. (1931) *London Street Games*, 2nd edn. London: Chatto & Windus.

Dudek, M. (2005) *Children's Spaces*. Oxford: Architectural Press.

Dunn, J. (2009) Keeping it real: an examination of the metacommunication processes used within the play of one group of preadolescent girls, *Play and Culture Series*, Vol. 9. Lanhan, MD: University Press of America.

Dunn, J. and O'Toole, J. (2009) When worlds collude: exploring the relationship between the actual, the dramatic and the virtual, in M. Anderson, J. Carroll and D. Cameron (eds) *Drama Education with Digital Technology* (pp. 20–37). London: Continuum Books.

Durost, W.N. (1932) *Children's Collecting Activity Related to Social Factors*. New York: Bureau of Publications, Teachers College, Columbia University.

Edgeworth, M. (1801) The purple jar, in M. Edgeworth, *Early Lessons*. London: Pickering & Chatto.

Edwards, R., Ribbens McCarthy, J. and Gillies, V. (2012) The politics of concepts: family and its (putative) replacements, *British Journal of Sociology*, 63(4): 730–46.

Enevold, J. (2012) Domesticating play, designing everyday life: the practice and performance of gender and gaming. Proceedings of 2012 DiGRA Nordic 2012. Available at www.digra.org/dl/db/12168.15073.pdf [Accessed 5 April 2013].

Epstein, D. (1996) Cultures of schooling, cultures of sexuality, *International Journal of Inclusive Education*, 1(1): 37–53.

Esfahani, N.N. (2012) 'Dresses are annoying. I like to design them myself': a post-phenomenological exploration of everyday artefacts. Unpublished PhD thesis, University of South Australia.

Factor, J. (2004) Tree stumps, manhole covers and rubbish tins: the invisible play-lines of a primary school playground, *Childhood*, 11: 142–54.

Factor, J. (2005) A forgotten pioneer, in K. Darian-Smith and J. Factor (eds) *Child's Play: Dorothy Howard and the Folklore of Australian Children* (pp. 1–19). Melbourne: Museum Victoria.

Faircloth, C. and Lee, E. (2010) Changing parenting culture, *Sociological Research Online*, 15(4). Available at <http://www.socresonline.org.uk/15/4/1.html> 10.5153/sro.2249 [Accessed 20 March 2013].

Fass, P.S. and Grossberg, M. (2012) *Reinventing Childhood after World War II.* Philadelphia, PA: University of Pennsylvania Press.

Fisher, K., McCulloch, A. and Gershuny, J. (1999) *British Fathers and Children: A Report for Channel 4 Dispatches.* University of Essex: Institute for Social and Economic Research. Available at http://www.timeuse.org/files/cckpub/british-fathersandchildren1999–1.pdf [Accessed 13 March 2013].

Fleming, D. (1996) *Power Play: Toys as Popular Culture.* Manchester: Manchester University Press.

Flynn, B. (2003) Geography of the digital hearth, *Information, Communication & Society*, 6(4): 551–76.

Formanek-Brunell, M. (1993) *Made to Play House: Dolls and the Commercialization of American Girlhood, 1830–1930.* New Haven, CT: Yale University Press.

Formanek-Brunell, M. (2012) Interrogating the meanings of dolls: new directions in doll studies, *Girlhood Studies*, 5(1): 3–13.

Francis, B. (2010) Re/theorising gender: female masculinity and male femininity in the classroom?, *Gender and Education*, 22(5): 477–90.

Freedgood, E. (2012) Cultures of commodities, cultures of things, in M. Hewitt, (ed.) *The Victorian World* (pp. 225–40). Abingdon: Routledge.

Frost, J.L. (2010) *A History of Children's Play and Play Environments: Toward a Contemporary Child Saving Movement.* New York: Routledge.

Gaunt, K.D. (2006) *The Games Black Girls Play: Learning the Ropes from Double-Dutch to Hip-Hop.* New York: New York University Press.

Gauthier, A.H., Smeeding, T.M. and Furstenberg, F. (2004) Are parents investing less time in children? Trends in selected industrialised countries. 24th General Conference of the International Union for the Scientific Study of Population. Salvador-Bahia, Brazil: Blackwell Publishing Inc.

Gee, J.P. (1999) *An Introduction to Discourse Analysis: Theory and Method.* London: Routledge.

Gibson, W. (1984) *Neuromancer.* London: Harper Collins.

Giddens, A. (2002) *Runaway World: How Globalisation is Reshaping Our Lives.* London: Profile Books.

Giddens, A. (2009) *Sociology*, 6th edn. Cambridge: Polity Press.

Giddings, S. (2007) I'm the one who makes the Lego Racers go: virtual and actual space in videogame play, in S. Weber and S. Dixon (eds) *Growing Up Online: Young People and Digital Technologies* (pp. 35–48). Basingstoke: Palgrave Macmillan.

Gilchrist, A.G. and Broadwood, L.E. (1915) Notes on children's game-songs, *Journal of the Folk-Song Society*, 5(19): 221–39.

Gill, T. (2007) *No Fear: Growing Up in a Risk Averse Society.* London: Calouste Gulbenkian Foundation.

Gillies, V. (2003) *Family and Intimate Relationships: A Review of the Sociological Literature*. London: Southbank University. Available at http://www.payonline.lsbu.ac.uk/ahs/downloads/families/familieswp2.pdf [Accessed 21 March 2013].

Gillington, A.E. (1909a) *Old Hampshire Singing Games*. London: Curwen.

Gillington, A.E. (1909b) *Old Isle of Wight Singing Games*. London: Curwen.

Gillington, A.E. (1909c) *Old Surrey Singing Games and Skipping-Rope Rhymes*. London: Curwen.

Gillington, A.E. (1913) *Old Dorset Singing Games*. London: Curwen.

Gillis, J. (1997) *A World of Their Own Making: Myth, Ritual and the Quest for Family Values*. Harvard, MA: Harvard University Press.

Gillis, J. (2003) Childhood and family time: a changing historical relationship, in A.M. Jenson and L. McKee (eds) *Children and the Changing Family: Between Transformation and Negotiation* (pp. 149–64). Abingdon: Routledge.

Gleave, J. and Cole-Hamilton, I. (2012) *'A World without Play': A Literature Review*. Available at http://www.playengland.org.uk/media/371031/a-world-without-play-literature-review–2012.pdf [Accessed 18 March 2013].

Goffman, E. (1974) *Frame Analysis: Essays on Face-to Face Behavior*. New York: Anchor.

Goffman, E. (1983) The interaction order, *American Sociological Review*, 48(1): 1–17.

Goldstein, K.S. (1971) Strategy in counting out: an ethnographic folklore fieldwork study, in E.M. Avedon and B. Sutton-Smith (eds) *The Study of Games* (pp. 161–78). New York: John Wiley.

Gomme, A.B. ([1894, 1898] 1984) *The Traditional Games of England, Scotland, and Ireland*. London: Thames and Hudson.

Gomme, A.B. and Sharp, C.J. (1909–12) *Children's Singing Games*, 5 vols. London: Novello.

Gottzén, L. (2012) Money talks: children's consumption and becoming in the family, in M. Hedegaard, K. Aronsson, C. Højholt and O. Skjær Ulvik (eds) *Children, Childhood and Everyday Life: Children's Perspectives* (pp. 91–108). Charlotte, NC: Information Age Publishing.

Gould, M. (2007) Sparing the rod, *Guardian*, 9 January. Available at http://www.guardian.co.uk/education/2007/jan/09/schools.uk1 [Accessed 18 March 2013].

Graham, J. (2010) The new wave of fan films, *Guardian*, 13 May. Available at http://www.guardian.co.uk/film/2010/may/13/fan-films-wes-anderson-spiderman [Accessed 29 January 2013].

Graham, M. (2012) Geography/internet: ethereal alternate dimensions of cyberspace or grounded augmented realities?, *The Geographical Journal, Online First*. Paper accepted for publication in November 2012. DOI: 10.1111/geoj.12009.

Griffin, H. (1984) The coordination of meaning in the creation of shared make-believe reality, in I. Bretherton (ed.) *Symbolic Play: The Development of Social Understanding* (pp. 73–100). New York: Academic Press.

Griffiths, M. and Machin, D. (2003) Television and playground games as part of children's symbolic culture, *Social Semiotics*, 13(2): 147–60.

Grugeon, E. (1988) Underground knowledge: what the Opies missed, *English in Education*, 22(2): 9–17.

Grugeon, E. (1993) Gender implications of children's playground culture, in P. Woods and M. Hammersley (eds) *Gender and Ethnicity in Schools*. Buckingham: Open University Press.

Grugeon, E. (2001) Girls' traditional games on two playgrounds, in J.C. Bishop and M. Curtis (eds) *Play Today in the Primary School Playground: Life, Learning and Creativity* (pp. 98–114). Buckingham: Open University Press.

Habermas, J. (1987) *The Theory of Communicative Action*, Vol. 2, (translated by T. McCarthy). Cambridge: Polity.

Halberstam, J. (1998) *Female Masculinity*. Durham, NC: Duke University Press.

Halliwell, J.O. (1842) *Nursery Rhymes of England*. London: T. Richards.

Halliwell, J.O. (1849) *Popular Rhymes and Nursery Tales*. London: J.R. Smith.

Hardy, J. (2011) Mapping commercial intertextuality: HBO's True Blood, *Convergence: The International Journal of Research into New Media Technologies*, 17(7): 7–17.

Harvey, F.J. and Chrisman, N.R. (2004) The imbrication of geography and technology: the social construction of geographic information systems, in S.D. Brunn, S.L. Cutter and J.W. Harrington, Jr (eds) *Geography and Technology* (pp. 65–80). Dordrecht: Kluwer.

Hayles, N.K. (1999) *How We Became Posthuman: Virtual Bodies in Cybernetics, Literature, and Informatics*. Chicago, IL: University of Chicago Press.

Haywood, C. and Mac an Ghaill, M. (2012) 'What's next for masculinity?': reflexive directions for theory and research on masculinity and education, *Gender and Education*, 24(6): 577–92.

Higson, A. (2013) Nostalgia is not what it used to be: heritage films, nostalgia websites and contemporary consumers, *Consumption Markets & Culture*, ahead-of-print (2013): 1–23.

Hill, J.A. (2011) Endangered childhoods: how consumerism is impacting child and youth identity, *Media, Culture and Society*, 33(3): 347–62.

Hjarvard, S. (2004) From bricks to bytes: the mediatization of a global toy industry, in I.Bjondeberg and P.Golding (eds) *European Culture and the Media* (pp. 43–63). Bristol: Intellect.

Holland, P. (2003) *We Don't Play with Guns Here: War, Weapon and Superhero Play in the Early Years*. Maidenhead: Open University Press.

Hollensen, S. (1998) *Global Marketing*. Harlow: Pearson Education.

Home, A. (1993) *Into the Box of Delights: A History of Children's Television*. London: BBC.

Howard, D. (1938) Folk jingles of American children: a collection and study of rhymes used by children today. Unpublished PhD thesis, New York University.

Inside Retail (2013) Disney targets children with QR codes, 15 March. Available at http://www.insideretailing.com.au/IR/IRnews/Disney-Targets-children-with-QR-codes-7779.aspx [Accessed 23 March 2013].

James, A., Jenks, C. and Prout, A. (1998) *Theorizing Childhood*. Cambridge: Polity Press.

James, N.C. and McCain, T. (1982) Television games preschool children play: patterns, themes and uses, *Journal of Broadcasting*, 26(4): 783–800.

Jenkins, H. (1992) *Textual Poachers: Television Fans and Participatory Culture*. London: Routledge.

Jenkins, H., Clinton, K., Purushotma, R., Robison, A. and Weigel, M. (2006) *Confronting the Challenges of Participatory Culture: Media Education for the 21st Century*. An Occasional Paper on Digital Media and Learning. Available at http://digitallearning.macfound.org/site/c.enJLKQNlFiG/b.2108773/apps/nl/content2.asp?content_id={CD911571–0240–4714–A93B–1D0C07C7B6C1} andnotoc=1. [Accessed 2 November 2012].

Jewitt, C. (ed.) (2009) *Routledge Handbook of Multimodal Analysis*. Abingdon: Routledge.

Jones, L., MacLure, M., Holmes, R. and MacRae, C. (2012) Children and objects: affection and infection, *Early Years*, 32(1): 49–60.

Jopson, L., Burn, A. and Robinson, J. (in press) The Opie recordings: what's left to be heard?, in A. Burn and C. Richards (eds) *Children's Games in the New Media Age: Childlore, Media and the Playground*. London: Ashgate Press.

Josselyn, I.M. (1956) Cultural forces, motherliness and fatherliness, *American Journal of Orthopsychiatry*, 26(2): 264–71.

Ju Choi, C. and Berger, R. (2009) Ethics of global Internet, community and fame addiction, *Journal of Business Ethics*, 85: 193–200.

Kane, P. (2004) *The Play Ethic: A Manifesto for a Different Way of Living*. London: Macmillan.

Karsten, L. (2005) It all used to be better? Different generations on continuity and change in urban children's daily use of space, *Children's Geographies*, 3(3): 275–90.

Kidson, F. (1916) *One Hundred Singing Games, Old, New and Adapted*. London: Bayley & Ferguson.

Kinder, M. (1993) *Playing with Power in Movies, Television, and Videogames: From Muppet Babies to Teenage Mutant Ninja Turtles*. Berkeley, CA: University of California Press.

Kline, S. (1993) *Out of the Garden: Toys and Children's Culture in the Age of TV Marketing*. London: Verso.

Kress, G. (2003) *Literacy in a New Media Age*. London: Routledge.

Kress, G. (2010) *Multimodality*. Abingdon: Routledge.

Kuijsten, A. (1995) Recent trends in household structure, in E.V. Imhofl (ed.) *Household Demography and Household Modelling*. New York: Plenum Press.

Lanclos, D.M. (2003) *At Play in Belfast: Children's Folklore and Identities in Northern Ireland*. New Brunswick, NJ: Rutgers University Press.

Langhamer, C. (2005) The meanings of home in postwar Britain, *Journal of Contemporary History*, 40: 341–62.

Latour, B. (2005) *Reassembling the Social: An Introduction to Actor-Network-Theory*. Oxford: Oxford University Press.

LEGO Group (2012) *The LEGO Group: A Short Presentation*. Available at http://cache.lego.com/r/aboutus/-/media/About%20Us/Company%20Profile/ts.20120420T123711.Company_profile_uk.pdf [Accessed 1 March 2013].

Lévi-Strauss, C. (1966) *The Savage Mind*. Chicago, IL: University of Chicago Press.

Levin, D. and Rosenquest, B. (2001) The increasing role of electronic toys in the lives of infants and toddlers: should we be concerned?, *Contemporary Issues in Early Childhood*, 2: 242–7.

Lichman, S. (2001) From hopscotch to *siji*: generations at play in a cross-cultural setting, in J.C. Bishop and M. Curtis (eds) *Play Today in the Primary School Playground: Life, Learning and Creativity* (pp. 152–66). Buckingham: Open University Press.

Lindsay, J. and Maher, J. (2013) *Consuming Families: Buying, Making, Producing Family Life in the 21st Century*. London: Routledge.

Livingstone, S. (2009) Half a century of television in the lives of our children, in E. Katz and P. Scannell (eds) *The End of Television? Its Impact on the World (so far). The Annals of the American Academy of Political and Social Science* (pp. 151–63). Los Angeles, CA/London/New Dehli: Sage Publications.

Lucas, E.V. (1902) *The Visit to London*. London: Methuen.

Lury, K. (2002) Children's channels, in D. Buckingham (ed.) *Small Screens: Television for Children*. London: Leicester University Press.

Machin, D. and Van Leeuwen, T. (2009) Toys as discourse: children's war toys and the war on terror, *Critical Discourse Studies*, 6(1): 51–63.

McKendrick, J., Bradford, M. and Fielder, A.V. (2000) Kid customer? Commercialization of playspace and the commodification of childhood, *Childhood*, 7: 295–314.

Mackenzie, C. (1912) *Kensington Rhymes*. London: Ballantyne. Available at http://archive.org/stream/kensingtonrhymes00mackiala#page/n7/mode/2up [Accessed 4 February 2013].

Maclagan, R.C. (1901) *The Games and Diversions of Argyleshire*. London: Nutt.

Maclean, C. (2009) Lego: play it again, *Telegraph*, 17 December. Available at http://www.telegraph.co.uk/finance/newsbysector/retailandconsumer/6825911/Lego-play-it-again.html [Accessed 4 February 2013].

McNeil, W.K. (1988) Introduction, in S.J. Bronner (ed.) *American Children's Folklore*. Little Rock, AR: August House.

Macrory, I. (2012) *Measuring National Well-being: Households and Families 2012*. Office for National Statistics. Available at http://www.ons.gov.uk/ons/dcp171766-259965.pdf [Accessed 15 May 2013].

Makman, L.H. (1999) Child's work is child's play: the value of George MacDonald's Diamond, *Children's Literature Quarterly*, 24(3): 119–29.

Marsh, J. (2002) Colloquium: electronic toys: why should we be concerned? A response to Levin and Rosenquest, *Contemporary Issues in Early Childhood*, 3(1): 132–7.

Marsh, J. (2005) Ritual, performance and identity construction: young children's engagement with popular cultural and media texts, in J. Marsh (ed.) *Popular Culture, New Media and Digital Literacy in Early Childhood* (pp. 28–50). London: RoutledgeFalmer.

Marsh, J. (2010a) Young children's play in online virtual worlds, *Journal of Early Childhood Research*, 8(1): 23–39.

Marsh, J. (2010b) *Childhood, Culture and Creativity: A Literature Review*. Creativity, Culture and Education Series: Newcastle Upon Tyne, UK. Available at http://www.creativitycultureeducation.org/research-impact/literature-reviews/ [Accessed 18 February 2013].

Marsh, J. (2010c) New literacies, old identities: young girls' experiences of digital literacy at home and school, in C. Jackson, C. Paechter and E. Reynolds (eds) *Girls and Education 3–16: Continuing Concerns, New Agendas* (pp. 197–209). Buckingham: Open University Press.

Marsh, J. (2011) Young children's literacy practices in a virtual world: establishing an online interaction order, *Reading Research Quarterly*, 46(2): 101–18.

Marsh, J. (2012) Children as knowledge brokers of playground games and rhymes in the new media age, *Childhood*, 19(4): 508–22.

Marsh, J. (in press, a) Online and offline play, in A. Burn and C. Richards (eds) *Children's Games in the New Media Age: Childlore, Media and the Playground*. London: Ashgate.

Marsh, J. (in press, b) Breaking the ice: play, friendships and social identities in young children's use of virtual worlds, in A. Burke and J. Marsh (eds) *Children's Virtual Play Worlds: Culture, Learning and Participation*. New York: Peter Lang.

Marsh, J. and Bishop, J.C. (2012) 'We're playing *Jeremy Kyle*!': television talk shows in the playground, *Discourse: Studies in the Cultural Politics of Education*. Article first published online: 23 November. DOI:10.1080/01596306.2012.739464.

Marsh, J., Hannon, P., Lewis, M. and Ritchie, L. (2009) *Family Digital Literacy Study*. Sheffield: University of Sheffield.

Marsh, K. (2006) Cycles of appropriation in children's musical play: orality in the age of reproduction, *The World of Music*, 48(1): 9–32.

Marsh, K. (2008) *The Musical Playground: Global Tradition and Change in Children's Songs and Games*. New York: Oxford University Press.

Massey, D. (2005) *For Space*. London: Sage Publications.

Maughan, B. and Gardner, F. (2012) Families and parenting, in D.J. Smith (ed.) *A New Response to Youth Crime* (pp. 247–86). Abingdon: Routledge.

Maybin, J. (2013) Evaluation in pre-teenagers' informal language practices around texts from popular culture, in A. Cekaite, S. Blum-Kulka, V. Aukrust and E. Teuba (eds) *Children's Peer Talk and Peer Learning in First and Second Language*. Cambridge: Cambridge University Press.

Meehan, E.R. (2005) Transindustrialism and synergy: structural supports for decreasing diversity in commercial culture, *International Journal of Media and Cultural Politics*,1(1): 123–6.

Mildon, K.H. (2009) An investigation into inequalities in parent–child involvement in active play. Unpublished MPhil thesis, University of York. Available at http://etheses.whiterose.ac.uk/965/1/Thesis_TheFinalVersion.pdf [Accessed 14 February 2013].

Miller, D. (2009) *Stuff*. Oxford: Polity.

Miller, F. and Gray, E. (2012) LEGO Friends petition: parents, women and girls ask toy companies to stop gender-based marketing, *The Huffington Post*, 15 January. Available at http://www.huffingtonpost.com/2012/01/15/lego-friends-girls-gender-toy-marketing_n_1206293.html [Accessed 14 February 2013].

Mitchell, W.J. (1997) *City of Bits: Space, Place, and the Infobahn*. Cambridge, MA: MIT Press.

Morgan, D.H.J. (2011) *Rethinking Family Practices*. Basingstoke: Palgrave Macmillan.

Moss, D. (2011) *Children and Social Change: Memories of Diverse Childhoods*. London: Continuum.

Mullin, K. (2005) Douglas, (George) Norman (1868–1952) *Oxford Dictionary of National Biography*, Oxford University Press. Available at http://www.oxforddnb.com/view/article/32874 [Accessed 5 April 2013].

Munroe, R. and Romney, A.K. (2006) Gender and age differences in same-sex aggregation and social behavior: a four-culture study, *Journal of Cross-Cultural Psychology*, 37(3): 3–19.

Myers, M. (1989) Socialising Rosamond: educational ideology and fictional form, *Children's Literature Association Quarterly*, 14(2): 52–8.

Newell, W.W. ([1883]1903/1963) *Games and Songs of American Children,* 2nd edn. New York: Dover.

Nicholson, E.W.B. (1897) *Golspie: Contributions to Its Folklore*. London: Nutt.

Ofcom (2007) *The Future of Children's Television Programming*. Available at http://stakeholders.ofcom.org.uk/binaries/consultations/kidstv/summary/kidstvresearch.pdf [Accessed 23 January 2013].

Ofcom (2012a) *Children and Parents: Media Use and Attitudes Report*. October. Available at http://stakeholders.ofcom.org.uk/binaries/research/media-literacy/oct2012/main.pdf [Accessed 23 January 2013].

Ofcom (2012b) *Public Service Broadcasting Annual Report 2012*. Available at http://stakeholders.ofcom.org.uk/binaries/broadcast/reviews-investigations/psb-review/psb2012/section-a.pdf [Accessed 23 January 2013].

Office for National Statistics (2013) *Summary of Labour Market Statistics*. Available at http://www.ons.gov.uk/ons/publications/re-reference-tables.html?edition=tcm%3A77–222531 [Accessed 23 January 2013].

Opie, I. (1988) Iona Opie 1923–. *Something about the Author Autobiography Series*, 6: 203–17.

Opie, I. (1989) The making of folklore books: chiefly the experiences of the Revd. John Brand and the Opies, *Folklore*, 100: 53–62.

Opie, I. (1993) *The People in the Playground*. Oxford: Oxford University Press.

Opie, I. (2001) Foreword, in J.C. Bishop and M. Curtis (eds) (2001) *Play Today in the Primary School Playground: Life, Learning and Creativity* (pp. x–xiv). Buckingham: Open University Press.

Opie, I. and Opie, P. (1951) *The Oxford Dictionary of Nursery Rhymes*. Oxford: Oxford University Press.

Opie, I. and Opie, P. (1955) *The Oxford Nursery Rhyme Book*. Oxford: Oxford University Press.

Opie, I. and Opie, P. (1959) *The Lore and Language of Schoolchildren*. Oxford: Oxford University Press.

Opie, I. and Opie, P. (1963) *The Puffin Book of Nursery Rhymes*. London: Puffin.

Opie, I. and Opie, P. (1969) *Children's Games in Street and Playground*. Oxford: Clarendon Press.

Opie, I. and Opie, P. (1985) *The Singing Game*. Oxford: Oxford University Press.

Opie, I. and Opie, P. (1997) *Children's Games with Things*. Oxford: Oxford University Press.

Opie, P. (1964) Proposal for a dictionary, arranged on historical principles, of English traditional lore, *Folklore*, 75(2): 73–90.

Orton, H., Halliday, W., Barry, M., Tilling, P. and Wakelin, M. (eds) (1962–71) *Survey of English Dialects (B): The Basic Material*, 4 vols. Leeds: Edward Arnold.

Oswell, D. (2002) *Television, Childhood and the Home: A History of the Making of the Child Television Audience in Britain*. Oxford: Clarendon Press.

Paechter, C. (2007) *Being Boys, Being Girls: Learning Masculinities and Femininities*. Buckingham: Open University Press.

Palmer, P. (1986) *The Lively Audience: A Study of Children around the TV Set*. Sydney: Allen and Unwin.

Palmer Bonte, E. and Musgrove, M. (1943) Influences of war as evidenced in children's play, *Child Development*, 14: 179–200.

Parker-Jenkins, M. (1991) *Sparing the Rod: Schools, Discipline and Children's Rights*. Stoke-on-Trent: Trentham Books.

Patte, M.M. and Brown, F. (2011) Playwork: a profession challenging societal factors devaluing children's play, *Journal of Student Wellbeing*, 5(1): 58–70.

Paulin, T. (1990) Introduction, *The Faber Book of Vernacular Verse*. London: Faber and Faber.

Pearce, G. and Bailey, R.P. (2011) Football pitches and Barbie dolls: young children's perceptions of their school playground, *Early Child Development and Care*, 181(10): 1361–79.

Pellegrini, A. and Blatchford, P. (2000) *The Child at School: Interactions with Peers and Teachers*. London: Edward Arnold.

Pieterse, J.N. (2001) Hybridity, so what? The anti-hybridity backlash and the riddles of recognition, *Theory, Culture and Society*, 18: 219–45.

Plumb, J.H. (1982) The new world of children in eighteenth-century England, in N. McKendrick, J. Brewer and J.H. Plumb (eds) *The Commercialization of Eighteenth-Century England* (pp. 286–315). Bloomington, IN: Indiana University Press.

Potts, A. (2004) Deleuze on Viagra (or, what can a Viagra-body do?), *Body & Society*, 10(1): 17–36.

Powell, A. (2012) Handclap, jump rope, and elastics rhymes. Available at http://www.cocojams.com/content/handclap-jump-rope-and-elastics-rhymes [Accessed 12 December 2012].

Prior, P. and Shipka, J. (2003) Chronotopic lamination: tracing the contours of literate activity, in C. Bazerman and D.R. Russell (eds) *Writing Selves/Writing Societies* (pp. 180–238). Fort Collins, CO: The WAC Clearinghouse.

Pugh, A.J. (2009) *Longing and Belonging: Parents, Children and Consumer Culture.* Berkeley, CA: University of California Press.

Qvortrup, J., Corsaro, W.A. and Honig, M.S. (eds) (2009) *The Palgrave Handbook of Childhood Studies.* Basingstoke: Palgrave Macmillan.

Reckwitz, A. (2002) Towards a theory of social practices, *European Journal of Social Theory*, 5(2): 243–63.

Renold, E. (2005) *Girls, Boys and Junior Sexualities: Exploring Children's Gender and Sexual Relations in the Primary School.* London: RoutledgeFalmer.

Renold, E. and Ringrose, J. (2008) Regulation and rupture: mapping tween and teenage girls' resistance to the heterosexual matrix, *Feminist Theory*, 9: 313–38.

Renold, E. and Ringrose, J. (2011a) Schizoid subjectivities: re-theorising teengirls' sexual cultures in an era of sexualisation, *Journal of Sociology*, 47(4): 389–409.

Renold, E. and Ringrose, J. (2011b) Phallic girls? Girls' negotiation of phallogocentric power, in J. Landreau and N.M. Rodriguez (eds) *Queer Masculinities* (pp. 47–67). New York: Springer.

Richards, C. (2012) Playing under surveillance: gender, performance and the conduct of the self in a primary school playground, *British Journal of Sociology of Education*, 33(3): 373–90.

Richards, C. (2013) Agonistic scenarios, in R. Willett, C. Richards, J. Marsh, A. Burn and J. Bishop, *Children, Media and Playground Cultures: Ethnographic Studies of School Playtimes* (pp 170–95). Basingstoke: Palgrave Macmillan.

Ritchie, J.T.R. (1964) *The Singing Street.* Edinburgh: Oliver & Boyd.

Ritchie, J.T.R. (1965) *Golden City.* Edinburgh: Oliver & Boyd.

Ritchie, J.T.R. (n.d.) The Bumbee Bell. Unpublished manuscript.

Robertson, R. (1995) Glocalization: time–space and homogeneity–heterogeneity, in M. Featherstone, S.Lash and R. Robertson (eds) *Global Modernities* (pp. 25–44). London: Sage Publications.

Roopnarine, J.L. (2012) What is the state of play?, *International Journal of Play*, 1(3): 228–30.

Roseneil, S. and Budgeon, S. (2004) Cultures of intimacy and care beyond 'the family': personal life and social change in the early 21st century, *Current Sociology*, 52(2): 135–49.

Ross, C. and Ryan, A. (1994) Changing playground society: a whole-school approach, in P. Blatchford and S. Sharp (eds) *Breaktime and the School* (pp. 175–87). London: Routledge.

Roud, S. (2010) *The Lore of the Playground: One Hundred Years of Children's Games, Rhymes and Traditions*. London: Random House.

Ryan, M.-L. (2003) *Narrative as Virtual Reality: Immersion and Interactivity in Literature and Electronic Media*. Baltimore, MD: Johns Hopkins University Press.

Schatzki, T.R. (2001) Introduction: practice theory, in T.R. Schatzki, K.K. Cetina and E. von Savigny (eds) *The Practice Turn in Contemporary Theory* (pp. 1–14). London: Routledge.

Singer, D.G. and Singer, J.L. (2005) *Imagination and Play in the Electronic Age*. Cambridge, MA: Harvard University Press.

Smith, P.K. (2013) Bullying, *Sociologia, Problemas e Practicas*, 71: 81–98.

Social Issues Research Centre (2008) *Childhood and Family Life: Socio-demographic Changes*. Oxford: Social Issues Research Centre. Available at https://www.education.gov.uk/. . ./Appendix-G_SIRC-report.pdf [Accessed 2 April 2013].

Sparrman, A., Sandin, B. and Sjoberg, J. (eds) (2012) *Situating Child Consumption: Rethinking Values and Notions of Children, Childhood and Consumption*. Lund: Nordic Academic Press.

Staples, T. (1997) *All Pals Together: The Story of Children's Cinema*. Edinburgh: Edinburgh University Press.

Stearns, P. (2009) Consumerism, in J. Pell and I. van Staveren (eds) *Handbook of Economics and Ethics* (pp. 62–8). Cheltenham: Edward Elgar Publishing.

Steemers, J. (2010) *Creating Preschool Television: A Story of Commerce, Creativity and Curriculum*. London: Palgrave.

Strauss, A.L. and Corbin, J. (1998) *Basics of Qualitative Research: Techniques and Procedures for Developing Grounded Theory*, 2nd edn. Thousands Oaks, CA: Sage Publications.

Street, B. (1995) *Social Literacies: Critical Approaches to Literacy in Development, Ethnography and Education*. London: Longman.

Strutt, J. (1801) *The Sports and Pastimes of the People of England*. London: J. White.

Sutton-Smith, B. (1997) *The Ambiguity of Play*. Cambridge, MA: Harvard University Press.

Sutton-Smith, B. (2008) Play theory: a personal journey and new thoughts, *American Journal of Play*, 1(1): 82–125.

Sutton-Smith, B. and Rosenberg, B.G. (1961) Sixty years of historical change in the game preferences of American children, *Journal of American Folklore*, 74(249): 17–46.

Swain, J. (2000) 'The money's good, the fame's good, the girls are good': the role of playground football in the construction of young boys' masculinity in a junior school, *British Journal of Sociology of Education*, 21(1): 95–109.

Taylor, A. and Taylor, J. (1809) *City Scenes: Or a Peep into London for Good Children*. London: Brown & Merritt. Available at http://books.google.co.uk/books?id=u

ZsNAAAAQAAJ&printsec=frontcover&source=gbs_ge_summary_r&cad=0#v= onepage&q&f=false [Accessed 11 February 2013].

Taylor, R. (2012) Messing about with metaphor: multimodal aspects to children's creative meaning making, *Literacy*, 46(3): 156–66.

Thompson, J. (1995) *The Media and Modernity: A Social Theory of the Media*. Stanford, CA: Stanford University Press.

Thomson, S. (2005) 'Territorialising' the primary school playground: deconstructing the geography of playtime, *Children's Geographies*, 3(1): 63–78.

Thorne, B. (1992) Girls and boys together . . . but mostly apart: gender arrangements in elementary schools, in J. Wrigley (ed.) *Education and Gender Equality* (pp. 117–32). London: Falmer Press.

Thorne, B. (1993) *Gender Play: Girls and Boys in School*. Buckingham: Open University Press.

Thrift, N. (2007) *Non-Representational Theory: Space, Politics, Affect*. London: Routledge.

Tobin, J. (ed.) (2004) *Pikachu's Global Adventure*. London: Duke University Press.

Trumpener, K. (2002) City scenes, commerce, Utopia and the birth of the picture book, in *The Victorian Illustrated Book* (pp. 332–84). Charlottesville, VA: University of Virginia Press.

Tylor, E.B. (1871) *Primitive Culture*. London: Murray.

Valentine, G. (2004) *Public Space and the Culture of Childhood*. London: Ashgate.

Van Tilburg, A.P. and Igou, E.R. (2012) On boredom: lack of challenge and meaning as distinct boredom experiences, *Motivation and Emotion*, 36(2): 181–94.

Verbeek, P. (2006) Materializing morality: design ethics and technological mediation, *Science, Technology & Human Values*, 31(3): 361–80.

Voida, A. and Greenberg, S. (2010) A gameroom of our own: exploring the domestic gaming environment. Technical Report 2010–961–10, Department of Computer Science, University of Calgary, Calgary, Alberta Canada. Available at http://grouplab.cpsc.ucalgary.ca/grouplab/uploads/ Publications/Publications/2010-Gameroom.Report2010–961–10.pdf [Accessed 15 March 2013].

Wallin, J.J. (2010) Rhizomania: five provocations on a concept, *Complicity: An International Journal of Complexity and Education*, 7(2): 83–9.

Walters, J. and Steemers, J. (2010) The bigger picture: preschool television in its critical and aesthetic contexts, in J. Steemers (ed.) *Creating Preschool Television: A Story of Commerce, Creativity and Curriculum* (pp. 191–211). Basingstoke: Palgrave Macmillan.

Warner, M. (2001) Introduction, in I. Opie and P. Opie, *The Lore and Language of Schoolchildren*. New York: New York Review of Books.

Wasko, J. (2001) *Understanding Disney: The Manufacture of Fantasy*. Cambridge: Polity.

Wells, C., MacLeod, A. and Frank, B. (2012) Queer theory, ethnography and education, in S. Delamont (ed.) *Handbook of Qualitative Research In Education* (pp. 108–25). Cheltenham: Edward Elgar Publishing.

Wheeler, S. (2011) The significance of family culture for sports participation, *International Review for the Sociology of Sport*, 47(2): 235–52.

Willett, R. (2011) An ethnographic study of preteen girls' play with popular music on a school playground in the UK, *Journal of Children and Media*, 5(4): 341–57.

Willett, R. (2013) Superheroes, naughty mums and witches: pretend family play among 7- to 10-year-olds, in R. Willett, C. Richards, J. Marsh, A. Burn and J.C. Bishop, *Children, Media and Playground Cultures: Ethnographic Studies of School Playtimes* (pp. 145–69). Basingstoke: Palgrave Macmillan.

Willett, R., Richards, C., Marsh, J., Burn, A. and Bishop, J. (2013) *Children, Media and Playground Cultures: Ethnographic Studies of School Playtimes.* Basingstoke: Palgrave Macmillan.

Williams, R. (1977) *Marxism and Literature.* Oxford: Oxford University Press.

Williams, R. (1981) *Politics and Letters: Interviews with New Left Review.* London: Verso.

Wilson, M. (1997) *Performance and Practice: Oral Narrative Traditions among Teenagers in Britain and Ireland.* Aldershot: Ashgate.

Withers, C. (1963) Introduction to Dover Edition of W.W. Newell ([1903]1963) *Games and Songs of American Children*, 2nd edn. New York: Dover.

Witty, P.A. and Lehman, H.C. (1930) Further studies of children's interest in collecting, *Journal of Educational Psychology*, 21: 112–27.

Witty, P.A. and Lehman, H.C. (1931) Sex differences: collecting interests, *Journal of Educational Psychology*, 22: 221–8.

Wohlwend, K. (2009) Damsels in discourse: girls consuming and producing identity texts through Disney princess play, *Reading Research Quarterly*, 44(1): 57–83.

Woodyer, T. (2010) Playing with toys: animated geographies of children's material culture. Unpublished PhD thesis, Royal Holloway University of London.

Woolgar, S. (2012) Ontological child consumption, in S. Sparrman, B. Sandin and J. Sjoberg (eds) *Situating Child Consumption: Rethinking Values and Notions of Children, Childhood and Consumption.* Lund: Nordic Academic Press.

Wright, J. and McLeod, K. (2012) Public memories and private meanings: representing the 'happy childhood' narrative in oral histories of adolescence and schooling in Australia, 1930s–1950s, *Oral History Forum d'histoire orale*, 32: 1–19. Available at http://www.oralhistoryforum.ca/index.php/ohf/article/view/424/488 [Accessed 5 April 2013].

Young, S. (2008) Lullaby light shows: everyday musical experience among under-two-year-olds, *International Journal of Music Education*, 26(1): 33–46.

Zelizer, V. (1985) *Pricing The Priceless Child: The Changing Social Value of Children.* Princeton, NJ: Princeton University Press.

Index